LEARN

THE FAST AND FUN WAY

SECOND EDITION

by Paul G. Graves, Ph.D.
University of Colorado

Heywood Wald, Coordinating Editor
Chairman, Department of Foreign Languages
Martin Van Buren High School, New York

To help you pace your learning, we've included stopwatches *like the one above* throughout the book to mark each 15-minute interval. You can read one of these units each day or pace yourself according to your needs.

CONTENTS

All inquiries should be addressed to:
Barron's Educational Series, Inc.
250 Wireless Boulevard
Hauppauge, New York 11788

Library of Congress Catalog Card No. 97-8267

International Standard Book No. 0-7641-0216-8 (book)
0-7641-7024-4 (package)

PRINTED IN THE UNITED STATES OF AMERICA
98765432

To my wife, Eva Alkalay Graves

Cover and Book Design Milton Glaser, Inc.
Illustrations Juan Suarez
Revised Edition Kathleen Luft

Library of Congress Cataloging-in-Publication Data

Graves, Paul G.
Learn German the fast and fun way / by Paul G. Graves. — 2nd ed.
p. cm.
ISBN 0-7641-0216-8. — ISBN 0-7641-7024-4
1. German language—Conversation and phrase books—English. I. Title.
PF3121.G72 1997
438.3'421—dc21 97-8267
CIP

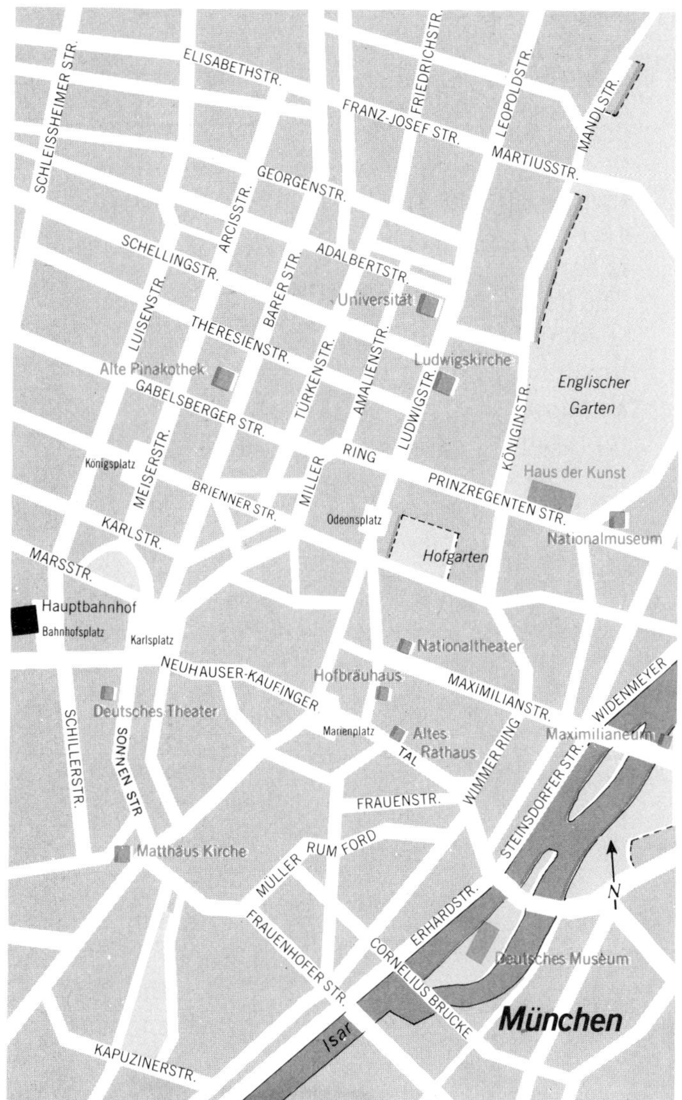

Major Sites, Munich

Congratulations, dear friend! Buying this book was a splendid idea. You will enjoy learning a new and beautiful language.

Beautiful? Yes, I know; people have been made to believe that Italian is more melodious, French more elegant, Spanish more virile—but who wants to sing, wear formal attire, or be macho all the time?

I have it on good authority (my own) that German is a down-to-earth, no-nonsense, yet surprisingly poetic language that you will love to learn.

Let's lay to rest some misconceptions.

No. **Donaudampfschiffahrtsgesellschaftskapitäswitwe** (widow of a captain of the Danube steamship company) is not the longest word known. There is a place in Wales whose Welsh name is longer by a couple of inches.

No. Speaking German won't give you a sore throat. I've been practicing it for years and to no ill effect. Like the Scots and the Dutch, Germans cherish their gutturals.

No. It's not true that the average German male wears short leather pants, likes to yodel, and feeds on sausages, potatoes, and sauerkraut.

On the other hand.

Yes. It's true that German is closely related to English, and that you will easily recognize hundreds of words.

Yes. It's true that Germans have a crush on their beer—but so will you, once you taste it. (Personally, I adore their wine, also.)

Yes. It's true that haggling in stores will get you nowhere, that service personnel are less tip-hungry than elsewhere, that hotel rooms are generally clean, and that trains run on time. True also that there's an abundance of theaters and opera houses, concerts and ballet.

Let's quickly talk about some of the major cities. Frankfurt is one of Germany's foremost transportation hubs, and also its financial center. It is served by a major international airport.

In the fall you can enjoy merry-making at Munich's Oktoberfest. The city is famous also for its great theaters, fine concerts, and rich art galleries.

If you seek elegance, Düsseldorf, a metropolis of the Rhine valley, takes first place. It is the fashion capital of Germany and one of its wealthiest cities as well.

Hamburg, the "Venice of the North," is one of the great seaports of the world. It is also an important cultural center noted especially for its major magazine and book publishing firms. The St. Pauli district in Hamburg is well known for its steamy nightlife.

The reunited city of Berlin was made the capital again in 1990, when the German Democratic Republic officially acceded to the Federal Republic. One of Europe's largest industrial centers, Berlin also is a cultural mecca, with three opera houses, several major orchestras, dozens of theaters, and world-renowned museums. It is the future seat of the federal government.

Bonn, the former unification capital of the Federal Republic of Germany, until 1949 was a little university town famous as the birthplace of the composer Ludwig van Beethoven. It was raised to eminence by political intrigue. Berlin, itself out of the running, promoted Bonn, fearing that Frankfurt would get the prize and keep it permanently, even if reunification were to occur. Bonn will continue to be an important administrative and scientific center even after Berlin becomes the seat of the federal government.

Dresden, now the capital of the Free State of Saxony, is increasingly important as a center of the microelectronics industry. A leading cultural center as well, Dresden is famed for its music, art collections, and baroque architecture.

Leipzig, also in Saxony, has a long tradition as a trade fair city. It was a focal point of peaceful resistance to the SED regime in the German Democratic Republic.

Away from the big, noisy cities, Germany's old-fashioned beauty is still intact. The enchanting valleys of the Rhine and the Mosel, the Neckar and the Danube, the vistas of the Black Forest, the Harz Mountains, and the Bavarian Alps, the ancient cathedrals, medieval towns, and legendary castles are wonders no tourist should miss.

Germany is governed under the Grundgesetz (Basic Law), adopted in 1949 as a provisional constitution. It became valid for the entire nation on October 3, 1990. This law guarantees rights to individuals and provides for a relatively decentralized form of government designed to prevent the emergence of a dictatorship like that of Adolf Hitler, who controlled Germany from 1933 to 1945. Germany is divided into 16 Länder (federal states). The head of state is the Bundespräsident (Federal President). The head of government is the Bundeskanzler (Federal Chancellor), who is elected by the lower house of parliament, called the Bundestag. The upper house, the Bundesrat, represents the interests of the Länder.

Why study German, you might ask.

Let's look at the practical application of it. Today, German is spoken by more than 100 million people living in Germany, Austria, and the greater part of Switzerland. It is used and understood by millions elsewhere in Europe and around the world.

German is one of the great international languages, particularly valuable in the fields of science, technology, and commerce. And speaking of commerce, did you know that the Federal Republic of Germany is a leading economic power, ranking second only to the United States among the world's trading nations?

You are now ready to set out on the exciting journey of learning a new language. This book is designed to make the learning process as easy, interesting, and convenient as possible. We have used verbs only in the present tense so that you can quickly gain a conversational knowledge of German.

PRONUNCIATION

We have tried to make the phonetic transcriptions in the text as self-explanatory as possible so that you do not have to learn a complex phonetic alphabet to use this book. Please read the pronunciation guide *before* you begin using the text so that you will know what the few unusual symbols mean.

Accent

German words of more than one syllable are usually stressed on the first syllable. However, there are many exceptions, and in this book the accented syllable is indicated by capital letters in the phonetic transcription of each word: *Moment* (mo-MENT) moment.

Syllabification

German words are divided before single consonants and between double ones:

sagen sa-gen (to say)
kommen kom-men (to come)

The consonant combinations, *sch, ch, ß* (ss), and *ph* are counted as single consonants. Compound words are divided into their individual parts:

Flugnummer Flug-num-mer (flight number)

By and large, German syllabification presents no problems for English speakers learning German.

VOWELS

German has **long vowels, short vowels,** and **diphthongs**. A vowel is usually long when doubled (*Boot* [boht] boat), when followed by an *h* (*Fehler* [FAY-leR] mistake), or when followed by a single consonant (*rot* [roht] red). Vowels generally are short when followed by two or more consonants (*essen* [ES-en] to eat). Diphthongs may be divided into three groups: *ai, ay, ei, ey* (*Eier* [EI-eR] eggs); *au* (*grau* [grow] gray); and *äu, eu* (*Beutel* [BOY-tel] bag).

The final *e* in German words is never silent as it is in such English words as *late* and *spoke.* It is always pronounced, and it sounds like the final *a* in the English *sofa.* To mark this unstressed mid-central vowel as different from a silent English *e* (and to remind you to pronounce this German sound!), we render it as *eh: bitte* (BI-teh) please; *Wände* (VEN-deh) walls.

The German vowels also include three with an umlaut (¨). They are *ä*, *ö*, and *ü*. These vowels with umlauts can also be either long or short. The *ä* presents no problems. The short *ä* is always pronounced like short *e*. For all practical purposes, you can pronounce the long *ä* like the long *e*.

The umlauts *ö* and *ü* are not easy for speakers of English and require some practice. The short *ö* is something like the vowel sounds in the English word *fur.* Try to say a long German *e* and round your lips at the same time. This rounding of the lips has to be still more extreme to produce the long *ö*.

The German *ü* is like *u* in the French word *une.* Say the English vowel sound *ee* as in *seen,* keep your tongue in that position, then round your lips into the English *oo* position, as in *boot.* As with the long and short *ö*, the long *ü* is "pushed farther forward" and the lips rounded a little more than with the short *ü*.

In German the vowel *y* is pronounced like the long *ü*: *Symphonie* (zǖm-foh-NEE).

The German diphthongs are easy for speakers of English.

SHORT VOWELS	English Equivalent	Symbol	LONG VOWELS	English Equivalent	Symbol
b*i*tten (to ask)	b*i*n	i	**b*ie*ten** (to offer)	b*ea*n	ee
B*e*tt (bed)	b*e*t	e	**B*ee*t** (flower bed)	b*ai*t	ay
St*a*dt (city)	h*o*t	a	**St*aa*t** (state)	f*a*ther	ah
L*o*ch (hole)	l*o*rry	o	**h*o*ch** (high)	l*oa*d	oh
Fl*u*ß (river)	p*u*t	u	**F*u*ß** (foot)	b*oo*t	oo

SHORT UMLAUT	English Equivalent	Symbol	LONG UMLAUT	English Equivalent	Symbol
W*ä*nde (walls)	b*e*t	e	**sp*ä*t** (late)	b*ai*t	ay
H*ö*lle (hell)	k*er*nel	ö	**H*ö*hle** (cave)	[none]	ȫ
H*ü*tte (hut)	[none]	ü	**H*ü*te** (hats)	[none]	ǖ

DIPHTHONGS		English Equivalent	Symbol
ai	**Hain** (grove)	h*igh*	ei
ei	**mein** (my)	h*igh*	ei
äu	**Häute** (skins)	*joy*	oy
eu	**heute** (today)	*joy*	oy
au	**auf** (on)	c*ow*	ow

CONSONANTS

Most German consonant sounds have very near equivalents in English. The following German consonants are spelled and pronounced as they are in English:

f, h, k, l,
m, n, p, t

The only consonant sounds in German that are unfamiliar to English speakers are the two represented by *ch* in words like *ich* and *Buch*.

GERMAN LETTERS	Symbols	Pronunciation/Example
ch	ch	Pronounced like the *ch* in the Scottish word *loch*. Make it by saying an *h*, then cutting off the flow of air by raising the back of your tongue. Occurs only after the vowels *a*, *o*, and *u* and the diphthong *au*. Example: *Buch* (booch) book.
ch	ç	The closest sound English has to the *ch* in *ich* is a strongly aspirated and drawn out *h*, as in *Hugh* or *Hubert*. Say *Hugh*, giving the initial *h* a long duration and a lot of air, and you will be very close to the *ich* sound. Example: *ich* (iç) I.
chs	ks	Pronounced like the English letter *x*. Example *Lachs* (laks) salmon.
c	ts	*c* before *e*, *i*, *ä*, or *ö* is pronounced *ts*. Example: *Celsius* (TSEL-zee-us).
	k	Otherwise it is pronounced like *k*. Example: *Café* (ka-FAY) coffee house.
b d g	p t k	The letters, *b*, *d*, *g* are pronounced as they are in English if they occur at the beginning of a syllable. Example: *gehen* (GAY-en). However, if they occur at the end of a syllable or before a *t*, they are pronounced like *p*, *t*, *k*. Examples: b *lieb, liebt* (leep, leept) dear, loves d *Lied* (leet) song g *flog, fliegt* (flohk, fleekt) flew, flies Note, too, that the combination *-ig* at the end of a word or syllable is pronounced like *ich*. Example: *windig* (VIN-diç) windy. Also, the second *g* in *Garage* (ga-RAH-žeh) is pronounced like that in the English word *garage*. The symbol for this kind of *g* is *ž*.
h	h	*h* is silent only when it indicates that a preceding vowel is long, as mentioned above. Example: *Stahl* (shtahl) steel. Otherwise, it is always pronounced as in English *house*. Example: *hoch* (hohch) high.
j	y	*j* is pronounced like English *y*. Example: *ja* (yah) yes.
kn	kn	In English, the *k* in *knee* is silent. In German, *both* the *k* and the *n* are sounded. Example: *Knie* (knee) knee.

GERMAN LETTERS	Symbols	Pronunciation/Example
ng	ng	Pronounced as in English *singer*, not as in *finger*. Example: *Ding* (ding) thing.
pf, ps	pf, ps	As in *kn*, both letters in the combinations *pf* and *ps* are pronounced in German. Examples: When you ask for pepper *(Pfeffer)* in German, don't ask for (FEF-eR) but for (PFEF-eR). And in *Psychologie*, the *p* is pronounced (psü-çoh-loh-GEE), not (sü-çoh-loh-GEE).
qu	kv	As in English, *q* in German is always followed by a *u*. However, this combination is pronounced *kv*. Example: *Qualität* (kvah-lee-TAYT) quality.
r	r	*R* not at the end of a word: You will not be misunderstood if you use an American *r*, but your German will sound much more authentic if you learn the German *r*. To make it, pronounce the back *ch* sound, then add voice to it. Some native speakers of German use a trilled, frontal *r* like the Spanish *r*. Example: *rot* (roht) red.
r	R	*R* at the end of a word (and in some other environments) is pronounced something like the final *r* in the British pronunciation of words like *mother* and *father* (mothah, fathah). Another similar sound is the Boston *r* as in *there* (''theyah''). Example: *Vater* (FAH-teR) father.
s	z	*S* can be pronounced in two ways. It is pronounced like *z* in *zoo* before and between vowels. Example: *sie* (zee) she. It is usually pronounced *sh* before *p* and *t*. Examples: *spät* (shpayt) late; *stehen* (SHTAY-en) to stand.
ß, ss	s	Both pronounced like English *s* in *soft*. Examples: *Maße* (MAHS-eh) measure; *Masse* (MAS-eh) mass. ß is a ligature of the letters *s* and *z*.
sch	sh	Pronounced like English *sh* in *shoot*. Example: *schon* (shohn) already.
tz	ts	Prounounced like English *ts* in *hats*. Example: *Platz* (plats) place, square.
v	f	Pronounced like English *f* in *father*. Example: *Vater* (FAH-teR) father.
w	v	Pronounced like English *v* in *vine*. Example: *Wasser* (VAS-eR) water.
z	ts	Pronounced like English *ts* in *hats*. Examples: *geizig* (GEI-tsiç) greedy, stingy; *Kreuz* (kroyts) cross.

HOW ENGLISH AND GERMAN ARE SIMILAR

English is a Germanic language, so you will find many similarities between English and German. Here are a few examples.

(bal)
der Ball
ball

NOUNS		ADJECTIVES		VERBS	
Arm	arm	**blau**	blue	**backen**	to bake
Ball	ball	**blind**	blind	**beginnen**	to begin
Bier	beer	**frei**	free	**binden**	to bind
Buch	book	**gut**	good	**bringen**	to bring
Freund	friend	**hart**	hard	**fallen**	to fall
Garten	garden	**kalt**	cold	**finden**	to find
Land	land	**lang**	long	**füllen**	to fill
Preis	price	**leicht**	light	**helfen**	to help
Schiff	ship	**rot**	red	**rollen**	to roll
Vater	father	**warm**	warm	**senden**	to send

(beeR)
das Bier
beer

(shif)
das Schiff
ship

(booch)
das Buch
book

(froynt)
der Freund
friend

(FAH-teR)
der Vater
father

(mohnt)
der Mond
moon

GETTING TO KNOW PEOPLE

(LOY-teh) (KEN-en-lern-en)
Leute kennenlernen

1 *(ein) (ge-SHPRAYÇ) (AN-fang-en)* Ein Gespräch anfangen

Starting a Conversation

Learning to greet people and to start a conversation is very important. Read over the following dialogue several times, pronouncing each line carefully. The dialogue contains basic words and expressions that you will find useful.

Mark and Mary Smith, their daughter Anne, and their son John have just arrived at Munich airport and are looking for their luggage. Mark approaches an airline employee:

MARK	*(GOO-ten) (tahk)* **Guten Tag.**	Hello.
CLERK	*(voh-MIT) (kan) (iç)* **Guten Tag. Womit kann ich** *(EEN-en) (DEEN-en)* **Ihnen dienen?**	Hello. What can I do for you? (*lit.* With what can I serve you?)
MARK	*(ZOO-cheh) (MEI-neh) (KOF-eR)* **Ich suche meine Koffer.**	I'm looking for my suitcases.
CLERK	*(eeR) (NAH-meh) (BIT-eh)* **Ah; Ihr Name, bitte?**	I see; your name, please?
MARK	*(ist)* **Mein Name ist Mark Smith.**	My name is Mark Smith.
CLERK	*(VO-heR) (KO-men) (zee)* **Woher kommen Sie?**	Where do you come from?

	(KO-meh) (ows) (dayn) (feR-EIN-ik-ten)	
MARK	**Ich komme aus den Vereinigten**	I come from the United States.
	(SHTAH-ten)	
	Staaten.	
	(EER-eh) (FLOOK-num-eR)	
CLERK	**Ihre Flugnummer?**	Your flight number?
	(DREI-hun-deRt-drei)	
MARK	**Dreihundertdrei aus New York.**	303 from New York.
	(EIN-en) (mo-MENT)	
CLERK	**Einen Moment, bitte.**	One moment, please.

As the clerk looks through some papers on his desk, Hans, a German business friend, runs into Mark.

	(vee) (gayts)	
HANS	**Tag, Mark. Wie geht's?**	Hi, Mark. How are you?
	(meeR) (unt) (deeR)	
MARK	**Hans! Mir geht's gut. Und dir?**	Hans! I'm O.K. And you?
	(zayR) (bist) (doo) (heeR) (owf)	
HANS	**Sehr gut. Bist du hier auf**	Very good. Are you here on a vacation?
	(FAYR-i-en)	
	Ferien?	
	(yah) (lăs) (miç) (fa-MEE-li-e)	
MARK	**Ja. Laß mich dir meine Familie**	Yes. Let me introduce my family to you. My
	(FOHR-stel-en) (frow)	
	vorstellen. Meine Frau Mary, meine	wife Mary, my daughter Anne, and my son John.
	(TOCH-teR) (zohn)	
	Tochter Anne und mein Sohn John.	
	(net) (KEN-en-tsoo-ler-nen)	
HANS	**Nett, Sie kennenzulernen.**	Nice to meet you.
CLERK	**Entschuldigen Sie, mein Herr,**	Excuse me, sir, the suitcases are coming
	(dee) (mit) (dayR)	
	die Koffer kommen mit der	with the next airplane.
	(NAYÇ-sten) (mah-SHEE-neh)	
	nächsten Maschine.	
	(tsum) (TOI-fel)	
MARK	**Zum Teufel!**	Heck! (*lit.* To the devil!)
	(ge-DULT)	
HANS	**Geduld, Mark!**	Patience, Mark!
	(das) (zoh) (ET-vas) (pas-EERT)	
MARK	**Daß so etwas passiert!**	That something like that happens.
	(DAN-keh)	
(to the clerk)	**Danke.**	Thanks.
CLERK	**Bitte.**	You're welcome.
	(owf) (VEE-deR-zay-en)	
MARK (to Hans)	**Auf Wiedersehen!**	So long.

(*AL-eh*)

HANS **Auf Wiedersehen, alle.** See you, all.

ALL **Auf Wiedersehen.** See you.

Now here is your first exercise, based on the dialogue you have just studied. Try to fill in the missing words without looking at the dialogue. To refresh your memory, the first letter of each missing word is given.

„Guten Tag."

„G____________ T____________. Womit kann ich Ihnen dienen?"

„Ich suche meine K________________."

„Ah. Ihr N________________ bitte?"

„M____________ N____________ ist Mark Smith."

„Woher k________________ Sie?"

„Ich komme aus den V________________ Staaten."

„Ihre F________________?"

„Dreihundertdrei."

„Einen M________________, b________________."

ANSWERS

Dialogue. Guten Tag Koffer Name Mein Name kommen Vereinigten Flugnummer Moment, bitte

Here is another exercise, which you may find more difficult. Try to rearrange the following groups of words to form sentences that are in the dialogue. Don't be discouraged if you can't make the words fit together properly. You're just beginning to learn a new language. Soon an exercise like this will be easy.

1. dir, meine, vorstellen, mich, laß, Familie
2. kommen, die, mit, Koffer, Maschine, nächsten, der
3. alle, Wiedersehen, auf

(LOY-teh) *(unt)* *(DING-eh)*

LEUTE UND DINGE

People and Things

One of the first things you will need to know in German is how to name people and things. This, of course, is the function of the noun. German nouns are divided into three genders. The gender of a word can be indicated by the definite article. The German singular noun is preceded by the definite article *der* if it is masculine, by *die* if it is feminine, or by *das* if it is neuter. *Die* is used with all plural nouns. In English, as you know, *the* performs all these functions. In German, nouns are always capitalized, no matter where they occur in the sentence. In English the plural is formed by adding an -s (dog, dogs, right?). In German there are a variety of plural endings. And some words add an umlaut in the plural.

As you learn each new noun, it is important that you

1. Always learn the definite article.
2. Always learn the plural.

Singular and Plural

SINGULAR	PLURAL
(dayR) (YUN-geh) **der Junge** the boy	*(dee) (YUN-gen)* **die Jungen** the boys
(dee) (KAT-seh) **die Katze** the cat	*(KAT-sen)* **die Katzen** the cats

ANSWERS

1. Laß mich dir meine Familie vorstellen.
2. Die Koffer kommen mit der nächsten Maschine.
3. Auf Wiedersehen, alle.

SINGULAR

(foos)
der Fuß
the foot

(BLOO-meh)
die Blume
the flower

(hows)
das Haus
the house

(AP-fel)
der Apfel
the apple

(OW-toh)
das Auto
the car

(MUT-eR)
die Mutter
the mother

(AR-beits-heft)
das Arbeitsheft
the workbook

PLURAL

(FǖÜ-seh)
die Füße
the feet

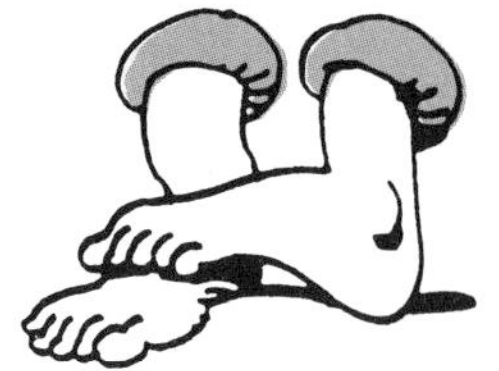

(BLOO-men)
die Blumen
the flowers

(HOY-zeR)
die Häuser
the houses

(EP-fel)
die Äpfel
the apples

(OW-tohs)
die Autos
the cars

(MÜT-eR)
die Mütter
the mothers

(AR-beits-hef-teh)
die Arbeitshefte
the workbooks

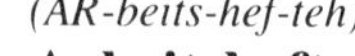

SINGULAR

(KOO-gel-shrei-beR)
der Kugelschreiber
the ballpoint pen

PLURAL

die Kugelschreiber
the ballpoint pens

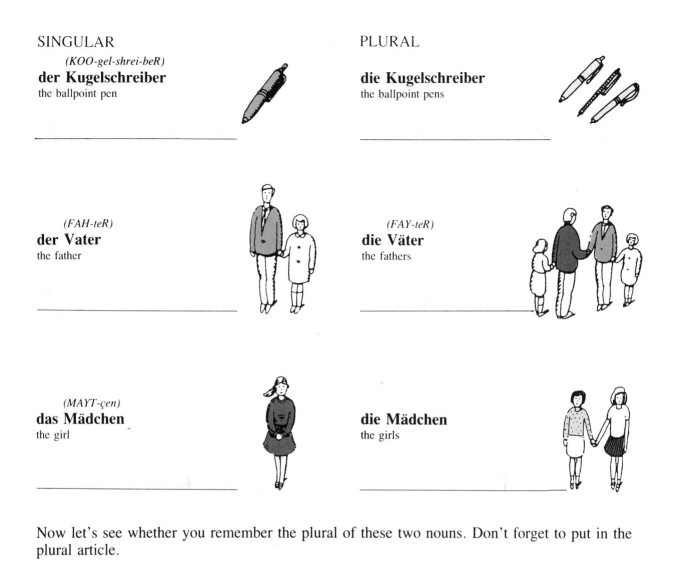

(FAH-teR)
der Vater
the father

(FAY-teR)
die Väter
the fathers

(MAYT-çen)
das Mädchen
the girl

die Mädchen
the girls

Now let's see whether you remember the plural of these two nouns. Don't forget to put in the plural article.

die Mutter
the mother

the mothers

der Junge
the boy

the boys

ANSWERS

die Mütter   die Jungen

(ein) *(EIN-eh)* *(ein)*
Ein, eine, ein

"A" and "An"

Now we come to the indefinite articles (in English *a* as in "a book," or *an* as in "an apple"). Again, there are three genders in German—*ein* is used with a masculine noun, *eine* with a feminine noun, and *ein* with a neuter noun. (Notice that the indefinite article can be the same for masculine and neuter nouns.)

Here are two feminine nouns:

(EIN-eh)
eine Mutter
a mother

(EIN-eh) (FROYN-din)
eine Freundin
a girlfriend

Here are two neuter nouns:

(ein)
ein Auto
an automobile

(ein)
ein Mädchen
a girl

Here are six masculine nouns:

(ein) (ON-kel)
ein Onkel
an uncle

(ein) (froynt)
ein Freund
a friend

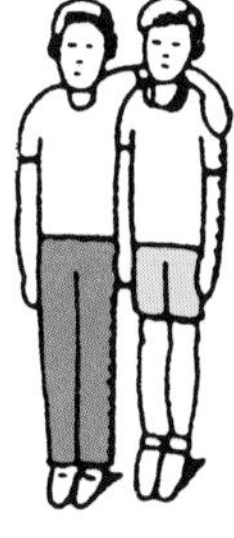

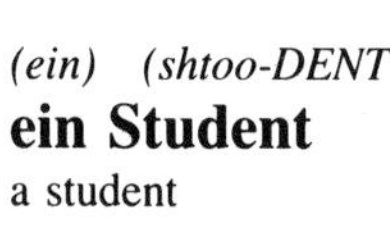

(ein) (shtoo-DENT)
ein Student
a student

(ein) (bowm)
ein Baum
a tree

ein Junge
a boy

ein Vater
a father

Got it? Now test yourself by putting the appropriate indefinite article in front of the following nouns:

1. ________________ Katze | 2. ________________ Baum
3. ________________ Freundin | 4. ________________ Freund
5. ________________ Mädchen | 6. ________________ Junge
7. ________________ Tante *(TAN-teh)* aunt | 8. ________________ Onkel
9. ________________ (masculine) Spiegel *(SHPEE-gel)* mirror | 10. ________________ Apfel

Here is another exercise. It may be difficult, but give it a try. Identify each picture by writing in the German word for it along with the proper indefinite article.

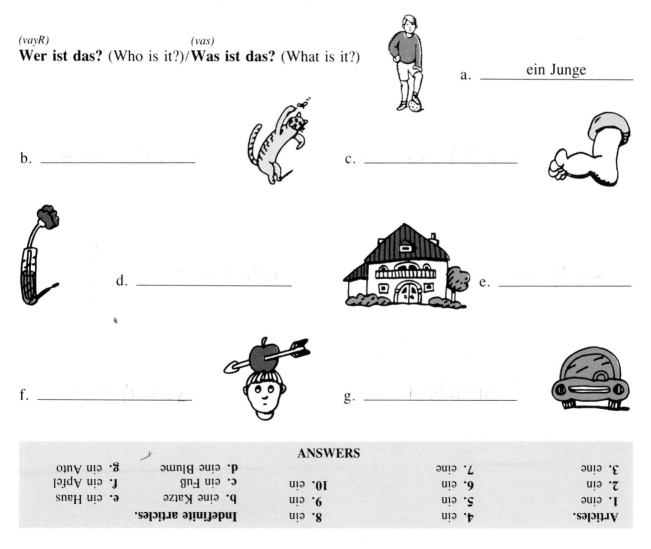

(vayR) **Wer ist das?** (Who is it?)/*(vas)* **Was ist das?** (What is it?)

a. ein Junge

b. ________________

c. ________________

d. ________________

e. ________________

f. ________________

g. ________________

ANSWERS

Articles. **1.** eine **2.** ein **3.** eine **4.** ein **5.** ein **6.** ein **7.** eine **8.** ein **9.** ein **10.** ein

Indefinite articles. **b.** eine Katze **c.** ein Fuß **d.** eine Blume **e.** ein Haus **f.** ein Apfel **g.** ein Auto

h. ______________ i. ______________

j. ______________ k. ______________

l. ______________

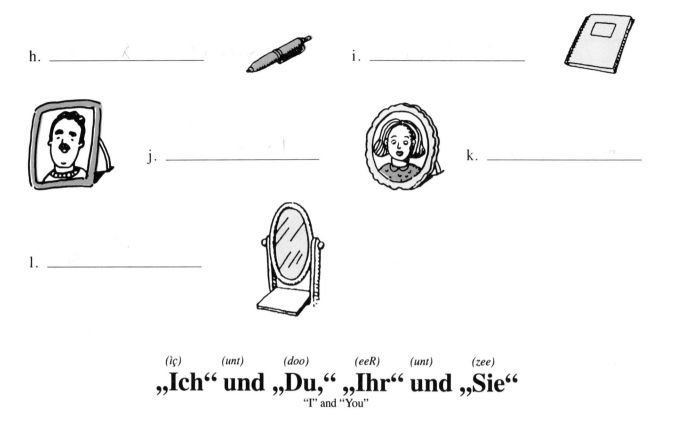

(iç) (unt) (doo) (eeR) (unt) (zee)

„Ich“ und „Du,“ „Ihr“ und „Sie“

“I” and “You”

It is very important to know how to say “I” and “you” in your new language.

“I” IS SIMPLY | **ICH** |

“YOU” IS GIVEN IN TWO WAYS

(a casual or familiar form and a polite form)

CASUAL		
DU *(doo)*	when addressing a family member or a friend	**Singular**
IHR *(eeR)*	when addressing family members or friends	**Plural**
POLITE		
SIE *(zee)*	when addressing strangers, superiors, etc.	**Singular** and **Plural**

In English, “I” is always capitalized. In German, *ich, du,* and *ihr* are not capitalized except at the start of a sentence, while *Sie* is always capitalized.

ANSWERS

h. ein Kugelschreiber **i.** ein Arbeitsheft **j.** ein Onkel **k.** eine Tante **l.** ein Spiegel *(fon)* *(feR-VAN-ten)* *(RAY-den)*

VON VERWANDTEN REDEN

Talking About Relatives

This is Hans' family tree. Note the word for each of the relatives.

(HIL-deh)
Hilde
(GROHS-mut-eR)
die **Großmutter**
grandmother

(LUT-viç)
Ludwig
(GROHS-fah-teR)
der **Großvater**
grandfather

(ZEEK-freet)
Siegfried
(FAH-teR)
der **Vater**
father

(BAYR-ta)
Berta
(MUT-eR)
die **Mutter**
mother

(klows)
Klaus
(ON-kel)
der **Onkel**
uncle

(LOT-eh)
Lotte
(TAN-teh)
die **Tante**
aunt

(hans)
Hans
(zohn)
der **Sohn**
son
(BROO-deR)
der **Bruder**
brother

(GEE-ze-la)
Gisela
(TOCH-teR)
die **Tochter**
daughter
(SHVES-teR)
die **Schwester**
sister

(PAY-teR)
Peter
(FET-eR)
der **Vetter**
or
(koo-ZAN)
der **Cousin**
cousin

(mah-REE)
Marie
(koo-ZEEN-eh)
die **Kusine**
cousin

Hans

Look carefully at the family tree and then try to answer the following questions about the relationships. Don't forget to use the correct form of the article: *der*, *die*, or *das*.

1. Peter ist der Vetter von Hans.
   of
2. Lotte ist __________ von Peter.
3. Gisela ist __________ von Hans.
4. Lotte ist __________ von Hans.
5. Hans ist __________ von Gisela.
6. Marie ist __________ von Hans.
7. Hans ist __________ von Siegfried.
8. Berta ist __________ von Marie.
9. Ludwig ist __________ von Gisela.
10. Hilde ist __________ von Peter.

Now here is an exercise that should be fun. Write in the plurals of the following words and find them in the word-search puzzle.

Haus __________

Arbeitsheft __________

Apfel __________

Kugelschreiber __________

Mutter __________

Mädchen __________

Vater __________

```
H Ä U S E R D T M Ä D C H E N P W E D R
P O I T O A R B E I T S H E F T E N V X
M Ü T T E R Q S T I Ä P F E L O J H G F
P I G F H K U G E L S C H R E I B E R D
W Y D V Ä T E R L I A U T O M O B I L E
```

ANSWERS

Relationships.
2. die Mutter **3.** die Schwester **4.** die Tante **5.** der Bruder **6.** die Kusine **7.** der Sohn **8.** die Tante **9.** der Großvater **10.** die Großmutter

Plurals.
Häuser Arbeitshefte Äpfel Kugelschreiber Mütter Mädchen Väter

Let's try another quick exercise. Fill in the blanks with German words so that the sentences make sense: Here are the words you can choose from: *Großmutter, Onkel, Bruder, Mutter, Tochter, Kusine, Sohn, Vetter.*

1. I am the son of my ____________.
2. My father has an only ____________.
3. The brother of my father is my ________.
4. The son of my mother is my __________.
5. The mother of my father is my ________.
6. My sister is our mother's __________.
7. The son of my uncle is my __________
8. The daughter of my aunt is my ________.

It's time to return to the Smiths, just beginning their trip to Germany. Test your readiness too by trying to understand the following short paragraph. Read the selection and then answer the questions that follow.

Herr Mark Smith wohnt in Chicago.

(ayR) (ZEI-neh) (fa-MEEL-i-eh) (zint) (yetst) (DOYTSH-lant)
Er und seine Familie sind jetzt in Deutschland.
he family

(zooçt)
Er sucht seine Koffer. Er, seine Frau,
looks for his

seine Tochter und sein Sohn sind auf Ferien.

(zahkt) (tsoo)
Er sagt zu Hans: „Laß mich dir meine
says to

Familie vorstellen."

TRUE or FALSE Please mark the following statements with T or F.

1. Herr Smith wohnt in Chicago. __________
2. Er und seine Kusine sind auf Ferien. __________
3. Er ist jetzt in Deutschland. __________
4. Er sagt zu Hans: „Laß mich dir meine Familie vorstellen." __________
5. Herr Smith sucht sein Auto. __________
6. Herr Smith und seine Familie sind auf Ferien. __________

ANSWERS

Relatives.
1. Mutter **2.** Sohn (could also be: Onkel, Bruder, Tochter, Kusine, Vetter) **3.** Onkel **4.** Bruder
5. Großmutter **6.** Tochter **7.** Vetter **8.** Kusine

True or false. 1. T **2.** F **3.** T **4.** T **5.** F **6.** T

Here are the German words for parts of a house. Study them and say them aloud.

(hows)
EIN HAUS
a house

(VASH-be-ken)
das Waschbecken
sink

(KÜL-shrank)
der Kühlschrank
refrigerator

(toy-LE-teh)
die Toilette
toilet

(KÜ-çeh)
die Küche
kitchen

(hayrt)
der Herd
stove

(TREP-eh)
die Treppe
stairway

(BAH-deh-van-eh)
die Badewanne
bathtub

(BAH-deh-tsim-eR)
das Badezimmer
bathroom

(VOHN-tsim-eR)
das Wohnzimmer
living room

(VANT-shrank)
der Wandschrank
closet

(SHLAHF-tsim-eR)
das Schlafzimmer
bedroom

(ZOH-fa)
das Sofa
sofa

(bet)
das Bett
bed

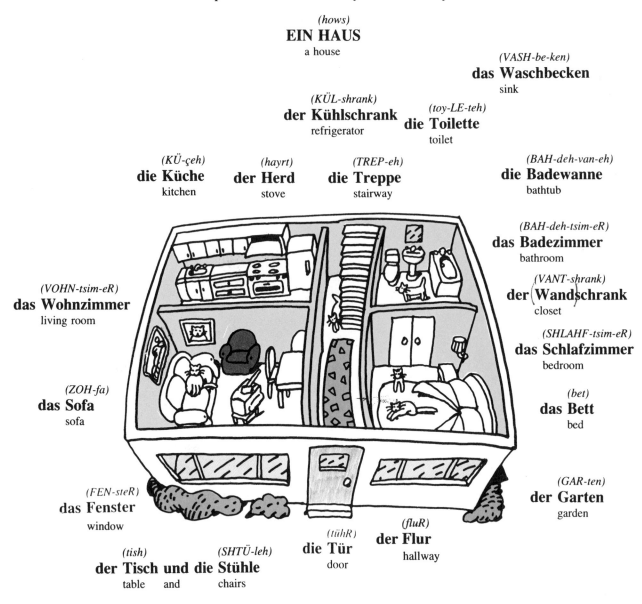

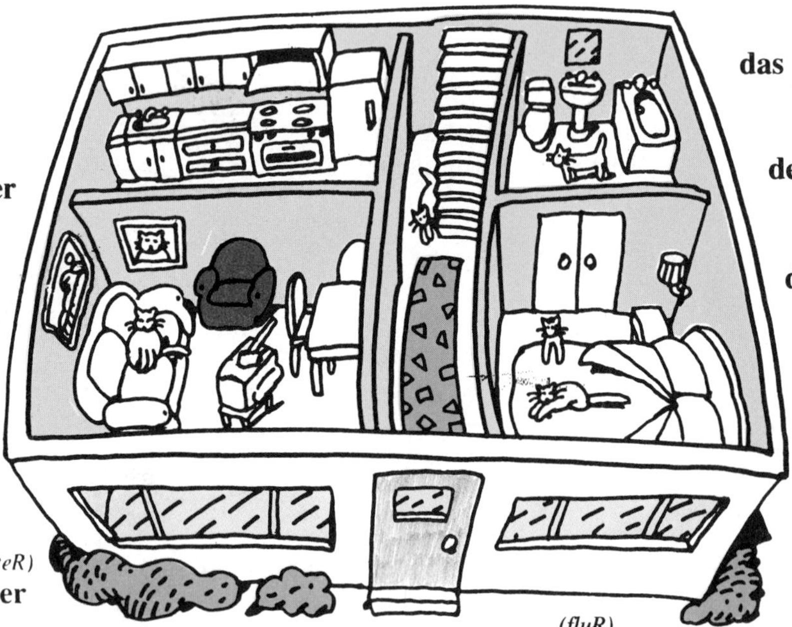

(FEN-steR)
das Fenster
window

(GAR-ten)
der Garten
garden

(tish) *(SHTÜ-leh)*
der Tisch und die Stühle
table and chairs

(tühR)
die Tür
door

(fluR)
der Flur
hallway

ARRIVAL

(AN-kunft)
Ankunft

2 *(UN-teR-kunft) (FIN-den)* Unterkunft finden

Finding a Place to Spend the Night

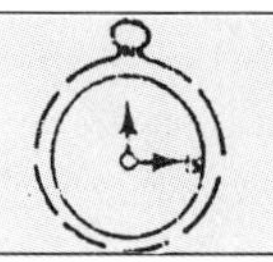

You'll probably book your hotel room from home—at least for your first night in Germany. But whether you have a reservation or not, you'll want to know some basic words that describe the services and facilities you expect to find at your hotel. Learn these words first, and notice how they are used in the dialogue you will read later.

(hoh-TEL)
das Hotel
hotel

(TSIM-eR)
das Zimmer
room

(preis)
der Preis
price

(BAH-deh-tsim-eR)
das Badezimmer
bathroom

(re-zer-VEER-ung)
die Reservierung
reservation

(re-zer-VEE-ren)
reservieren
to reserve

(tührR)
die Tür
door

(AN-ge-shtel-teh)
die Angestellte
clerk

(TSIM-eR-mayt-çen)
das Zimmermädchen
maid

(pas)
der Paß
passport

(FEN-steR)
das Fenster
window

(SHTUN-deh)
die Stunde
hour

Singular and Plural

We already learned quite a bit about forming the plural in German. Here are a few more forms . . . and then an easy quiz.

SINGULAR	PLURAL
der Freund	die Freunde
die Freundin	die Freundinnen
der Paß	die Pässe
der Spiegel	die Spiegel
die Großmutter	die Großmütter
der Großvater	die Großväter
der Sohn	die Söhne
die Tochter	die Töchter
der Bruder	die Brüder
die Schwester	die Schwestern
der Vetter	die Vettern
die Kusine	die Kusinen
das Hotel	die Hotels
das Zimmer	die Zimmer
der Baum	die Bäume

Now let's see whether you remember:

SINGULAR		PLURAL
eine	__________	*(tsvei)* zwei ____________________ two
ein	__________	zwei ____________________
ein	__________	zwei ____________________
eine	__________	zwei ____________________
ein	__________	zwei ____________________
ein	__________	zwei ____________________

ANSWERS

Katze, Katzen
Spiegel, Spiegel

Junge, Jungen
Blume, Blumen

Zimmer, Zimmer
Hotel, Hotels

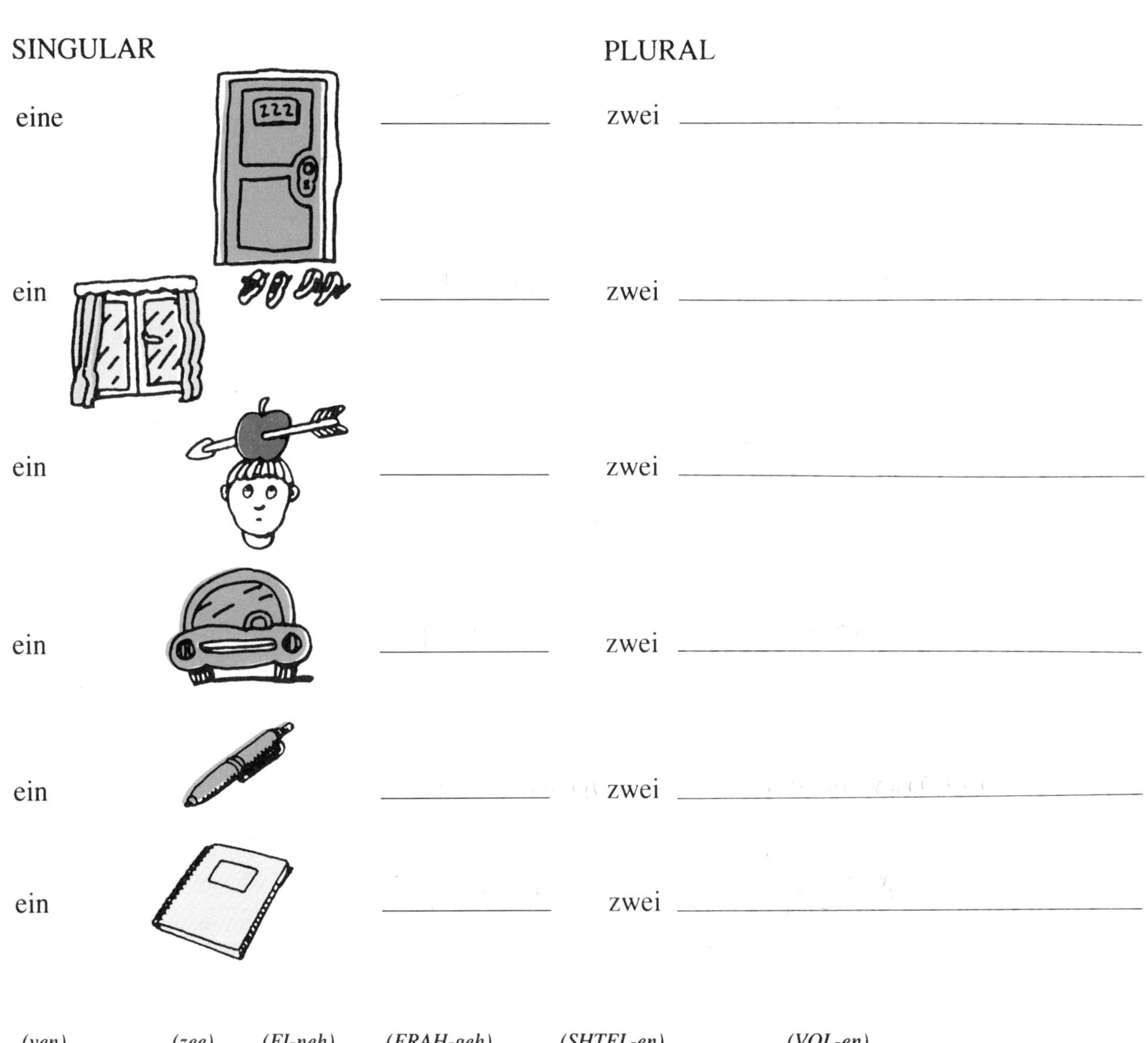

(ven) (zee) (EI-neh) (FRAH-geh) (SHTEL-en) (VOL-en)

WENN SIE EINE FRAGE STELLEN WOLLEN . . .

If You Want to Ask a Question . . .

When you're traveling, you'll need to ask a lot of questions. It's very important to learn the following words so you can form questions in German.

(vas) was	what	*(vee)* wie	how
(vayR) wer	who	*(vee-FEEL)* wieviel	how much

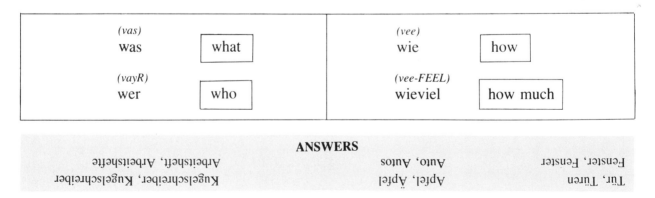

ANSWERS

Tür, Türen
Fenster, Fenster
Apfel, Äpfel
Auto, Autos
Kugelschreiber, Kugelschreiber
Arbeitsheft, Arbeitshefte

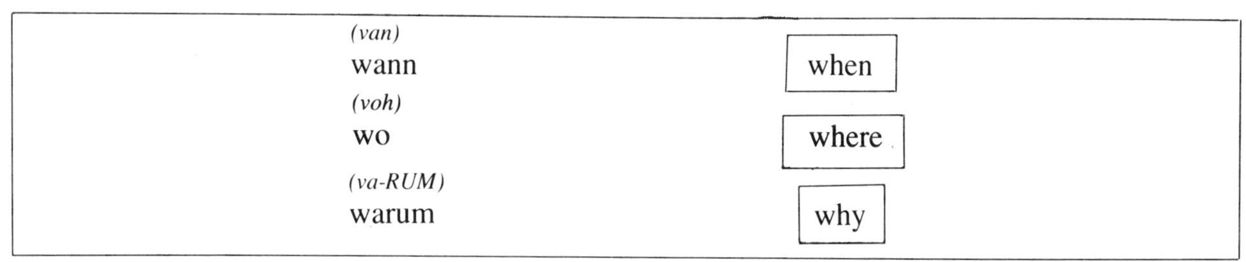

(van) wann	when
(voh) wo	where
(va-RUM) warum	why

(vee-FEEL) (gelt)
Wieviel Geld?
how much money

(broht)
Wieviel Brot?
how much bread

In the plural we add an -e to *wieviel.*

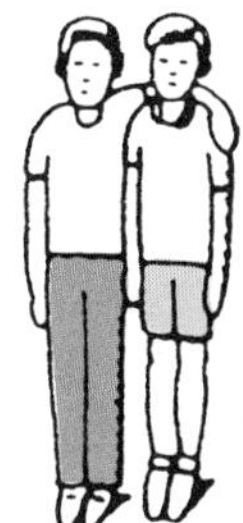

(vee-FEE-leh)
Wieviele Jungen?

Wieviele Mädchen?

To form a question, you simply reverse the word order:

(ist)
Der Junge ißt Brot.
eats

Ißt der Junge Brot?

In the question, the verb comes first, followed by the subject.

Now try to match up each question with its answer.

1. Was ißt Mary?
2. Wann kommen die Koffer?
3. Wo sind Mark und Marie?
4. Wer ist hier?
5. *(VET-eR)* Wie ist das Wetter? (weather)
6. *(KOST-et) (das)* Wieviel kostet das? (costs that)
7. Ißt das Mädchen jetzt?

A. *(zee)* Sie sind in Deutschland. (they)
B. Mary ißt Brot.
C. Hans ist hier.
D. Das kostet zwei Mark.
E. *(MOR-gen)* Die Koffer kommen morgen. (tomorrow)
F. Ja, das Mädchen ißt.
G. *(goot)* Das Wetter ist gut. (good)

ANSWERS

1. B **2.** E **3.** A **4.** C **5.** G **6.** D **7.** F

In the following dialogue you will learn some words and expressions that might come in handy when looking for a room. Always read each dialogue line carefully and out loud.

MARK (to hotel employee) **Entschuldigen Sie, bitte. Ich habe eine Reservierung** *(re-zer-VEER-ung)* **für zwei Zimmer für heute nacht. Ich heiße Mark Smith.**

Excuse me, please. I have a reservation for two rooms for tonight. My name is Mark Smith.

ANGESTELLTER **Guten Morgen, Herr Smith. Ja, ich habe Ihre Reservierung für zwei Zimmer mit Bad** *(baht)***. Aber wir stehen vor einem Problem** *(pro-BLAYM)***.**

Good morning, Mr. Smith. Yes, I do have your reservation for two rooms with bath. But we are faced with a problem.

MARK **Was ist los?**

What's the matter?

ANGESTELLTER **Die Dusche** *(DU-sheh)* **in einem der Zimmer ist kaputt.**

The shower in one of the rooms is broken.

MARK **Das macht nichts. Wir können die Wanne** *(VAN-eh)* **benutzen.**

That doesn't matter. We can use the bathtub.

ANGESTELLTER **Noch eine Schwierigkeit** *(SHVEE-riç-keit)***, Herr Smith. In einem der Zimmer kann man das Fenster nicht öffnen** *(ÖF-nen)***.**

(There's) another difficulty, Mr. Smith. In one of the rooms the window cannot be opened.

MARK (to his wife Mary) **Was sollen wir tun? Zimmer sind unmöglich zu bekommen. Die Stadt ist von** *(tu-RI-sten)* *(ü-beR-SHVEMT)* **Touristen überschwemmt.**

What are we going to do? It's impossible to get any rooms. The city is flooded with tourists.

MARY *(dah)* **Bleiben wir da. Ich bin viel zu** *(MÜ-deh)* **müde, um jetzt auf** *(TSIM-er-zoo-cheh)* **Zimmersuche zu gehen.**

Let's stay here. I am much too tired to go room-hunting now.

ANGESTELLTER **Sehr gut. Das kommt auf** *(TSVEI-hun-deRt)* **200 Mark pro Tag.**

Very good. That amounts to 200 marks per day.

MARK **Ist das** *(in-kloo-ZEE-veh)* **inklusive Frühstück?**

Does this include breakfast?

ANGESTELLTER *(ya-VOHL)* **Jawohl.**

Yes, sir.

MARK **Also gut. Hier sind unsere** *(REI-zeh-pes-eh)* **Reisepässe.**

Well then. Here are our passports.

ANGESTELLTER **Wollen Sie bitte dieses** *(for-mu-LAHR)* **Formular ausfüllen? Hier sind die Schlüssel. Die Zimmer sind im dritten** *(shtok)* **Stock.**

Would you please fill out this form? Here are the keys. The rooms are on the fourth floor.*

MARK **Haben Sie einen** *(OWF-tsook)* **Aufzug?**

Is there an elevator?

ANGESTELLTER *(na-TÜR-liç)* **Natürlich. Dort drüben.**

Of course. Over there.

MARK **Danke schön.**

Thank you.

ANGESTELLTER **Bitte sehr. Ich hoffe, unsere Stadt gefällt Ihnen.**

You're welcome. I hope you enjoy our city.

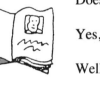

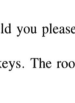

*Note that Germans designate floors in a building differently than Americans. In Germany, the street-level floor is called *das* *(ERT-ge-shos)* *Erdgeschoß*, not the first floor. The German first floor is above *das Erdgeschoß* and is the same as the American second floor. Thus, when the German hotel clerk in our dialogue speaks of the third floor *(dritten Stock)*, he is referring to what is known as the fourth floor in America.

Did you understand the German dialogue? Try to fill in the missing words from memory:

1. Ich habe eine ______________________ für zwei Zimmer.
2. Wir stehen vor einem ______________________.

3. Wir können die Wanne ______________________.
4. Im anderen Zimmer kann man das ______________________ nicht öffnen.
5. Die Stadt ist von ______________________ überschwemmt.
6. Ist das inklusive ______________________?
7. Wollen Sie bitte dieses ______________________ ausfüllen?
8. Die Zimmer sind im dritten ______________________.
9. Der ______________________ ist dort drüben.

Can you make sentences out of these scrambled words?

1. kaputt, ist, Dusche, die 2. sollen, was, wir, machen 3. Schlüssel, hier, die, sind

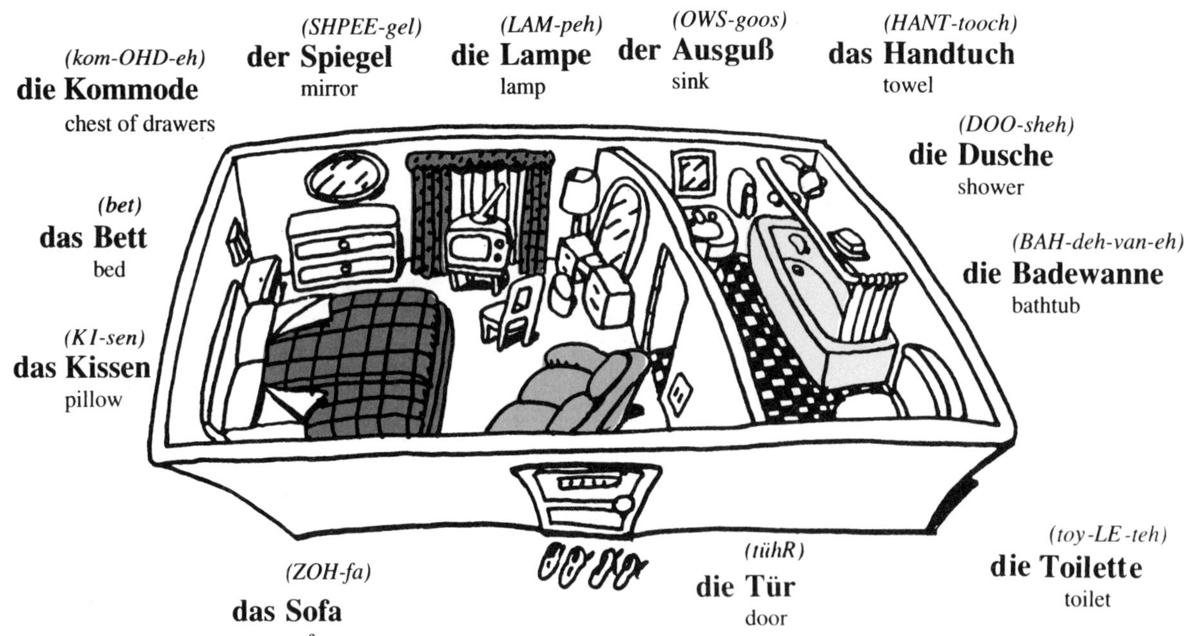

ANSWERS

Dialogue. 1. Reservierung **2.** Problem **3.** benutzen **4.** Fenster **5.** Touristen **6.** Frühstück **7.** Formular **8.** Stock **9.** Aufzug

Scrambled Words. 1. Die Dusche ist kaputt. **2.** Was sollen wir machen? **3.** Hier sind die Schlüssel.

(proh-NOH-men) (unt) (VAYR-ben)

Pronomen und Verben

Pronouns and Verbs

You've already learned how to say "I" and "you" in German. Now it's time to move on to other pronouns—the words for "he," "she," "it," "we," and "they."

PRONOUNS			
SINGULAR		PLURAL	
ich	I	*(veeR)* **wir**	we
(doo) **du**	you (familiar)	*(eeR)* **ihr**	you (familiar)
Sie	you (polite)	**Sie**	you (polite)
(ayR) **er**	he	**sie**	they
sie	she		
es	it		

It's pretty difficult to get along without verbs. Verbs are words that often express action—like talking, singing, or arriving (in Germany!). You can't get too far without first learning the different forms a verb can take. Now let's conjugate the verb *sagen* *(ZAH-gen)* (to say). The *-en* denotes the infinitive. This is the verb form that you find listed in the dictionary.

SAGEN to say			
SINGULAR			
1st person:	**ich**	*(ZAH-geh)* **sag*e***	I say I am saying I do say
2nd person: (familiar form)	**du**	*(zahkst)* **sag*st***	you say you are saying you do say
3rd person:	**er** **sie** **es**	*(zahkt)* **sag*t***	he/she/it says he/she/it is saying he/she/it does say

PLURAL			
1st person:	**wir**	**sag*en***	we say we are saying we do say
2nd person: (familiar form)	**ihr**	**sag*t***	you say you are saying you do say
3rd person:	**sie**	**sag*en***	they say they are saying they say

POLITE FORM: Singular and Plural			
2nd person:	**Sie**	**sag*en***	you say you are saying you do say

VERB ENDINGS Present Tense					
ich	(verb) ________	**-e**	**wir**	________	**-en**
du	________	**-st**	**ihr**	________	**-t**
er **sie** **es**	________	**-t**	**sie**	________	**-en**
Sie	________	**-en**			

(ET-vas)

Der Junge sagt etwas.
The boy says something.

Die Jungen sagen etwas.
The boys say something.

Now try to put on the right endings.

(ZING-en)
singen
to sing

ich sing ________________

du sing ________________

er sing ________________

wir sing ________________

ihr sing ________________

sie sing ________________

Sie sing ________________

ANSWERS

singen. ich singe, du singst, er singt, wir singen, ihr singt, sie singen, Sie singen

(KOM-en)
kommen
to come

ich komm ______________ wir komm ______________

du komm ______________ ihr komm ______________

er komm ______________ sie komm ______________

Sie komm ______________

Now put on the right endings according to each sentence.

Das Mädchen sag________ etwas.

Die Onkel komm________ morgen.

Mary sing________ sehr gut.

Du komm________ und ich sing________.

Wir sing________ und ihr sing________.

To put any action in the negative just put *nicht* after the verb:

Affirmative
Ich singe. I sing.
Wir singen. We sing.

Negative
Ich komme nicht. I don't come.
Sie kommen nicht. They don't come.

Here is an easy review—you should be able to do it quickly. Fill in vertically the German equivalent of the words listed on the left.

1. to say
2. in
3. number
4. to give
5. he
6. name

1.	2.	3.	4.	5.	6.
S	I	N	G	E	N
☐	☐	☐	☐	☐	☐
☐		☐	☐		☐
☐		☐	☐		☐
☐		☐	☐		
		☐			

ANSWERS

kommen. ich komme, du kommst, er kommt, wir kommen, ihr kommt, sie kommen, Sie kommen
Endings. sagt kommen singt kommst, singe singen, singt
Puzzle. **1.** sagen **2.** in **3.** Nummer **4.** geben **5.** er **6.** Name

Now try to put the correct article form in front of these plural nouns.

7. ________ Fenster	8. ________ Türen	9. ________ Hotels
10. ________ Zimmer	11. ________ Freundinnen	12. ________ Freunde
13. ________ Spiegel	14. ________ Onkel	15. ________ Pässe
16. ________ Badezimmer.		

Are you surprised by the answers?

The following brief passage lets you test your comprehension of what you have learned in this unit about requesting a room in a hotel.

(KEI-neh) (SHÖ-nen)
Herr Jones hat keine Reservierung im Hotel. Sie haben keine schönen Zimmer mehr. Frau
(MÜ-deh) no nice
Jones sagt dem Angestellten: „Wir sind sehr müde." Der Angestellte sagt: „Es tut mir leid.
(nooR) tired
Ich habe nur ein kleines Zimmer im dritten Stock. Das Zimmer hat kein Bad und
only
kostet 60 Mark."

Did you understand the passage? Try answering the following multiple-choice questions. Circle the correct answer.

1. Was hat Herr Jones nicht?
   a. Brot b. einen Schlüssel c. eine Reservierung.
2. Das Zimmer im dritten Stock ist
   a. klein b. groß c. schön
3. Herr Jones spricht mit
   a. Paul b. Peter c. dem Angestellten
4. Frau Jones sagt, wir sind sehr
   a. Deutsche b. müde c. Engländer
5. Der Angestellte sagt:
   a. „Ich habe ein schönes Zimmer." b. „Wir sind arm." c. „Es tut mir leid."
6. Das Zimmer kostet
   a. 70 Mark b. 60 Mark c. 50 Mark

ANSWERS

Articles.
7. die **8.** die **9.** die **10.** die **11.** die **12.** die **13.** die **14.** die **15.** die **16.** die

Reading.
1. c **2.** a **3.** c **4.** b **5.** c **6.** b

SEEING THE SIGHTS

(ZAY-ens-vür-diç-kei-ten) *(be-ZIÇ-ti-gen)*
Sehenswürdigkeiten besichtigen

3 *(tsu-REÇT-fin-den)* *(tsu)* *(foos)* Zurechtfinden zu Fuß

Finding Your Way on Foot

(vee) *(KOM-eh)* *(iç)* *(tsum)*
Wie komme ich zum . . .?

How Do I Get to . . .?

"How do I get to. . . ?" "Where is the nearest subway?" "Is the museum straight ahead?" You'll be asking directions and getting answers wherever you travel. In the following dialogue John and Anne are trying to find a museum. Acquaint yourself with the words and phrases that will make getting around easier. Don't forget to read each line out loud several times to practice your pronunciation, and act out each part to be certain you understand the new words.

(FRAH-gen) *(dayn)* *(po-lee-TSIST-en)*
ANNE **John, fragen wir den Polizisten**
(man) *(moo-ZAY-um)*
wie man das Museum findet.

John, let's ask the policeman how one finds the museum.

(ent-SHUL-di-gen)
JOHN (to the policeman) **Entschuldigen Sie bitte, können Sie mir sagen, wie ich das Museum finde?**

Excuse me please, can you tell me how to find the museum?

(ge-VIS) *(GAY-en)* *(ge-rah-deh-OWS)*
POLIZIST **Gewiß. Gehen Sie geradeaus**
(tsooR) *(SHIL-leR-shtrah-seh)* *(dan)* *(reçts)*
zur Schillerstraße, dann rechts in die
(HEI-neh)
Heinestraße und dann rechts in die
(MOH-tsaRt) *(feR-KAYRS-am-peln)*
Mozartstraße, wo die Verkehrsampeln sind.

Certainly. Go straight ahead to Schillerstraße, then right into Heinestraße, then right into Mozartstraße, where there are traffic lights.

(SHTRAH-sen-tsü-geh) (nach)
Zwei Straßenzüge nach den Verkehrsampeln finden Sie das Museum.

Two blocks after the traffic lights you'll find the museum.

JOHN **Vielen Dank.**

Thanks a lot.

(zayR)
POLIZIST **Bitte sehr.**

You're very welcome.

(After having followed the directions)

ANNE **Das ist nicht das Museum.**

That isn't the museum.

(POST-amt)
Es ist das Postamt.

It's the post office.

(ge-DULT)
JOHN **Geduld, Anne. Es ist spät.**

Patience, Anne. It's late.

(tsoo-RÜK)
Gehen wir zum Hotel zurück.

Let's go back to the hotel.

Fill in the missing dialogue parts:

1. „Fragen wir den P________________, wie man das M________________ findet."
2. „Entschuldigen Sie, bitte, können Sie mir sagen, wie ich das Museum f________________?"
3. „Gewiß. Geradeaus zur Schillerstraße, dann r________________ in die Heinestraße, dann r________________ in die Mozartstraße. Zwei Straßenzüge nach den V________________ finden Sie das M________________."
4. „Vielen ________________."

(NÜTS-li-çeh) (KLEI-neh) (VÖR-teR)
Nützliche kleine Wörter
Helpful Little Words

in
in

Herr Smith wohnt *in* Amerika.

(ows)
aus
from

Er kommt *aus* A________________________

ANSWERS

Dialogue parts. **1.** Polizisten, Museum **2.** finde **3.** rechts, rechts, Verkehrsampeln, Museum **4.** Dank

Helpful words. Amerika

mit
with

1. Er kommt *mit* der F ________________

(*OH-neh*)
ohne
without

2. Er kommt *ohne* K ________________

(*fühR*)
für
for

3. Wir brauchen das Zimmer *für* eine W ________________

(*fohR*)
vor
in front of

4. Marks Katze ist *vor* dem H ________________

(*HIN-teR*)
hinter
behind

5. Die Katze ist *hinter* dem H ________________

(*links*)
links
left

6. Die Katze ist *links* vom H ________________

rechts
right

7. Die Katze ist *rechts* vom H ________________

(*TSVI-shen*)
zwischen
between

8. Die Katze ist *zwischen* H ________________ #1

und H ________________ #2

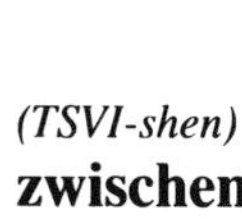

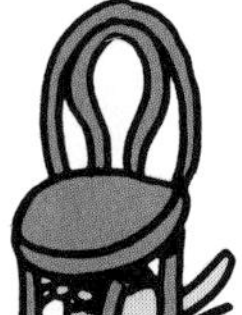

(*UN-teR*)
unter
under

9. Die Katze ist *unter* dem S ________________

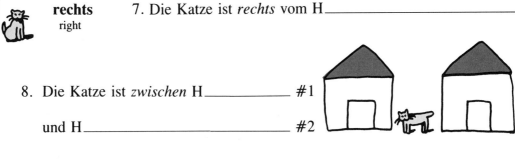

ANSWERS

1. Freundin **2.** Koffer **3.** Woche **4.** Haus **5.** Haus **6.** Haus **7.** Haus **8.** Haus, Haus **9.** Stuhl

(Ü-beR)
über
over

10. Die Katze springt *über* den *M*________________ (*(shprinkt)* springt = jumps; M… = moon)

(noch) (EIN-mal) (VAYR-ben)

Noch einmal Verben

Verbs Again

In the previous unit we conjugated the verb *sagen* (to say). Now you will learn to conjugate verbs that differ a little from *sagen*.

(SHPRE-çen) **SPRECHEN** to speak			
	SINGULAR	PLURAL	SINGULAR AND PLURAL POLITE
1st person:	*(SHPRE-çeh)* **ich spreche**	**wir sprech*en***	**Sie sprech*en***
2nd person:	*(shpriçst)* **du spr*i*ch*st***	*(shpreçt)* **ihr sprech*t***	
3rd person:	**er / sie / es** } *(shpriçt)* **spr*i*ch*t***	**sie sprech*en***	

The endings are the same as in *sagen* or *singen* or *kommen*. But the vowel *e* changes to *i* in the second and third person singular.

(ZAY-en) **SEHEN** to see			
	SINGULAR	PLURAL	SINGULAR AND PLURAL POLITE
1st person:	*(ZAY-eh)* **ich seh*e***	**wir seh*en***	**Sie seh*en***
2nd person:	*(zeest)* **du *sie*h*st***	*(zayt)* **ihr seh*t***	
3rd person:	**er / sie / es** } *(zeet)* **s*ie*h*t***	**sie seh*en***	

Here the *i* in the second person singular becomes an *ie,* which makes it a long *i* (ee). Do you remember how to form the negative? Review the following examples.

Ich spreche nicht. I do not speak. **Er sieht nicht.** He does not see.

ANSWERS

Endings. 10. Mond

Can you add the correct endings to the following verbs? The only two verbs used are *sprechen* and *sehen*.

a. Der Angestellte sprich____________________.

b. Das Mädchen sieh____________________.

c. Ich seh____________________ nicht.

d. Ich sprech____________________.

e. Die Katzen seh____________________ nicht.

f. Die Jungen seh____________________ die Apotheke nicht.

g. Wir sprech____________________.

h. Ihr seh____________________.

i. Du sprich____________________.

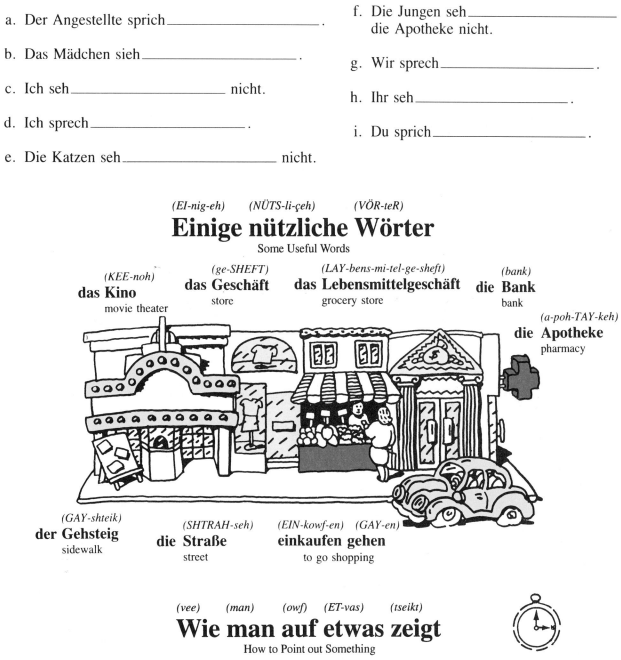

(EI-nig-eh) (NÜTS-li-çeh) (VÖR-teR)

Einige nützliche Wörter

Some Useful Words

(vee) (man) (owf) (ET-vas) (tseikt)

Wie man auf etwas zeigt

How to Point out Something

Words like "this" and "these" are important to know, particularly when you go shopping. The German forms are easy to learn. They vary just a little, depending on whether the noun is masculine, feminine, or neuter and whether it is singular or plural. Nouns of all three genders form the plural in the same way.

ANSWERS

a. spricht **b.** sieht **c.** sehe **d.** spreche **e.** sehen **f.** sehen **g.** sprechen **h.** seht **i.** sprichst

„DIES" UND „DIESE"

"This" and "These"

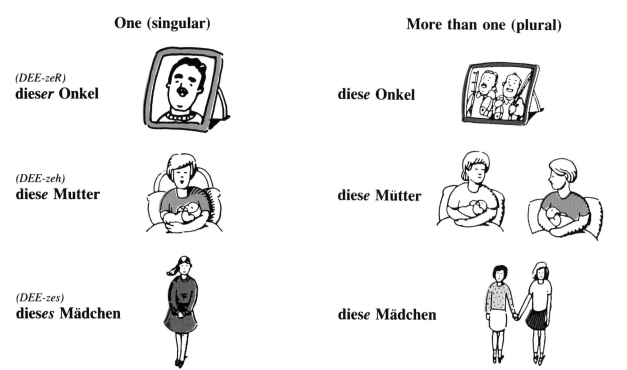

One (singular)		More than one (plural)	
(DEE-zeR) **dies*er* Onkel**		**dies*e* Onkel**	
(DEE-zeh) **dies*e* Mutter**		**dies*e* Mütter**	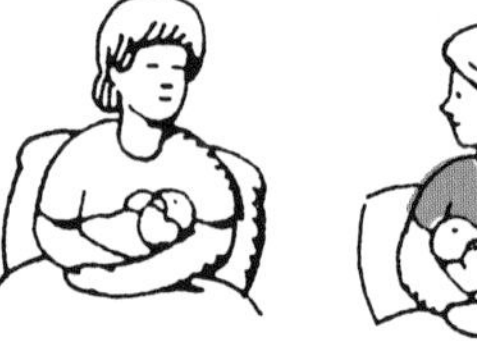
(DEE-zes) **dies*es* Mädchen**		**dies*e* Mädchen**	

Instead of using *dieser, diese, dieses* we can also use the definite article *der, die, das* if we want to point out something:

One (singular)		More than one (plural)	
der Fuß		**die Füße**	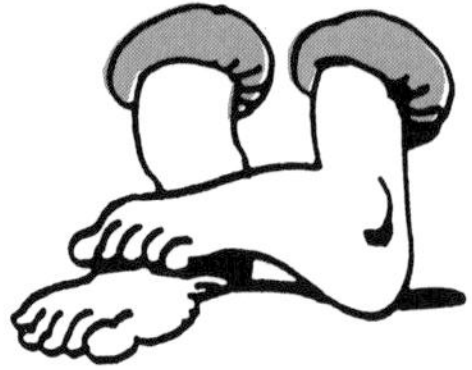
die Katze		**die Katzen**	
das Auto		**die Autos**	

Now let's try the following exercise. Put the appropriate form in each slot:

Here's a chance to test your knowledge of the verbs and prepositions you've learned up to now.

Fill in the blanks with the appropriate endings:

1. Marie sieh_______ Karl nicht.
2. Wir seh_______ das Haus.
3. Ihr seh_______ Marys* Haus.
4. Die Jungen seh_______ die Blumen.
5. Ich seh_______ Mary nicht.
6. Du sieh_______ Marks* Onkel.

*The s in **Marys** or **Marks** is the same as is used in English: "Mary'*s*" or "Mark'*s*" (the house of Mary; the uncle of Mark). But in German the apostrophe is not used.

ANSWERS

This and these.

SINGULAR	PLURAL	SINGULAR	PLURAL
dieses Auto, das Auto	diese Autos, die Autos	diese Katze, die Katze	diese Katzen, die Katzen
dieser Onkel, der Onkel	diese Onkel, die Onkel	dieses Haus, das Haus	diese Häuser, die Häuser

Endings.

1. sieht **2.** sehen **3.** seht **4.** sehen **5.** sehe **6.** siehst

Fill in the blanks with the appropriate words:

1. Mark kommt ________ Amerika.
from

2. Er kommt ________ Koffer.
without

3. Er kommt ________ Frau Smith.
with

4. Wir brauchen das Zimmer ________ eine Woche.
for

5. Die Katze ist ________ dem Haus.
in front of

6. Die Katze ist ________ vom Haus.
left

7. Die Katze ist ________ vom Haus.
right

8. Die Katze ist ________ Haus #1 und Haus #2.
between

9. Die Katze ist ________ dem Haus.
under

10 Die Katze springt ________ den Mond.
over

11. Die Katze ist ________ dem Haus.
behind

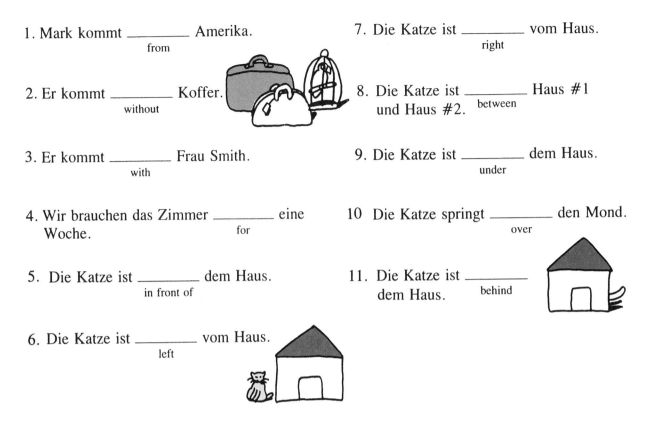

Fill in vertically the German equivalent of the words listed on the left.

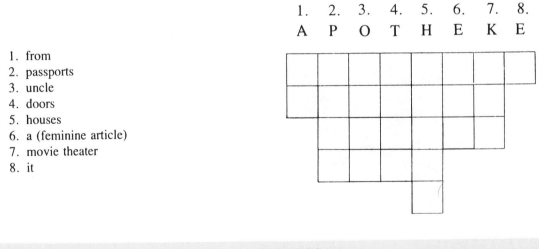

1. from
2. passports
3. uncle
4. doors
5. houses
6. a (feminine article)
7. movie theater
8. it

1.	2.	3.	4.	5.	6.	7.	8.
A	P	O	T	H	E	K	E

ANSWERS

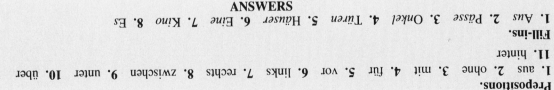

Prepositions.
1. aus **2.** ohne **3.** mit **4.** für **5.** vor **6.** links **7.** rechts **8.** zwischen **9.** unter **10.** über
11. hinter

Fill-ins.
1. *Aus* **2.** *Pässe* **3.** *Onkel* **4.** *Türen* **5.** *Häuser* **6.** *Eine* **7.** *Kino* **8.** *Es*

What's Mary doing? Read this passage to review German words for directions. Then try to answer the questions that follow.

Mary fragt den Polizisten: „Wo ist die Bank?" Der Polizist sagt ihr: „Gehen Sie rechts und dann links." Mary kommt zu den Verkehrsampeln und sieht die Bank nicht. Aber sie sieht das Postamt. Dann geht sie zum Hotel zurück.

Now try to answer the following questions:

1. Wer fragt den Polizisten, wo die Bank ist?

____

2. Was sagt der Polizist?

____

(voh-HIN)
3. Wohin (to where) kommt sie?

____

4. Was sieht sie?

____

5. Wohin geht sie zurück?

____

ANSWERS

Questions. **1.** Mary fragt den Polizisten. **2.** Gehen Sie rechts und dann links. **3.** Sie kommt zu den Verkehrsampeln. **4.** Sie sieht die Bank. **5.** Sie geht zum Hotel zurück.

4 Öffentliche Verkehrsmittel

(ÖF-ent-li-çeh) *(feR-KAYRS-mit-el)*

Public Transportation

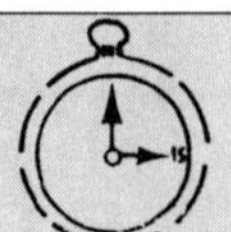

1 Frauenkirche
2 Neues Rathaus
3 Peterskirche
4 Residenz
5 Nationaltheater
6 Theatinerkirche
7 Karlstor
8 Propyläen
9 Lenbachhaus
10 Alte Pinakothek
11 Neue Pinakothek
12 Universität
13 Siegestor
14 Monopteros
15 Haus der Kunst
16 Nationalmuseum
17 Friedensengel
18 Maximilianeum
19 Völkerkundemuseum
20 Isartor
21 Deutsches Museum
22 Maria-Hilf-Kirche
23 Gärtnerplatztheater
24 Sendlinger Tor
25 Paulskirche
26 Circus Krone
27 Olympiastadion
28 Olympiaturm

Bahn
Tram
Bus
Fremdenverkehrsamt im Hauptbahnhof
500 Meter

Kartographie Huber & Oberländer

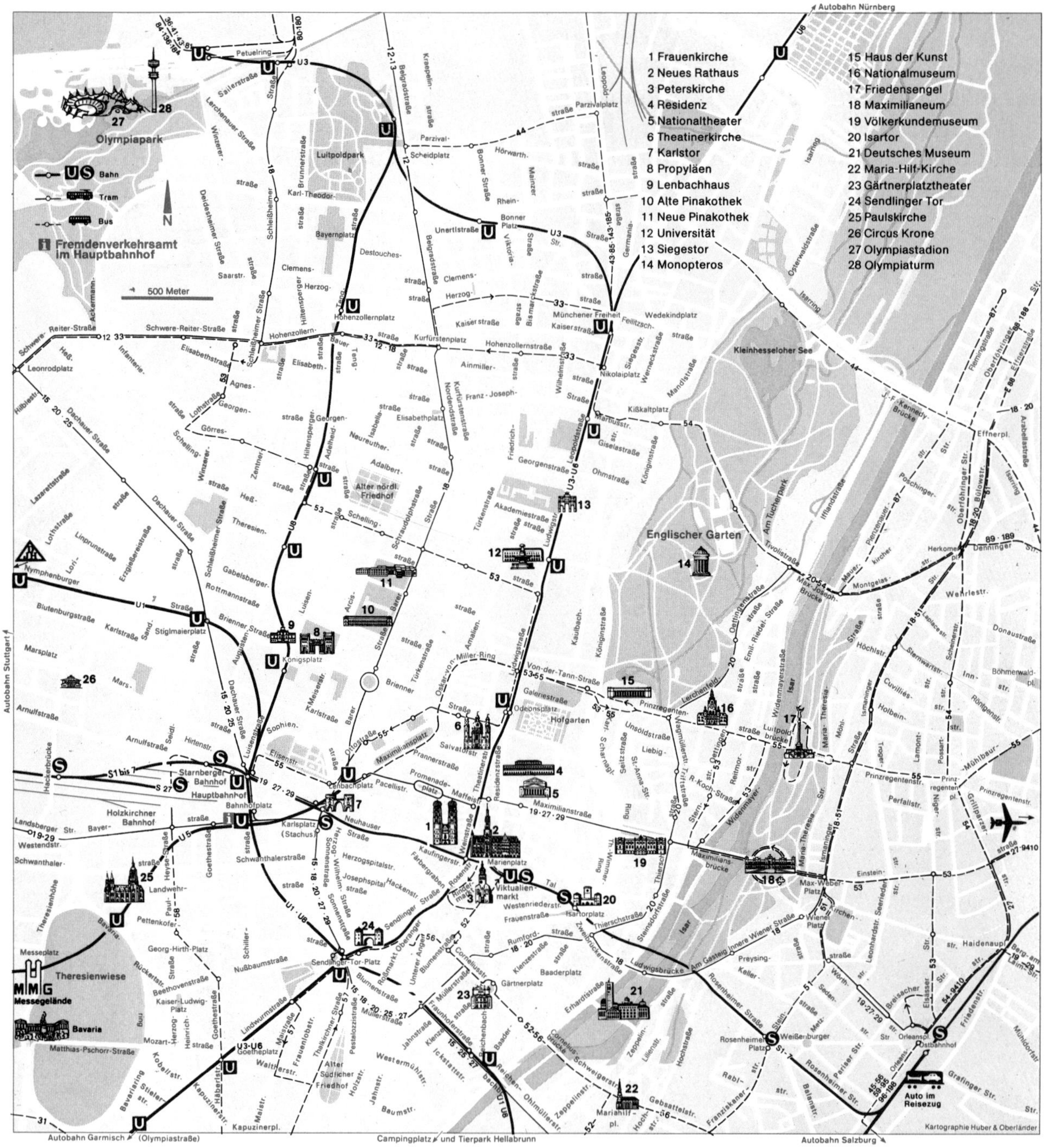

Munich *(Courtesy of Munich Tourist Office)*

The following dialogue contains useful words and expressions that you might find helpful when using public transportation. Always read the dialogue of a unit several times out loud.

MARY	*(SOL-en) (TAK-si) (tsoom) (NAY-men)* **Sollen wir ein Taxi zum Kino nehmen?**	Shall we take a taxi to the movie theater?
MARK	*(KOST-et) (tsoo-FEEL)* **Nein. Das kostet zuviel.**	No. It costs too much.
MARY	*(OO-bahn)* **Dann nehmen wir die U-Bahn.**	Then let's take the subway.
MARK	**Nein. Dann kann ich die** *(shtat)* **Stadt nicht sehen.**	No. then I can't see the city.
MARK	*(RIÇ-tiç)* **Richtig. Wir nehmen** *(BE-seR) (bus)* **besser den Bus.**	Right. It's better if we take the bus.
MARK	*(goot)* **Gut.**	Good.

	(They get on a bus) **Entschuldigen Sie, bitte, wieviel kostet eine Fahrkarte?** *(FAHR-kar-teh)*	Excuse me, please, how much is a ticket?*
(FAHR-eR) FAHRER driver	**Eine Mark.**	One mark.
MARK	*(SHTEI-gen) (beim)* **Wir steigen beim Kino in der Schillerstraße aus.**	We are getting off at the movie theater on the Schillerstraße.
FAHRER	**Gut, mein Herr.**	All right, sir.
MARK	*(HÖHF-liç) (DOY-tshen)* **Wie höflich die Deutschen sind!**	How polite the Germans are!

Did you read the dialogue several times? Out loud? Test your understanding by filling in the missing dialogue parts in the following sentences.

„Nehmen wir ein T__________________ zum Kino?"

„Nein. Das kostet z__________________."

„Dann nehmen wir die U-__________________."

*In many German cities bus and subway tickets must be purchased in advance. Tickets often are not collected, but nonuniformed personnel make spot-checks, and people without proper tickets must pay a substantial fine. You should always find out about the system used in the city you're visiting.

ANSWERS

Dialogue. Taxi, zuviel, Bahn

„Nein. Dann kann ich die S__________________ nicht sehen."

„Richtig. Wir nehmen besser den B__________________."

„Gut!"

„Entschuldigen Sie, bitte, wieviel kostet eine __________________?"

„Eine Mark."

„Wir s__________________ beim Kino in der Schillerstraße aus."

„Gut, mein Herr."

„Wie h__________________ die Deutschen sind!"

Was ist das?

a. __________________

c. __________________

b. __________________

d. __________________

ANSWERS

Dialogue.
Stadt, Bus, Fahrkarte, steigen, höflich

Was ist das?
a. ein Taxi b. ein Bus c. eine U-Bahn d. ein Auto

(mayR) (VAYR-ben)

Mehr Verben

More Action Words

In the previous dialogue we used the verb *nehmen* (to take) and the verb *kosten* (to taste, to cost). Both are conjugated somewhat irregularly:

NEHMEN to take	**KOSTEN** to taste, to cost	
ich nehm*e* **du *nimmst*** **er / sie / es *nimmt***	**ich kost*e*** **du kost*est*** **er / sie / es kost*et***	Singular
wir nehm*en* **ihr nehm*t*** **sie nehm*en***	**wir kost*en*** **ihr kost*et*** **sie kost*en***	Plural
Sie nehm*en*	**Sie kost*en***	Polite, Singular and Plural

Other verbs that take an *e* between stem and ending are *arbeiten* *(AR-bei-ten)* (to work), *antworten* *(ANT-vor-ten)* (to answer), *bitten* *(BIT-en)* (to ask), *finden* *(FIN-den)* (to find), *senden* *(ZEN-den)* (to send), and *reden* *(RAY-den)* (to talk).

Many German verbs have a vowel change in the second and third person singular. Such verbs include *schlafen* *(SCHLAH-fen)* (to sleep) and *fahren* *(FAH-ren)* (to go, travel, ride, drive).

SCHLAFEN to sleep	**FAHREN** to go	
(SCHLAH-feh) **ich schlafe** *(schlayfst)* **du schl*ä*fst** **er / sie / es schl*ä*ft**	*(FAH-reh)* **ich fahre** *(fayRst)* **du f*ä*hrst** **er / sie / es f*ä*hrt**	Singular
wir schlafen **ihr schlaft** **sie schlafen**	**wir fahren** **ihr fahrt** **sie fahren**	Plural
Sie schlafen	**Sie fahren**	Polite, Singular and Plural

Other verbs having a vowel change in the second and third person singular are

(FAL-en) **fallen** (to fall)	*(FAN-gen)* **fangen** (to catch)	*(TRAH-gen)* **tragen** (to carry)
(VAK-sen) **wachsen** (to grow)	*(VA-shen)* **waschen** (to wash)	

(SHAF-neR)

WAS MAN DEM SCHAFFNER SAGT

What to Say to the Conductor

Eine Karte, bitte.	One ticket please.
(EIN-shteig-en) **einsteigen**	to get on
(OWS-shteig-en) **aussteigen**	to get off
(UM-shteig-en) **umsteigen**	to transfer
(AN-hal-ten) **anhalten**	to stop
(HALT-eh-shtel-eh) **die Haltestelle**	the stop
(SHTAY-en-bleib-en) **stehenbleiben**	to remain standing (not move)

PLEASE NOTE: All five of the above-mentioned verbs have separable prefixes. That means that the two parts they consist of have to be separated in certain sentence patterns. Mark says „Wir *steigen* beim Kino *aus*." ("We get off at the movie theater"). Most of the time this kind of verb combines a preposition (*aus*, *ein*, *um*) with a verb (*steigen*). Sometimes two verbs are combined in one word (*stehen* and *bleiben*). If a conjugated form of the verb is used, the first part always stands at the end of the sentence: Ich steige ein; er steigt aus; wir steigen aus; sie steigen aus; der Autobus bleibt stehen.

(HOWPT-vör-tern) *(ar-TEE-keln)*

Von Hauptwörtern und Artikeln

On Nouns and Articles

Let's backtrack a little. We have learned about articles, and we know that in German there is *der, die, das,* whereas in English we are much more stingy. All we use is the word *the.* In English we do not divide nouns into genders.

German also is more complicated in identifying the function of a noun in a sentence. The function is shown by the noun's *case.* As you'll see on the accompanying tables, there are four cases in German. The case is indicated by the article and in some instances by the spelling of the noun. Let's look at cases involving masculine, feminine, and neuter nouns.

MASCULINE NOUNS

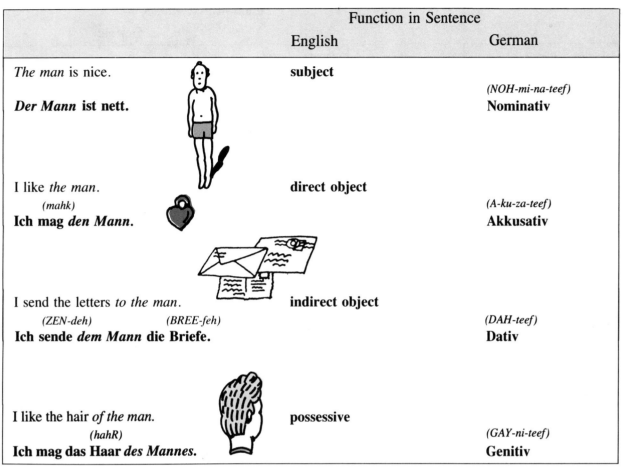

	Function in Sentence English	German
The man is nice. **_Der Mann_ ist nett.**	**subject**	*(NOH-mi-na-teef)* **Nominativ**
I like *the man.* *(mahk)* **Ich mag _den Mann_.**	**direct object**	*(A-ku-za-teef)* **Akkusativ**
I send the letters *to the man.* *(ZEN-deh)* *(BREE-feh)* **Ich sende _dem Mann_ die Briefe.**	**indirect object**	*(DAH-teef)* **Dativ**
I like the hair *of the man.* *(hahR)* **Ich mag das Haar _des Mannes_.**	**possessive**	*(GAY-ni-teef)* **Genitiv**

The table below shows the four cases, **in the singular**, of the masculine word *Mann*:

der Mann	den Mann	dem Mann	des Mannes
subject	direct object	indirect object	possessive

In the plural the forms are:

die Männer	die Männer	den Männer*n*	der Männer

FEMININE NOUNS

	Function in Sentence English	German
The woman is pretty. *(hüpsh)* **_Die Frau_ ist hübsch.**	**subject**	**Nominativ**
I like *the woman.* **Ich mag _die Frau_.**	**direct object**	**Akkusativ**

FEMININE NOUNS

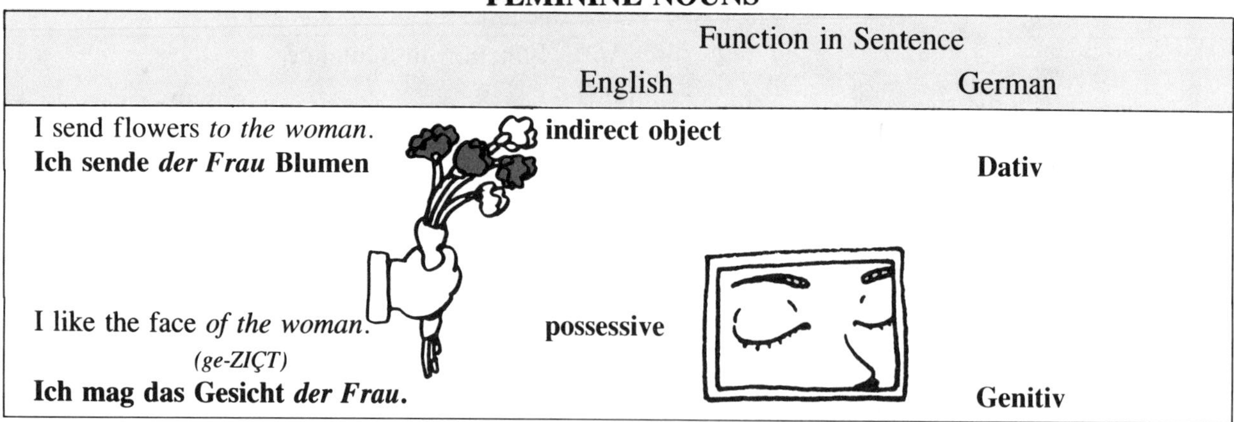

	Function in Sentence	
	English	German
I send flowers *to the woman.* **Ich sende *der Frau* Blumen**	**indirect object**	**Dativ**
I like the face *of the woman.* *(ge-ZIÇT)* **Ich mag das Gesicht *der Frau.***	**possessive**	**Genitiv**

Again we have four cases, this time the **singular** of a feminine noun:

die Frau	die Frau	der Frau	der Frau
subject	direct object	indirect object	possessive

In the plural, the forms are:

die Frauen	die Frauen	den Frauen	der Frauen

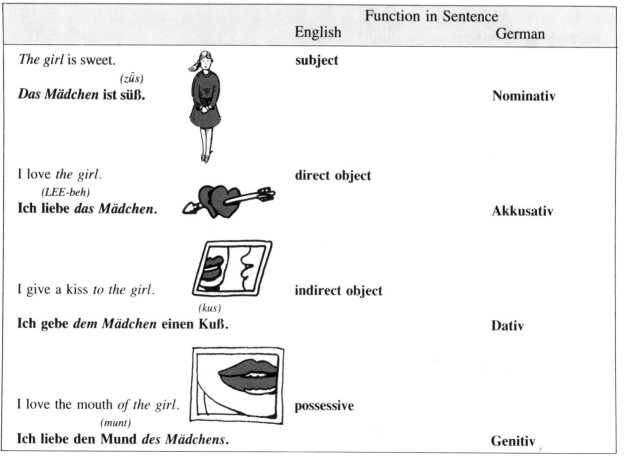

NEUTER NOUNS

	Function in Sentence	
	English	German
The girl is sweet. *(zūs)* ***Das Mädchen* ist süß.**	**subject**	**Nominativ**
I love *the girl.* *(LEE-beh)* **Ich liebe *das Mädchen.***	**direct object**	**Akkusativ**
I give a kiss *to the girl.* *(kus)* **Ich gebe *dem Mädchen* einen Kuß.**	**indirect object**	**Dativ**
I love the mouth *of the girl.* *(munt)* **Ich liebe den Mund *des Mädchens.***	**possessive**	**Genitiv**

And here we have the four cases of a neuter noun:

das Mädchen	das Mädchen	dem Mädchen	des Mädchens
subject	direct object	indirect object	possessive

Of course, other nouns (and adjectives) have other endings. Watch out for those endings in the dialogues. In the dialogues you learn the language as it is actually spoken.

SUMMARY						
ARTICLES*						
	Singular			Plural		
	M	F	N	M	F	N
Subject	**der**	**die**	**das**	**die**	**die**	**die**
Direct Object	**den**	**die**	**das**	**die**	**die**	**die**
Indirect Object	**dem**	**der**	**dem**	**den**	**den**	**den**
Possessive	**des**	**der**	**des**	**der**	**der**	**der**

*M = masculine; F = feminine; N = neuter.

Did you notice? All nouns use the same articles in the plural. The plural of the noun itself can be formed in several ways. As a rule, nouns add an *-n* in the dative (indirect object) plural (den Männer*n*) unless the plural form already has a final *-n* (den Frauen).

Here are two very important irregular verbs you should learn. They are *sein* (to be) and *haben* (to have).

(zein)
SEIN
to be

GERMAN	ENGLISH	EXAMPLE		
(bin) **ich bin**	I am	**Ich bin ein**	____________.	(man)
(bist) **du bist**	you are	**Du bist eine**	____________.	(woman)
er, sie, *(ist)* **es ist**	he, she, it is	**Er ist ein**	____________.	(boy)
(zint) **wir sind**	we are	**Wir sind**	____________.	(2 girls)
(zeit) **ihr seid**	you are	**Ihr seid**	____________.	(2 girls)
sie sind	they are	**Sie sind**	____________.	(2 girls)
Sie sind	you are (polite)	**Sie sind**	____________.	(professor)

ANSWERS

Sein. Mann Frau Junge zwei Mädchen zwei Mädchen zwei Mädchen ein Professor

(HAH-ben)
HABEN
to have

GERMAN	ENGLISH	EXAMPLE		
(HAH-beh) **ich habe**	I have	**Ich habe einen**	______________.	(key)
(hast) **du hast**	you have	**Du hast einen**	______________.	(suitcase)
(hat) **er, sie, es hat**	he, she, it has	**Er hat ein**	______________.	(book)
(HAH-ben) **wir haben**	we have	**Wir haben**	______________.	(flowers)
(hapt) **ihr habt**	you have	**Ihr habt**	______________.	(cats)
sie haben	they have	**Sie haben**	______________.	(cars)
Sie haben	you have (polite)	**Sie haben**	______________.	(sons)

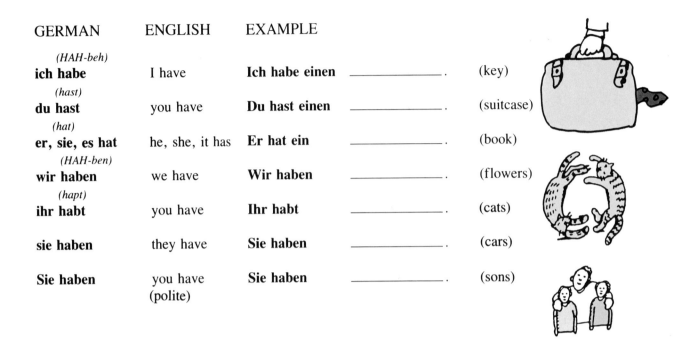

(fer-SHTAN-den)
Verstanden? (Did you understand?) Now here's a change of pace. A little puzzle that should be easy. Just fill in the correct German words vertically:

1. questions
2. right
3. all
4. and
5. he
6. no

1	2	3	4	5	6
F	R	A	U	E	N

ANSWERS

Haben.
Schlüssel Koffer Buch Blumen Katzen Autos Söhne

Puzzle.
1. Fragen **2.** rechts **3.** alle **4.** und **5.** er **6.** nein

In English we frequently use contractions—for instance, "do not" is shortened to "don't." Contractions are common in German, too. For example, a preposition and an article are frequently combined and shortened. *Bei dem* (near the) becomes *beim*, *in dem* (in the) becomes *im*. But not all combinations of a preposition and an article are shortened to form a contraction. Thus, *in der* (in the) is never shortened, nor is *auf dem* (on the). Study the following table of frequently used German contractions of a preposition and an article.

(kon-trak-tsee-OH-nen)

Einige Kontraktionen

Some Contractions

Preposition and Article		Contraction	Example
an dem	=	**am**	he stands *at the bed*: *am Bett*
auf das	=	**aufs**	he puts the paper *on the* sofa: *aufs* Sofa *(ZOH-fa)*
bei dem	=	**beim**	they arrive *near the* market: *beim* Markt
hinter das	=	**hinters**	the cat goes *behind the* house: *hinters* Haus
in dem	=	**im**	the dog is *in the* house: *im* Haus
in das	=	**ins**	the man goes *into the* house: *ins* Haus
über das	=	**übers**	the mouse jumps *over the* girl: *übers* Mädchen
von dem	=	**vom**	he comes *from the* movie theater: *vom* Kino
vor das	=	**vors**	the boy runs *in front of the* girl: *vors* Mädchen
zu dem	=	*(tsum)* **zum** (masc.)	the dog walks *to the* man: *zum* Mann
zu der	=	*(tsooR)* **zur** (fem.)	the cat walks *to the* mother: *zur* Mutter

Got the idea? Contractions aren't very hard to learn. Let's practice a few:

1. Der ____Hund____ ist ______________.

2. Der ______________ geht ______________.

3. Die ______________ springt ______________.

4. Der ______________ geht ______________.

ANSWERS

1. im Haus **2.** Mann, ins Haus **3.** Katze, übers Mädchen **4.** Junge, zur Mutter

The following brief passage will allow you to test your comprehension of what you have learned in this unit about transportation.

(nahch)
Herr Schmidt und seine Frau nehmen den Bus. Nach zwei Haltestellen nehmen sie die
After
U-Bahn.

Sie steigen bei der Schillerstraße aus. Sie kommen am Markt an und kaufen
(MEN-geh)
eine Menge.
lot

Now try to answer the following questions:

1. Was nehmen Herr Schmidt und seine Frau?

____

2. Was nehmen sie nach zwei Haltestellen?

____

3. Wo kommen sie an?

____

4. Was kaufen sie auf dem Markt?

____

ANSWERS

1. den Bus **2.** die U-Bahn **3.** am Markt **4.** eine Menge

5 Von Zeit und Zahlen

(fon) (tseit) (unt) (TSAH-len)

All about Time and Numbers

WIEVIEL UHR IST ES?

(ooR)

What Time Is It?

Es ist acht Uhr.

Es ist ein Uhr.

Es ist drei Uhr.

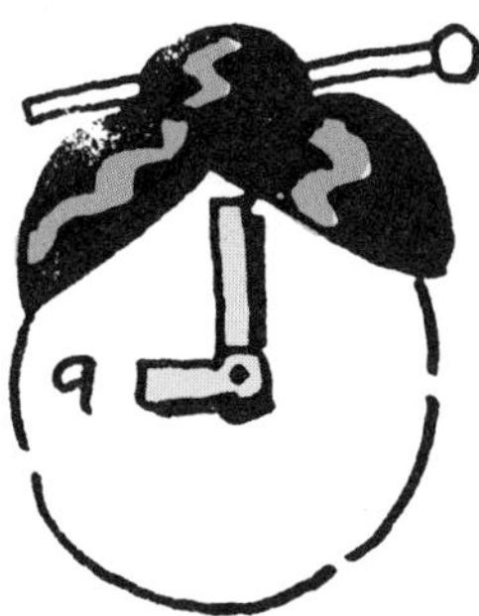

Es ist neun Uhr.

German indicates "A.M." by adding **morgens** (MOHR-gens) (in the morning) to the time: *zwei Uhr morgens*. **Vormittags** (FOHR-mi-taks) indicates the later morning hours "before midday." **Mittags** means "in the period around midday." **Nachmittags** (NACH-mi-taks), "after midday," indicates P.M. hours, as does **abends** (AH-bents), "in the evening:" **sieben Uhr abends** (seven in the evening).

(TSAY-len)

WIR ZÄHLEN AUF DEUTSCH

We Count in German

(GRUNT-tsah-len)

Die Grundzahlen 1–1.000.000

Cardinal Numbers 1–1,000,000

0 *(nul)* **null**	1 *(eins)* **eins**	2 *(tsvei)* **zwei**	3 *(drei)* **drei**	4 *(feeR)* **vier**	5 *(fünf)* **fünf**	6 *(zeks)* **sechs**
7 *(ZEE-ben)* **sieben**	8 *(acht)* **acht**	9 *(noyn)* **neun**	10 *(tsayn)* **zehn**			
11 *(elf)* **elf**	12 *(tsvölf)* **zwölf**	13 *(DREI-tsayn)* **dreizehn**	14 *(FEER-tsayn)* **vierzehn**	15 *(FÜNF-tsayn)* **fünfzehn**	16 *(ZEÇ-tsayn)* **sechzehn**	
17 *(ZEEP-tsayn)* **siebzehn**	18 *(ACHT-tsayn)* **achtzehn**	19 *(NOYN-tsayn)* **neunzehn**	20 *(TSVAN-tsiç)* **zwanzig**	21 *(EIN-unt-tsvan-tsiç)* **einundzwanzig,** etc.		
30 *(DREI-siç)* **dreißig**	40 *(FEER-tsiç)* **vierzig**	50 *(FÜNF-tsiç)* **fünfzig**	60 *(ZEÇ-tsiç)* **sechzig**	70 *(ZEEP-tsiç)* **siebzig**		
80 *(ACHT-tsiç)* **achtzig**	90 *(NOYN-tsiç)* **neunzig**	100 *(HUN-deRt)* **hundert**	101 *(hun-deRt-EINS)* **hunderteins**	200 *(ZWEI-hun-deRt)* **zweihundert,** etc.		
1000 *(TOW-zent)* **tausend**	1.000.000 *(mil-YOHN)* **eine Million**					

(ORD-nungs-tsah-len)

Die Ordnungszahlen 1–10

Ordinal Numbers 1–10

1st *(AYRS-teh)* **der Erste**	2nd *(TSVEI-teh)* **der Zweite**	3rd *(DRIT-teh)* **der Dritte**	4th *(FEER-teh)* **der Vierte**	5th *(FÜNF-teh)* **der Fünfte**
6th *(ZEÇS-teh)* **der Sechste**	7th *(ZEE-ben-teh)* **der Siebente**	8th *(ACH-teh)* **der Achte**	9th *(NOYN-teh)* **der Neunte**	10th *(TSAYN-teh)* **der Zehnte**

Now you are ready to learn more about telling time. You will note that a particular time can be expressed in more than one way in German.

Es ist sechs Uhr zehn.
six o'clock and ten (minutes)

(mi-NOO-ten)
Es ist zehn Minuten nach sechs.
ten minutes after six

(fünf) *(feeR-unt-FÜNF-tsiç)*
Es ist fünf Uhr vierundfünfzig.
five fifty-four

Es ist sechs Minuten vor sechs.
six minutes before six

Es ist zwei Uhr dreißig.
two thirty

(halp)
Es ist halb drei.
half before three

Es ist ein Uhr fünfzehn.
one fifteen

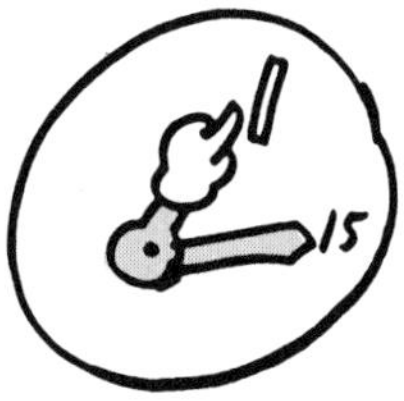

(FEER-tel)
Es ist ein Viertel nach eins.
quarter after one

Es ist Viertel zwei.
quarter of the way to two

Es ist zwei Uhr fünfundvierzig.
two forty-five

Es ist ein Viertel vor drei.
a quarter of three

Es ist dreiviertel drei.
three quarters of the way to three

The twenty-four hour system is being used more and more, not only in Germany but all over Europe. It is more practical because it makes the German equivalents of A.M. and P.M. unnecessary.

(tsook) *(FEER-tsayn)* Der Zug kommt um 14 Uhr (vierzehn Uhr) an.	The train arrives at 2 P.M.
(ZEÇ-tsayn) Er fährt um 16.30 (sechzehn Uhr dreißig) ab.	It leaves at 4:30 P.M.

1 P.M. = 13 – dreizehn Uhr.

2 P.M. = 14 – vierzehn Uhr.

8 P.M. = 20 – zwanzig Uhr.

To understand the 24-hour system, just deduct 12 from any number of 12 hours or later. Thus, 13.25 is equivalent to 1:25 P.M., 19.27 equals 7:27 P.M., and 0.37 is the same as 12:37 A.M.

Now test yourself on telling time. Remember, there is more than one way of expressing time.

Wieviel Uhr ist es?

a. 2:24 Es ist zwei Uhr vierundzwanzig.

b. 6:15 ______________________

c. 7:30 ______________________

d. 9:40 ______________________

e. ______________ f. ______________ g. ______________

(FAHR-plan) **FAHRPLAN** Timetable	*(BRÜ-sel)* *(veen)* **Brüssel—Wien** Brussels Vienna			
7.00	**ab**	**Brüssel**	**an**	20.00
13.30	**an**	**Frankfurt**	**ab**	15.00
15.00	**ab**	**Frankfurt**	**an**	13.30
20.15	**an**	*(MÜN-çen)* **München**	**ab**	8.30
8.30	**ab**	**München**	**an**	20.00
10.30	**an**	*(ZALTS-burk)* **Salzburg**	**ab**	18.00
10.45	**ab**	**Salzburg**	**an**	17.45
12.00	**an**	*(lints)* **Linz**	**ab**	16.00
12.30	**ab**	**Linz**	**an**	15.30
15.00	**an**	**Wien**	**ab**	13.00

ab = departs
an = arrives

ANSWERS

b. Sechs Uhr fünfzehn *or* ein Viertel nach sechs *or* viertel sieben **c.** sieben Uhr dreißig *or* halb acht **d.** neun Uhr vierzig *or* zwanzig Minuten vor zehn **e.** viertel zwei **f.** halb zwölf **g.** zehn Uhr fünfundzwanzig

Referring to the timetable, complete the following sentences:

1. Der Zug nach Wien verläßt *(fayR-LEST)* leaves Brüssel um ______________ und kommt in Wien um ______________ an.

2. Wie lange braucht der Zug von Wien nach Salzburg? ______________.

3. Der Zug verläßt München um ______________ und kommt in Brüssel um ______________ an.

Now let's look at numbers in a different context—shopping.

Mr. Smith goes to a department store in Munich.

Er kauft:

einen Hut *(hoot)* hat (dreißig Mark),
ein Hemd *(hemt)* shirt (siebenundzwanzig Mark),
Schuhe *(SHOO-eh)* shoes (neunzig Mark).

Aber der Angestellte irrt *(irt)* makes a mistake sich und sagt: „Es tut mir leid, das Hemd kostet nur *(nooR)* only zweiundzwanzig Mark.“ Wieviel zahlt *(tsahlt)* pays Herr Smith?

4. DM ______________

The following dialogue contains some expressions useful in telling time.

Read it aloud a few times.

MARK	**Entschuldigen Sie, bitte, wieviel Uhr ist es?**	Excuse me, please, what time is it?
EIN MANN	**Es ist Mitternacht.** *(MIT-eR-nacht)*	It is midnight.
MARK	**Wie kann das sein? Es ist noch immer Tag.** *(zein) (noch) (IM-eR)*	How can it be? It is still daytime.

ANSWERS

1. sieben Uhr, fünfzehn Uhr **2.** vier und dreiviertel Stunden **3.** acht Uhr dreißig, zwanzig Uhr
4. DM 142

EIN MANN **Entschuldigen Sie, dann ist es Mittag.** — Excuse me, then it is noon.

(SHPAH-sen)
MARK **Spaßen Sie?** — Are you joking?

(too-RIST)
EIN MANN **Nein. Ich habe keine Uhr. Sind Sie ein Tourist?** — No. I don't have a watch. Are you a tourist?

MARK **Ja.** — Yes.

(VO-len) *(KOW-fen)*
EIN MANN **Wollen Sie eine Uhr kaufen? Zwanzig Mark.** — Do you want to buy a watch? 20 marks.

MARK **Aber Sie sagen, daß Sie keine Uhr haben.** — But you say that you don't have a watch.

EIN MANN **Fünfzehn Mark.** — Fifteen marks.

MARK **Nein, danke.** — No, thank you.

(AYR-li-çeR) (TASH-en-deep)
EIN MANN **Hier ist Ihre Uhr. Ich bin ein ehrlicher Taschendieb.** — Here is your watch. I am an honest pickpocket.

See if you remember the dialogue by filling in the blanks:

1. „Entschuldigen Sie, mein Herr, wieviel ________________ ist es?"
2. „Es ist ________________ ."
3. „Wie kann das sein, es ist noch immer ________________ ."
4. „Entschuldigen Sie, dann ist es ________________ ."
5. „________________ Sie?"
6. „Nein. Ich habe keine ________________ . Sind Sie ein ________________ ?"
   „Ja."
7. „Wollen Sie eine Uhr ________________ ? ________________ Mark."

ANSWERS

1. Uhr 2. Mitternacht 3. Tag 4. Mittag 5. Spaßen 6. Uhr, Tourist 7. kaufen, Zwanzig

8. „Aber Sie ____________________, daß Sie keine Uhr haben."

9. „Fünfzehn ____________________."

10. „Nein, ____________________."

(UN-zer-eh) *(REI-ze-play-neh)*

Unsere Reisepläne

Our Travel Plans

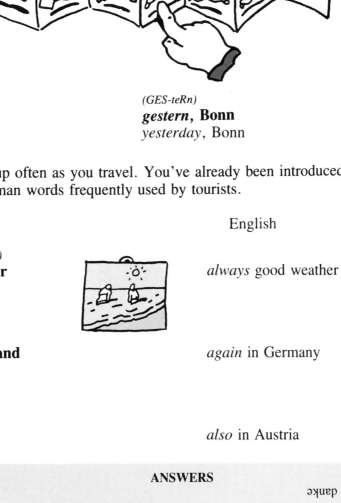

(HOY-teh)
***heute,* München**
today, Munich

(GES-teRn)
***gestern,* Bonn**
yesterday, Bonn

***morgen,* Wien**
tomorrow, Vienna

Some words come up often as you travel. You've already been introduced to quite a few. Here are some more German words frequently used by tourists.

German		English
(VE-teR) ***immer* gutes Wetter**	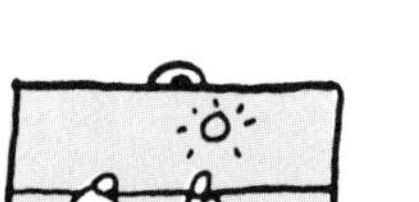	*always* good weather
(VEE-deR) ***wieder* in Deutschland**		*again* in Germany
(owch) *(ÖS-te-reiç)* ***auch* in Österreich**		*also* in Austria

ANSWERS

8. sagen **9.** Mark **10.** danke

German	English
(shohn) (FRANK-furt) ***schon* in Frankfurt**	*already* in Frankfurt
(dort) (varm) ***dort* ist es warm**	*there* it is warm
(heeR) (kalt) ***hier* ist es kalt**	*here* it is cold
(gelt) **ich brauche *viel* Geld**	I need *much, a lot of* money
(VAY-niç) (HAH-reh) **er hat *wenig* Haare**	he has *little* hair
(yetst) ***jetzt* gehe ich schlafen**	*now* I go to bed
***jetzt* schlafe ich**	*now* I go to sleep
***gut,* ich auch**	*good, okay,* me too
(BES-seR) **dieses Bier ist *besser***	this beer is *better*
(dan) ***dann* ins Kino**	*then* to the movies
(SHTROO-del) ***zuviel* Strudel!**	*too much* strudel!
(gern) **ich komme *gern***	I come *gladly*
(nee) ***nie(mals)* wieder!**	*never* again!
(niçts) (tsoo) ***nichts* zu sehen**	*nothing* to see
(NEE-mant) ***niemand* dort**	*nobody* there

Here's a little exercise. See if you can remember the meaning of the underlined words. Match the German sentences with their English equivalents.

1. Heute sind wir in Wien.
2. Er ist schon in München.
3. Morgen sind wir in Linz.
4. Wir essen immer zeitig. *(TSEI-tiç)* early
5. Jetzt kommt der Bus.
6. Er hat wenig Geld.
7. Sie ist nie dort.
8. Dann fahren wir nach Bonn.
9. Das kostet zuviel.

a. The bus is coming now.
b. Tomorrow we are in Linz.
c. Today we are in Vienna.
d. He is already in Munich.
e. We always eat early.
f. She is never there.
g. That costs too much.
h. He has little money.
i. Then we will go to Bonn.

Verben

Action Words

Tun (to do) and *wissen* (to know) are two more irregular verbs that you should learn.

(toon) **Tun** to do	
(TOO-eh) ich tue	I do
(toost) du tust	you do
er tut	he does
wir tun	we do
ihr tut	you do
sie tun	they do
Sie tun	you do (polite)

(VIS-en) **Wissen** to know	
(veis) ich weiß	I know
(veist) du weißt	you know
er weiß	he knows
wir wissen	we know
(vist) ihr wißt	you know
sie wissen	they know
Sie wissen	you know (polite)

ANSWERS

Matching. 1-c, 2-d, 3-b, 4-e, 5-a, 6-h, 7-f, 8-i, 9-g

Now let's review some of the verb forms we have learned lately:

ich ______ (am)	du ______ (are)	er ______ (is)
wir ______ (are)	ihr ______ (are)	Sie ______ (are)
ich ______ (have)	du ______ (have)	er ______ (has)
wir ______ (have)	ihr ______ (have)	sie ______ (have)
du ______ (sleep)	er ______ (takes)	er ______ (works)
du ______ (eat)	er ______ (sees)	wir ______ (do)
ihr ______ (do)	du ______ (do)	er ______ (does)
ich ______ (know)	du ______ (know)	er ______ (knows)

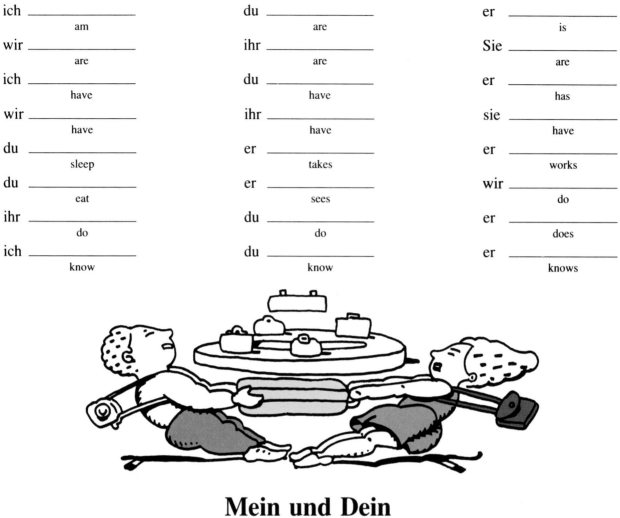

Mein und Dein

Mine and Yours

Here you have a short summary of the possessive adjectives, words that tell you what belongs to you and what belongs to him or her. They always precede the noun, and their endings reflect the *gender* and *case* of the nouns they modify. In the singular, the endings are the same as those for the indefinite article *ein*.

John ist *mein* Mann.	Mary ist *meine* Frau.	Das ist *mein* Buch.
masculine	feminine	neuter

ANSWERS

Verbs.

ich bin	du bist	er ist
wir sind	ihr seid	Sie sind
ich habe	du hast	er hat
wir haben	ihr habt	sie haben
du schläfst	er nimmt	er arbeitet
du ißt	er sieht	wir tun
ihr tut	du tust	er tut
ich weiß	du weißt	er weiß

Here is a list of the possessive adjectives. The forms shown here are in the nominative case.

POSSESSIVE ADJECTIVES—NOMINATIVE CASE

possessive adjective in English	with masculine nouns	with feminine nouns	with neuter nouns
my	mein Sohn	meine Tochter	mein Zimmer
your	dein Vater	deine Mutter	dein Haus
his	sein Freund	seine Schwester	sein Bild
her	ihr Freund	ihre Schwester	ihr Bild
our	unser Baum	unsere Katze	unser Kino
your	euer Vetter	eure Tür	euer Postamt
their	ihr Spiegel	ihre Straße	ihr Bier
your (polite)	Ihr Onkel	Ihre Bank	Ihr Auto

The possessive adjectives all take the same ending in the **plural** for all three genders. For example,

mein*e* Söhne, mein*e* Freundinnen, mein*e* Zimmer (nominative)
mein*er* Söhne, mein*er* Freundinnen, mein*er* Zimmer (genitive)

In the **singular**, the endings vary according to gender and case.

Examples:

Genitive:	das Buch mein*es* Mannes	my husband's book
Dative:	Sie gibt ihr*em* Mann ein Buch.	She gives her husband a book.
Accusative:	Sie liebt ihr*en* Mann.	She loves her husband.
Genitive:	das Buch mein*er* Frau	my wife's book
Dative:	Er gibt sein*er* Frau ein Buch.	He gives his wife a book.
Accusative:	Er liebt sein*e* Frau.	He loves his wife.

(ka-PEERT)
Kapiert? Did you get it? Try to apply your new knowledge of German possessive adjectives to the following little exercise.

SINGULAR		PLURAL	
1. ______________ (my)	Blume	______________ (my)	Blumen
2. ______________ (your)	Haus (familiar)	______________ (your)	Häuser (familiar)
3. ______________ (his)	Freund	______________ (his)	Freunde
4. ______________ (her)	Freundin	______________ (her)	Freundinnen

ANSWERS

Possessives. **1.** meine, meine **2.** dein, deine *or* euer, eure **3.** sein, seine **4.** ihre, ihre

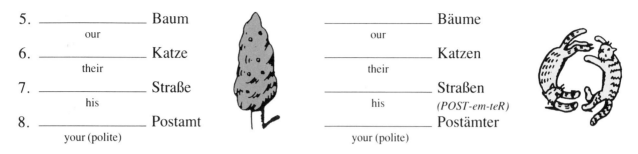

	SINGULAR		PLURAL
5.	______________ Baum our		______________ Bäume our
6.	______________ Katze their		______________ Katzen their
7.	______________ Straße his		______________ Straßen his
8.	______________ Postamt your (polite)		*(POST-em-teR)* ______________ Postämter your (polite)

Uhrzeit. The following brief passage will test your comprehension of what you have learned in this unit about telling time.

„Wieviel Uhr ist es?" fragt der Vater seine Tochter.
„Drei Uhr," sagt die Tochter.
(fleekst)
„Um wieviel Uhr fliegst du nach Deutschland?"
(ANT-vor-tet)
„Um fünf Uhr zwanzig," antwortet die Tochter.
„Auf Wiedersehen und gute Reise!"
(FAH-tee)
„Auf Wiedersehen, Vati."

Now try to answer the following questions:

1. Was fragt der Vater seine Tochter?

____

2. Was sagt die Tochter?

____

3. Um wieviel Uhr fliegt die Tochter nach Deutschland?

____

True or False?

4. Die Mutter spricht mit ihrer Tochter. __________

5. Sie fliegt nach England. __________

6. Es ist jetzt sieben Uhr. __________

ANSWERS

5. unser, unsere **6.** ihre, ihre **7.** seine, seine **8.** Ihr, Ihre

Dialogue.

1. Wieviel Uhr ist es? **2.** Drei Uhr. **3.** Um fünf Uhr zwanzig **4.** F **5.** F **6.** F

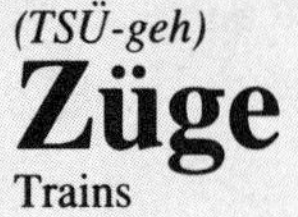

6 (TSÜ-geh) Züge
Trains

Trains are a very important form of transportation in Germany, for people as well as freight. You'll probably take a train when in Germany, so the following dialogue should prove very useful. Be sure to read it aloud.

(AL-es) (EIN-shtei-gen)
Alles einsteigen!
All aboard!

(AL-zoh) (BAHN-hohf)
MARY **Also das ist der Bahnhof.** — Well, this is the train station.

(SCHNEL-tsook) (HAM-burk)
ANNE **Vati, nehmen wir den Schnellzug nach Hamburg?** — Dad, do we take the express train to Hamburg?

MARK **Nein, der kostet zu viel.** — No, that costs too much.

(EIL-tsook)
ANNE **Nehmen wir den Eilzug?** — Do we take the limited-stop train?

(RÜK-fahR-kar-teh) (peR-ZOH-nen)
MARK **Ja.** (to a ticket clerk) **Entschuldigen Sie, bitte, wieviel kostet eine Rückfahrkarte für vier Personen nach Hamburg?** — Yes. Excuse me, please, how much is a return ticket for four persons to Hamburg?

(SHAL-ter-be-amteR)
SCHALTERBEAMTER **Eilzug?** — Limited-stop train?
ticket clerk

MARK **Ja.** — Yes.

SCHALTERBEAMTER **Zweihundert Mark.** 200 marks. Here are the tickets.

Hier sind die Fahrkarten.

MARK **Vielen Dank. Gibt es** Many thanks. Are there nonsmoking sections?
(NIÇT-row-cheR-ap-tei-leh)
Nichtraucherabteile?

SCHALTERBEAMTER **Ja. Der Zug hat** Yes. The train has smoking and nonsmoking sections.
(ROW-cheR)
Raucher- und Nichtraucherabteile.

Now fill in the missing dialogue parts:

1. „Also das ist der B__________________."
2. „Vati, nehmen wir den S__________________ nach Hamburg?"
3. „Nein, das k__________________ zu viel."
4. „Nehmen wir den E__________________?"

   „Ja."
5. „Entschuldigen Sie, wieviel k__________________ eine R__________________ für vier P__________________ nach Hamburg?"

   „Eilzug?"

   „Ja."
6. „Zweihundert Mark. Hier sind die F__________________."

There are various types of trains, the fastest being the *TEE-Zug* (Trans-Europe-Express). Also fast is the *IC-Zug* (Intercity-Zug). Less expensive is the *D-Zug* or *Schnellzug*, but this train is less speedy and makes more stops. The *Eilzug* is somewhat slower than the *D-Zug*. The *Personenzug* is the cheapest and slowest. It stops at all stations. Freight is transported by the *Güterzug*.

Tickets can be purchased beforehand from a travel agent or at the railroad station. There usually is no problem getting a seat. There are a number of reduced-fare plans.

ANSWERS

Dialogue.
1. Bahnhof **2.** Schnellzug **3.** kostet **4.** Eilzug **5.** kostet, Rückfahrkarte, Personen **6.** Fahrkarten

(köln)

Here is a train schedule from Köln (Cologne) to several other European cities. For example, if you want to go to København (Copenhagen) from Köln, there are six trains possible. If you leave Köln at 10 A.M., you will arrive in København at 7:45 P.M. (remember, the train schedules in Europe use the 24-hour system).

Köln

Genova

	ar / an	Observations / Bemerkungen
6 57	20 07	IC ✕ ⊠ Milano
15 20	8 06	⊠ Milano C Ⓢ
18 46	9 07[1]	🛌 🛏

[1] Ⓦ ar/an 9 56

Hamburg Hbf

	ar / an	Observations / Bemerkungen
Ⓒ 5 32	9 48	IC ✕
7 00	11 14	IC ✕
Ⓒ 8 03	12 14	IC ✕
9 00	13 14	IC ✕
10 00	14 14	IC ✕
10 08	14 57	
Ⓒ 11 00	15 14	IC ✕
12 03	16 14	IC ✕
13 00	17 16	IC ✕
14 00	18 14	IC ✕
15 00	19 14	IC ✕
Ⓑ 16 03	20 16	IC ✕
17 00	21 14	IC ✕
18 00	22 16	IC ✕
Ⓑ 19 00	23 16	IC ✕
20 03	0 16	IC ✕
Ⓓ 23 26	5 44	🛌 🛏

Ⓑ ①-⑤, ⑦
Ⓒ ①-⑥
Ⓓ Ⓢ; Ⓦ: ①-⑤, ⑦

Hannover

	ar / an	Observations / Bemerkungen
5 50	9 13	
6 14	9 51	✕
Ⓒ 7 03	9 59	IC ✕
Ⓒ 8 02	10 58	IC ✕
9 03	11 57	IC ✕
Ⓓ 10 03	12 57	IC ✕
Ⓓ 11 03	13 57	IC ✕
12 02	14 57	IC ✕
13 03	15 57	IC ✕
13 25	16 46	✕
Ⓐ 14 03	16 57	IC ✕
15 03	17 57	IC ✕
Ⓑ 16 02	18 58	IC ✕
Ⓑ 17 03	19 59	IC ✕
18 03	20 57	IC ✕
19 03	22 00	IC ✕
20 02	23 00	IC ✕

Ⓐ ①-⑥
Ⓑ ①-⑤, ⑦
Ⓒ ①-⑥, except/sauf/ohne 18 VI, 26 XII, 21, 23 IV
Ⓓ ①-⑥

Heidelberg

	ar / an	Observations / Bemerkungen
Ⓒ 5 57	8 39	IC ✕
6 57	9 39	IC ✕ ⊠ Mannheim IC ✕
7 38	10 29	✕
7 57	10 39	IC ✕
8 24	11 24	✕
Ⓒ 8 57	11 39	IC ✕
Ⓒ 9 57	12 39	IC ✕ ⊠ Mannheim IC ✕
10 57	13 39	IC ✕
11 57	14 39	IC ✕
12 57	15 39	IC ✕
13 57	16 39	IC ✕
14 57	17 39	IC ✕
15 57	18 39	IC ✕
16 57	19 39	IC ✕ ⊠ Mannheim IC ✕
17 57	20 39	IC ✕
Ⓑ 18 57	21 39	IC ✕
19 57	22 42	IC ✕ ⊠ Mannheim IC ✕

Ⓑ ①-⑤, ⑦
Ⓒ ①-⑥

Innsbruck

	ar / an	Observations / Bemerkungen
7 57	16 38	IC ✕
Ⓒ 8 57	17 26	IC ✕ ⊠ München TEE ✕
9 03	18 36	IC ✕ ⊠ München
10 03	19 00	IC ✕
15 57	1 30	IC ✕ ⊠ München Ⓡ
23 28	9 50	🛌 🛏 ⊠ München Ⓡ ✕

Ⓒ ①-⑥

København

	ar / an	Observations / Bemerkungen
3 28	14 09	⊠ Hamburg
7 00	16 29	IC ✕ ⊠ Hamburg
10 00	19 45	IC ✕
13 00	22 45	IC ✕ ⊠ Hamburg
Ⓑ 19 00	6 45	IC ✕ ⊠ Hamburg 🛌 🛏
22 39	9 09	🛌 🛏

Ⓑ ①-⑤, ⑦

Koblenz

	ar / an	Observations / Bemerkungen
5 36	6 37	✕
Ⓒ 5 57	6 49	IC ✕
6 57	7 49	IC ✕
7 00	13 55	🚢
7 38	8 38	✕
7 57	8 49	IC ✕
8 24	9 23	✕
9 03	9 55	IC ✕
9 20	10 24	✕
9 57	10 49	IC ✕
10 49	11 40	TEE ✕
10 57	11 49	IC ✕
11 57	12 49	IC ✕
12 32	13 33	
12 57	13 49	IC ✕
13 57	14 49	IC ✕
14 14	15 20	
14 57	15 49	IC ✕
15 20	16 21	
15 57	16 49	IC ✕
16 22	17 28	
16 57	17 49	IC ✕
17 17	18 21	
17 57	18 49	IC ✕
18 46	19 45	
Ⓓ 18 57	19 49	IC ✕
19 57	20 49	IC ✕
20 47	21 43	
Ⓓ 21 03	21 55	IC ✕
21 35	22 32	
22 36	23 43	
23 28	0 31	

Ⓒ ①-⑥, except/sauf/ohne 18 VI, 26-31 XII, 21, 23 IV
Ⓓ ①-⑤, ⑦, except/sauf/ohne 17 VI, 25 XII, 20, 22 IV

Liège

	ar / an	Observations / Bemerkungen
4 47	6 39	
7 05	8 41	
Ⓒ 8 09	9 27	IC ✕
8 21	10 07	
9 07	10 41	
11 12	12 37	
13 20	14 48	IC ✕
15 08	16 34	
16 35	18 10	IC ✕
17 06	18 43	✕
18 18	19 45	✕
20 20	21 51	
23 37	1 14	

Ⓒ 29 V-19 XI, 12 XII-7 I, 5 III-2 VI;
①-⑥ 21 XI-10 XII, 9 I-3 III

Courtesy of Swiss Federal Railways

Now use the schedule to complete the following questions:

Leave Köln at 3:08 P.M. Arrive in Liège at ________.

Leave Köln at ________ and arrive in Heidelberg at 4:39 P.M.

Leave Köln at 8:47 P.M. and arrive in Koblenz at ________.

(Vee) (man) (um) (ET-vas) (BIT-et)

Wie man um etwas bittet

Asking for Something

There are two ways you can say "I want" in German. The second way is more polite.

(vil)

ICH WILL

Ich will ein Glas Bier. I want a glass of beer.

du willst, er will—

but watch out for the plural:

(VOL-en) (volt)

wir wollen, ihr wollt, sie wollen

(möç-teh)

ICH MÖCHTE

A little more polite:

Ich möchte ein Glas Bier. I would like a glass of beer.

du möchtest, er möchte

wir möchten, ihr möchtet, sie möchten

Sie möchten

See if you can match up the verb forms with their meanings in English:

1. ich will
2. er möchte
3. sie wollen
4. sie will
5. ihr wollt
6. sie möchten

A. they want
B. she wants
C. I want
D. he would like
E. they would like
F. you want

ANSWERS

4:34 P.M., 1:57 P.M., 9:43 P.M.

Matching. 1. C 2. D 3. A 4. B 5. F 6. E

Here's a further exercise. Fill in the missing word.

1. Er ____________________ jetzt essen. *(ES-en)*
   wants (to eat)
2. Sie ____________________ ins Kino gehen.
   they would like (to go)
3. Wir ____________________ zum Bahnhof fahren.
   want (to drive)
4. Sie ____________________ den D-Zug nehmen.
   she wants (to take)
5. ____________________ Blumen?
   would you (familiar) like
6. Er ____________________ ein Glas Milch.
   would like — milk

You got them all correct?

(zehR) (goot)
Sehr gut!
Very good

ALLES EINSTEIGEN!

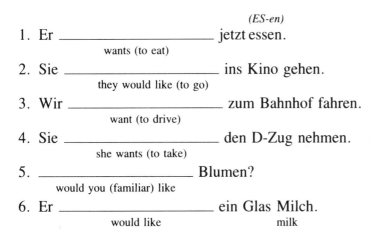

reisen
to travel

(AP-teil)
das Abteil
compartment

(tsook)
der Zug
train

(SHLEES-fach)
das Schließfach
locker

(sich NEE-der-zets-en)
sich niedersetzen
to sit down

(FAHR-gast)
der Fahrgast
passenger

ANSWERS

Fill-ins. **1.** will **2.** möchten **3.** wollen **4.** will **5.** Möchtest du **6.** möchte

(ge-PEK-an-nah-meh-shte-leh)
die Gepäckannahmestelle
baggage checking counter

(ge-PEK-ap-fer-ti-gung)
die Gepäckabfertigung
baggage dispatch

(VAR-teh-zahl)
der Wartesaal
waiting room

(KOW-fen)
Fahrkarten kaufen
to purchase tickets

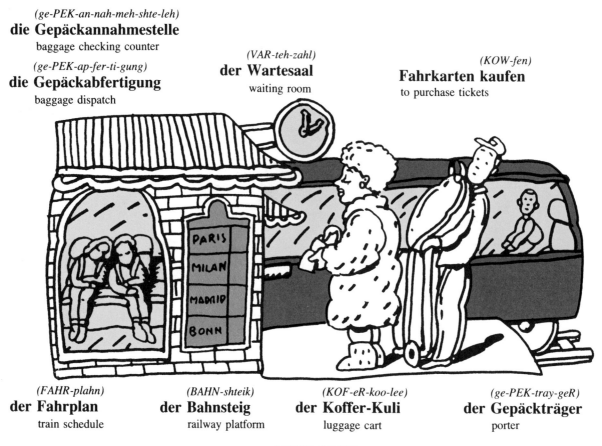

(FAHR-plahn)
der Fahrplan
train schedule

(BAHN-shteik)
der Bahnsteig
railway platform

(KOF-eR-koo-lee)
der Koffer-Kuli
luggage cart

(ge-PEK-tray-geR)
der Gepäckträger
porter

WORD HUNT
Can you find these eight words in German that are hidden away in this puzzle?

1. to travel
2. train schedule
3. waiting room
4. compartment
5. we
6. movie theater
7. to fall
8. all

N	Z	L	W	I	R	G	K	A
R	I	N	A	M	P	F	I	B
F	A	H	R	P	L	A	N	G
E	A	B	T	E	I	L	O	E
S	B	O	E	B	P	L	L	I
R	E	I	S	E	N	E	B	Z
N	Z	N	A	F	O	N	C	I
O	L	Z	A	R	L	M	G	G
E	D	R	L	G	N	A	A	L

ANSWERS

Word Hunt.
1. reisen **2.** Fahrplan **3.** Wartesaal **4.** Abteil **5.** wir **6.** Kino **7.** fallen **8.** alle

(ray-fleks-IF-proh-noh-men)

Reflexivpronomen

Reflexive Pronouns

A reflexive verb refers or "reflects" the action back to the subject of a sentence. This is done by means of reflexive pronouns, such as "myself" and "yourself." Here are the reflexive pronouns in German.

Example:

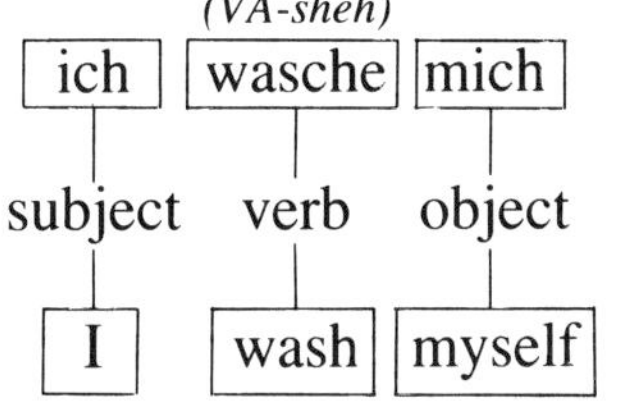

ich wasche mich	I wash myself
(vesht) du wäscht dich	you wash yourself
(vesht) (ziç) er, sie, es wäscht sich	he, she, it washes himself, herself, itself
(VA-shen) wir waschen uns	we wash ourselves
(vasht) ihr wascht euch	you wash yourselves
sie waschen sich	they wash themselves
Sie waschen sich (polite)	you wash yourself, yourselves

There are no special words for the reflexive pronouns in the first and second persons; we use the personal pronouns *mich, dich, uns, euch.* The reflexive pronoun for all three genders in the third person singular is *sich,* and *sich* is also the reflexive pronoun for the third person plural and for the formal *Sie* (you).

SUMMARY

Subject	Verb	Reflexive Pronoun (object)
ich	__________	**mich**
du	__________	**dich**
er, sie, es	__________	**sich**
wir	__________	**uns**
ihr	__________	**euch**
sie	__________	**sich**
Sie	__________	**sich**

(a-mü-ZEE-ren)
Let's practice using reflexive pronouns with the verb *amüsieren*, which in its reflexive form is *sich amüsieren*, which means—you guessed it—to amuse oneself, to enjoy oneself.

ich amüsiere ______________	du amüsierst ______________
er amüsiert ______________	wir amüsieren ______________
ihr amüsiert ______________	sie amüsieren ______________

Here are some more reflexive verbs. Study them and then complete the short exercise that follows. It should be easy. You're well into your new language.

(rah-ZEE-ren) sich rasieren:	to shave oneself
sich entschuldigen:	to excuse oneself, to apologize
(eR-IN-ern) sich erinnern:	to remember

1. Wann rasiert er ______________?
2. Entschuldigst du ______________?
3. Ihr erinnert ______________.
4. Wir rasieren ______________.
5. Sie amüsiert ______________.
6. Erinnert sie ______________?
7. Ich entschuldige ______________.
8. Amüsierst du ______________?

ANSWERS

sich amüsieren.
mich dich sich uns euch sich
Reflexive pronouns.
1. sich **2.** dich **3.** euch **4.** uns **5.** sich **6.** sich **7.** mich **8.** dich

7 Länder und Sprachen

(LEN-deR) *(SHPRAH-chen)*

Countries and Languages

Ich bin . . .

(iç) *(bin)*

I Am . . .

As you travel, you'll meet people from a variety of countries. Here are some ways nationality is identified in German.

(a-may-ree-KAH-neR)
Ich bin Amerikaner.
I am American.

(ÖS-teR-rei-çeR)
Ich bin Österreicher.
Austrian

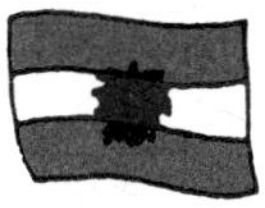

(ows-TRAH-lee-eR)
Ich bin Australier.
Australian

(BEL-gee-eR)
Ich bin Belgier.
Belgian

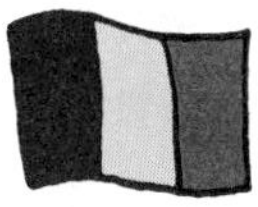

(ENG-len-deR)
Ich bin Engländer.
English

(ka-NAH-dee-eR)
Ich bin Kanadier.
Canadian

(çi-NAY-zeh)
Ich bin Chinese.
Chinese

(DAY-neh)
Ich bin Däne.
Danish

(HOL-en-deR)
Ich bin Holländer.
Dutch

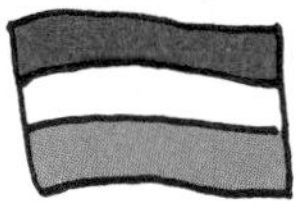

(fran-TSOH-zeh)
Ich bin Franzose.
French

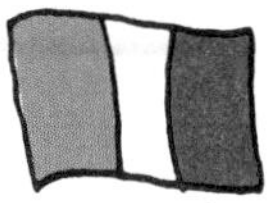

(DOY-tsheR)
Ich bin Deutscher.
German

(i-ta-lee-AY-ner)
Ich bin Italiener.
Italian

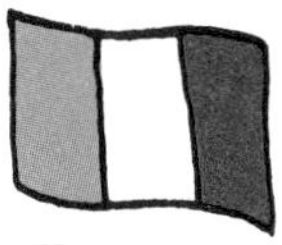

(ya-PAH-neR)
Ich bin Japaner.
Japanese

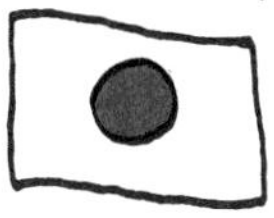

(mek-si-KAH-neR)
Ich bin Mexikaner.
Mexican

(NOHR-vay-geR)
Ich bin Norweger.
Norwegian

(POH-leh)
Ich bin Pole.
Polish

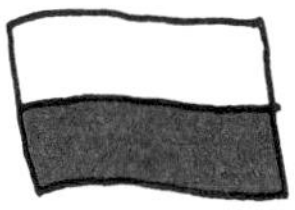

(RUS-eh)
Ich bin Russe.
Russian

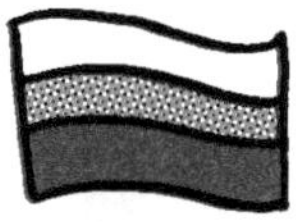

(SHPAHN-ee-eR)
Ich bin Spanier.
Spanish

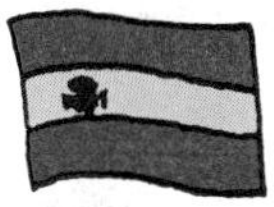

(SHVAY-deh)
Ich bin Schwede.
Swedish

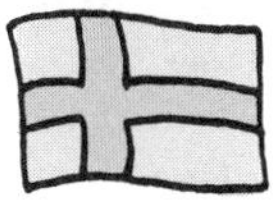

(SHVEI-tseR)
Ich bin Schweizer.
Swiss

(TÜR-keh)
Ich bin Türke.
Turkish

In the preceding examples nationality was given in the masculine form. The feminine form usually, but not always, ends with *-in*. For instance, a woman would say „Ich bin Amerikanerin" *(a-may-ree-KAH-ner-in)* or „Ich bin Chinesin" *(çi-NAY-zin)* or „Ich bin Deutsche." *(DOY-tsheh)*

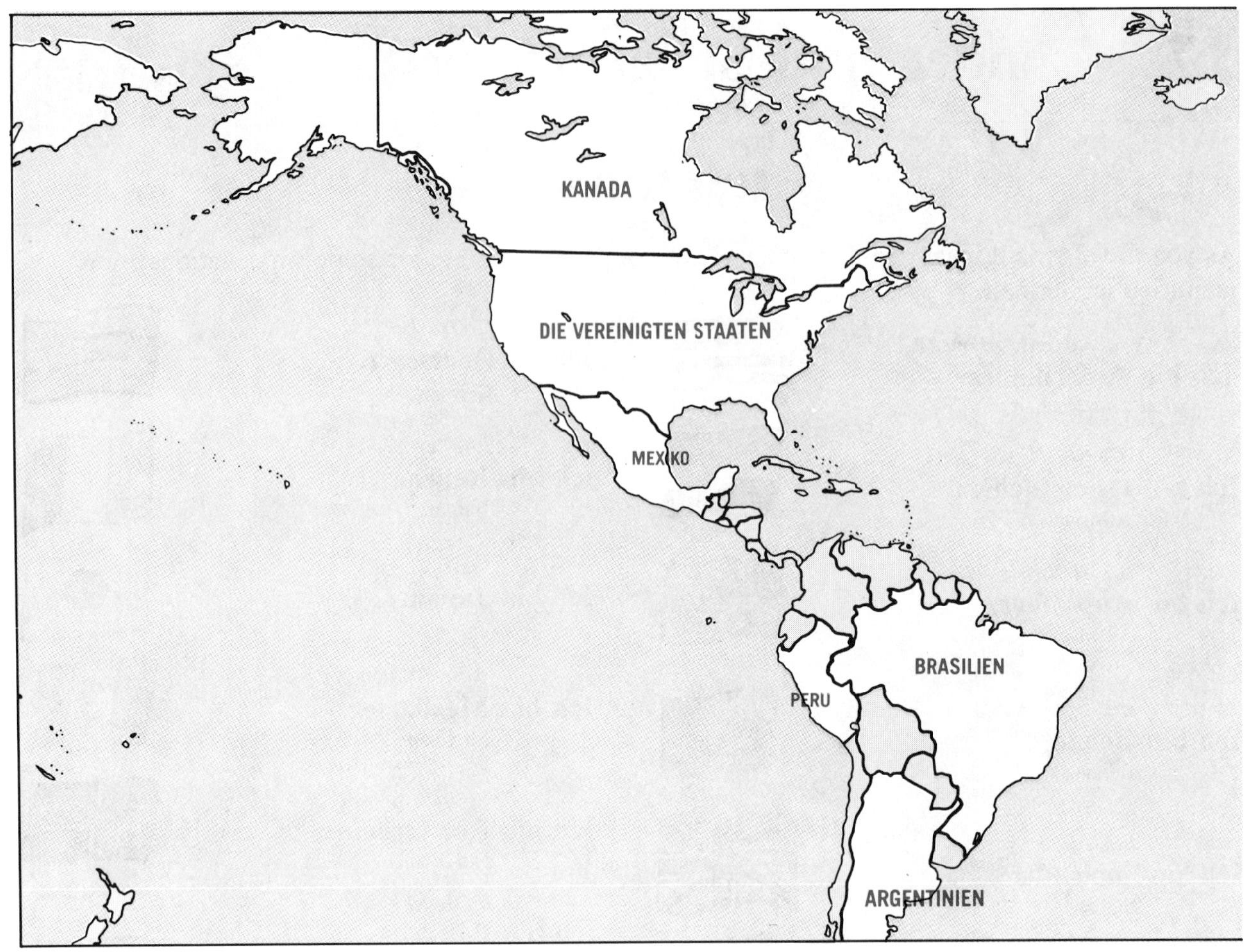

All of the following countries except two are classified as neuter. The definite or indefinite article is hardly ever used with the "neuter" countries. The article is used, however, with the "feminine" countries (die Schweiz, for instance) and the "plural" countries (die Vereinigten Staaten, for example).

(ows-TRAL-ee-en)
Australien Australia

(ÇEE-na)
China China

(DOYTSH-lant)
Deutschland Germany

(i-TAL-i-en)
Italien Italy

(MEKS-ee-ko)
Mexiko Mexico

(SHPAHN-i-en)
Spanien Spain

(feR-EI-niç-ten) (SHTAH-ten)
die Vereinigten Staaten
(a-MAY-ree-kah)
von Amerika U.S.A.
or
(oo-es-ah)
die U.S.A.

(shveits)
die Schweiz Switzerland

(KA-na-da)
Kanada Canada

(FRANK-reiç)
Frankreich France

(GROHS-bri-tah-ni-en)
Großbritannien Great Britain

(ÖS-teR-reiç)
Österreich Austria

(YAH-pan)
Japan Japan

(RUS-lant)
Rußland Russia

(ma-ROK-oh)
Marokko Morocco

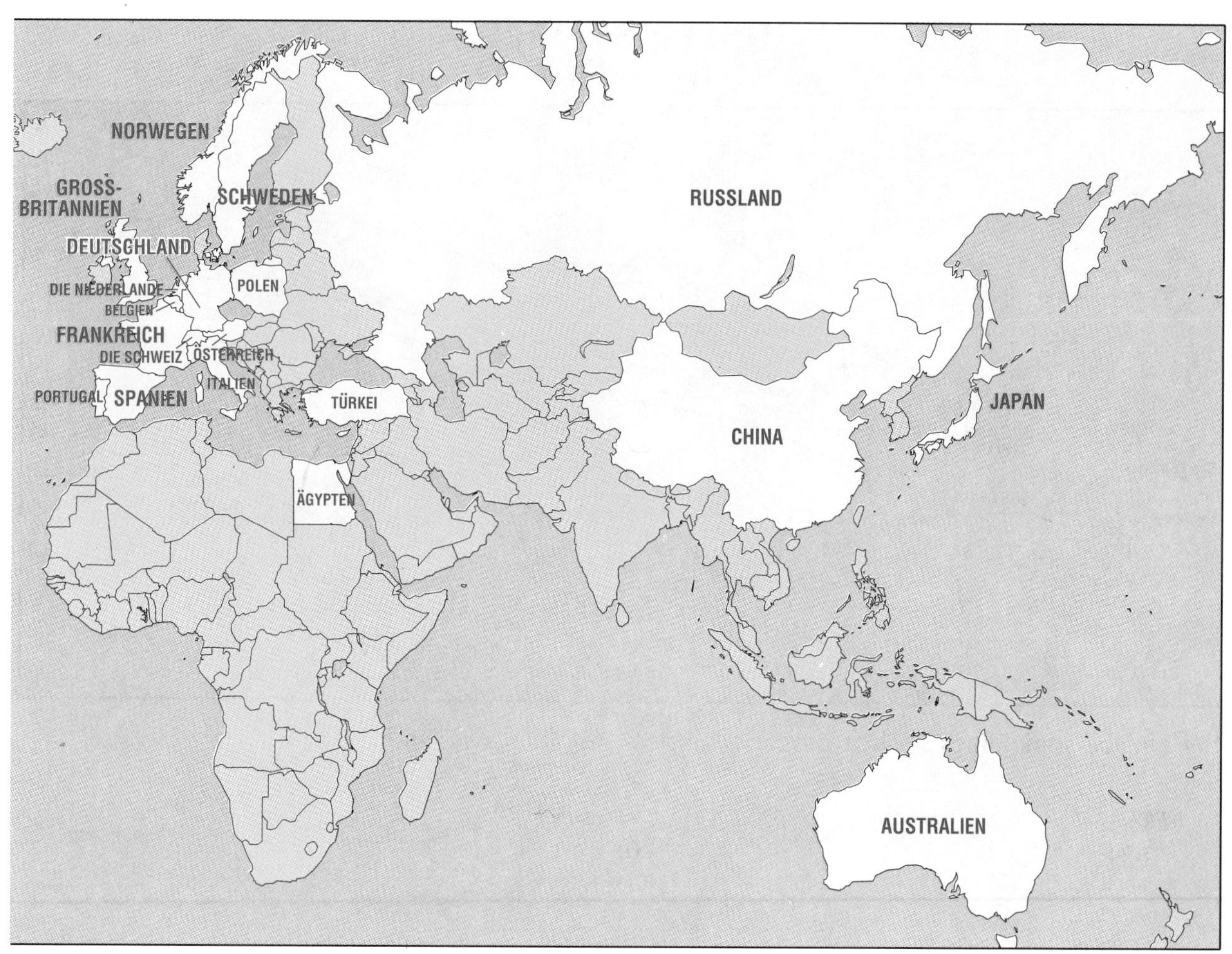

(iç) *(SHPRE-çeh)*

Ich spreche . . .

I Speak . . .

Let's learn to say the names of some languages. As in English, the name of the language is often very similar to the name of the country.

(ENG-lish)
Ich spreche Englisch.

(doytsh)
Ich spreche Deutsch.

(fran-TSÖ-zish)
Ich spreche Französisch.

(SHPAH-nish)
Ich spreche Spanisch.

(RU-sish)
Ich spreche Russisch.

(çi-NAY-zish)
Ich spreche Chinesisch.

(ya-PAH-nish)
Ich spreche Japanisch.

(iç) *(REI-zeh)* *(nach)*

Ich reise nach

I am traveling to . . .

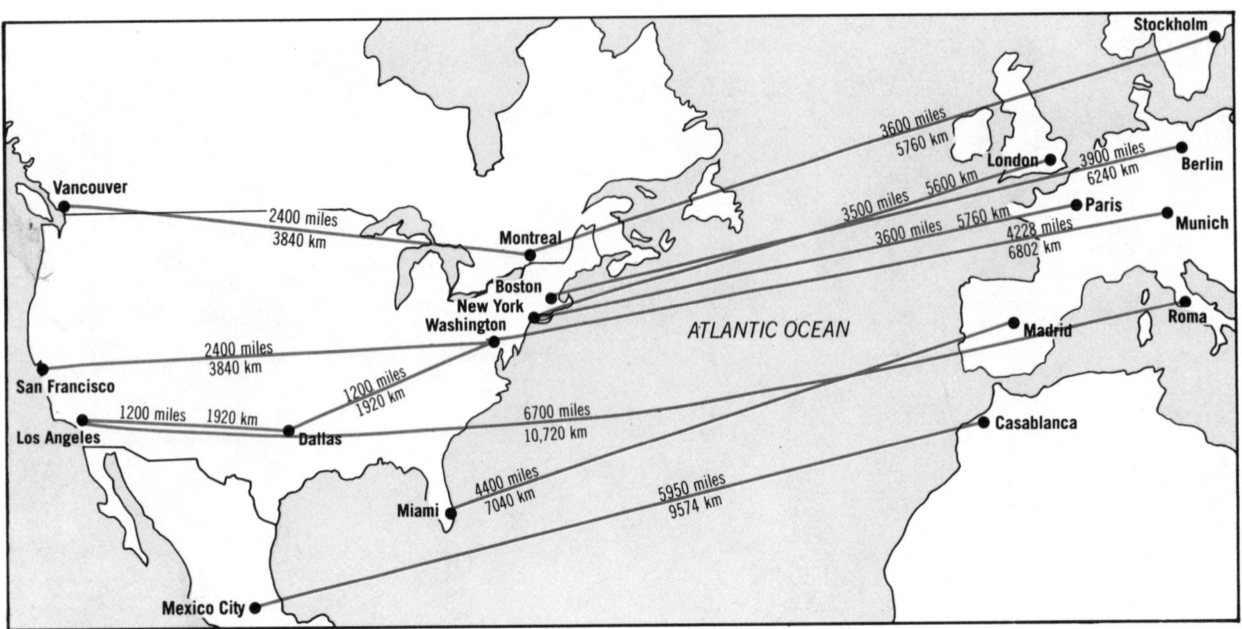

Let's place some cities in their proper countries. *Auf Deutsch, bitte.*

(FRAH-geh) Frage question	*(ANT-vort)* Antwort answer
1. Wo ist Vancouver?	Vancouver ist in Kanada.
2. Wo ist Los Angeles?	
3. Wo ist Stockholm?	
4. Wo ist *(pa-REES)* Paris?	
5. Wo ist Madrid?	
6. Wo ist London?	
7. Wo ist *(rohm)* Rom?	
8. Wo ist Casablanca?	

ANSWERS

2. in den Vereinigten Staaten **3.** in Schweden **4.** in Frankreich **5.** in Spanien **6.** in England
7. in Italien **8.** in Marokko

(feR-LOHR-en) *(OO-bahn)*

Verloren in der U-Bahn

Lost in the Subway

Knowing the frustrations of not being understood, can you imagine how Anne felt when she lost her purse?

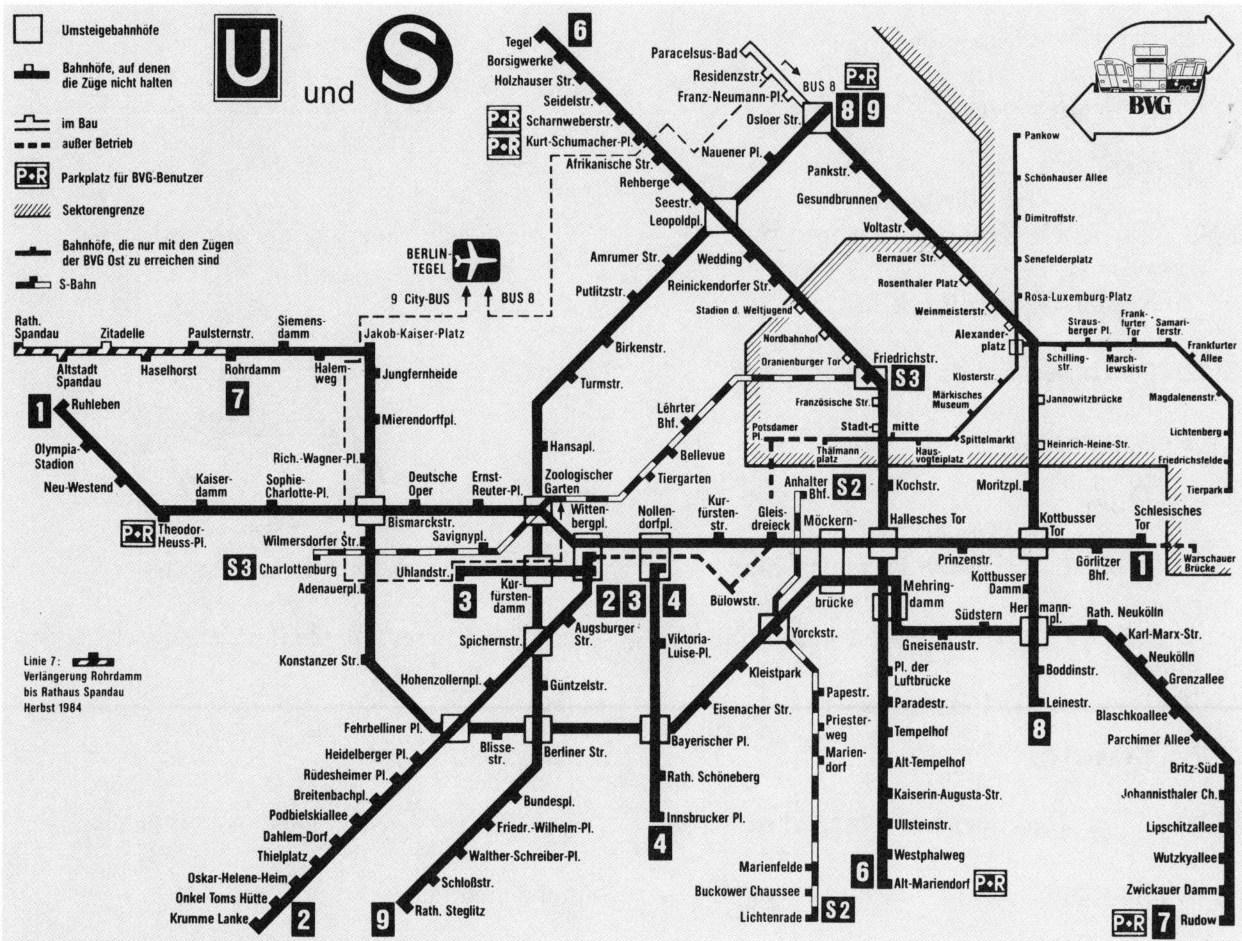

BERLIN (Bus and Subway System)

From Berliner Verkehrs-Betriebe (BVG). Reprinted by permission.

ANNE (to policeman at desk in police station)

	Entschuldigen Sie bitte, sprechen Sie Englisch?	Excuse me, please, do you speak English?
POLIZIST	**Ein wenig.** *(VAY-niç)* **Womit kann ich Ihnen behilflich** *(be-HILF-liç)* **sein?**	A little. How can I help you?
ANNE	**My purse—**	
POLIZIST	**Ihre Handtasche?** *(HANT-ta-sheh)*	Your purse?
ANNE	**Ja. Die ist weg!** *(vek)* **In der U-Bahn . . . .**	Yes. It is gone. In the subway . . . .

POLIZIST	*(leit)* *(BAHR-gelt)* **Das tut mir leid. Viel Bargeld? Cash?**	I am sorry. Much cash?
ANNE	**Cash—nur ein paar Mark. Aber tausend Mark in—in—**	Only a few marks. But 1,000 marks in—in—
POLIZIST	*(REI-zeh-sheks)* **Reiseschecks? Traveler's checks?**	
ANNE	*(kre-DIT-kar-ten)* **Ja. Auch Kreditkarten und mein** *(REI- zeh-pas)* **Reisepaß. Was soll ich tun?**	Yes. Also credit cards and my passport. What shall I do?
POLIZIST	**Haben Sie die Nummern der Reiseschecks?**	Do you have the numbers of the traveler's checks?
ANNE	**O ja.**	Oh yes.
POLIZIST	*(bü-ROH)* *(gleiç)* **Gut. Ein Büro ist gleich hier** *(er-ZETST)* **um die Ecke. Dort ersetzt man** *(HO-fent-liç)* **hoffentlich die Reiseschecks.**	Good. An office is right around the corner. There they can replace the travelers checks, I hope.
ANNE	**Ersetzt?**	Replace them?
POLIZIST	**Ja. Und dort kann man Ihnen** *(fee-LEIÇT)* **vielleicht auch mit den Kreditkarten helfen.**	Yes. And there they can possibly also help you with the credit cards.
ANNE	**Und mein Reisepaß?**	And my passport?
POLIZIST	**Da müssen Sie zum** *(kon-zu-LAT)* **amerikanischen Konsulat. Möchten** *(for-moo-LAR)* **Sie bitte dieses Formular ausfüllen?** *(HIN-zets-en)* **Sie können sich dort hinsetzen.**	With this you have to go to the American consulate. Would you please fill out this form? You can sit there.
ANNE	**Vielen Dank.**	Many thanks.
POLIZIST	*(ge-SHAY-en)* **Gern geschehen. Und es tut** *(VIRK-liç)* **mir wirklich leid.**	Don't mention it. And I am truly sorry.

8	*(OW-tohs)* *(KLEIN-bus-seh)* **Autos und Kleinbusse** Cars and Vans *(SHTRAH-sen-shil-deR)* **Straßenschilder** Road Signs

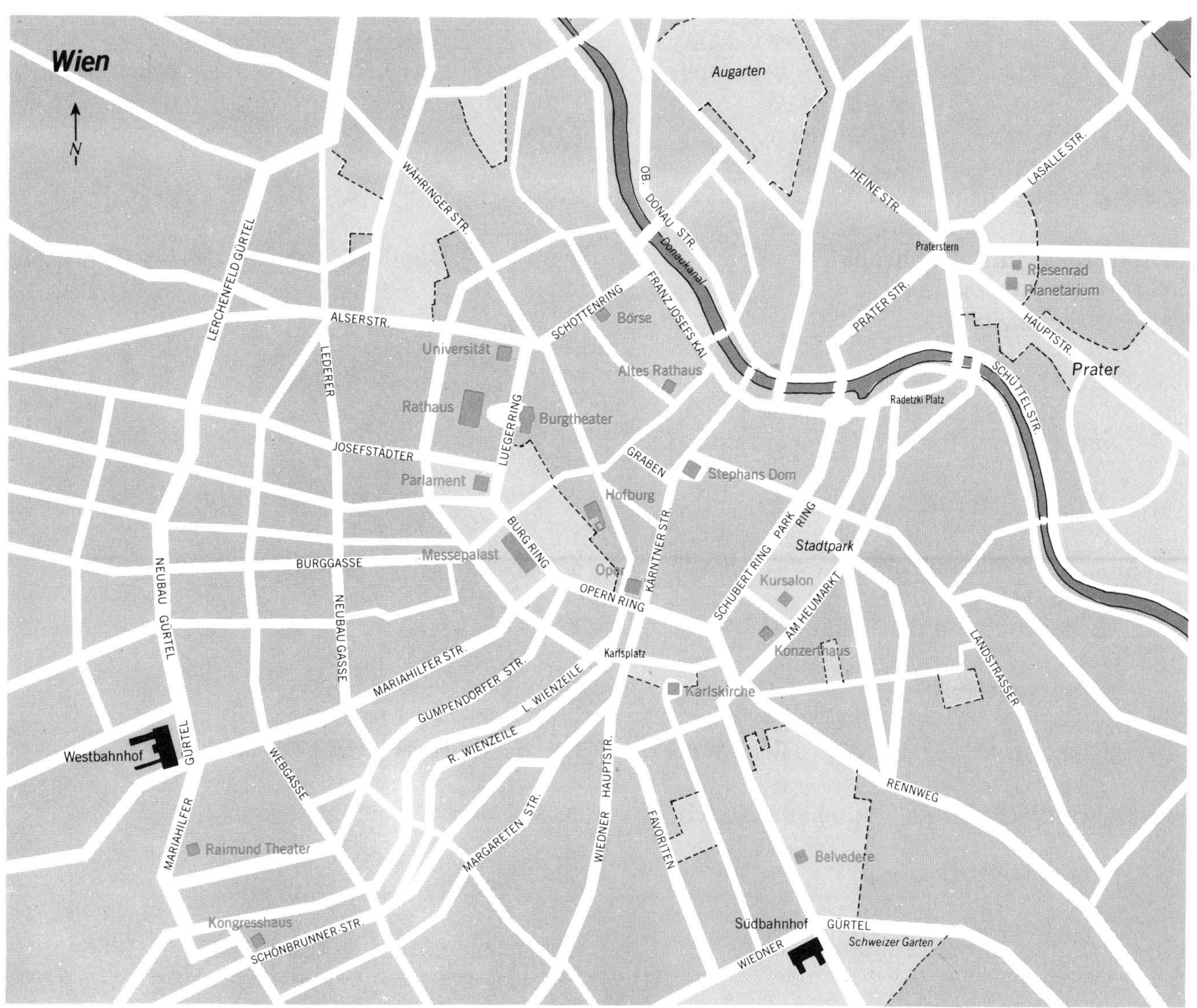

(bei) *(dayR)* *(OW-toh-feR-mee-tung)*

BEI DER AUTOVERMIETUNG

At the Car Rental Office

Read the following dialogue closely. It should prove useful if you want to rent a car — perhaps to see the many sights of Vienna (Wien). As always, say each German line out loud several times.

MARK **Guten Morgen. Ich möchte einen Wagen mieten.** *(MEE-ten)*	Good morning. I would like to rent a car.
ANGESTELLTER **Für wie lange?** *(LAN-geh)*	For how long?"
MARK **Zwei Wochen.**	Two weeks.
ANGESTELLTER **Warten Sie mal . . . wir haben einen Opel und einen Volkswagen. Der Volkswagen ist kleiner.** *(VAR-ten) (OH-pel) (FOLKS-vah-gen) (KLEIN-eR)*	Let's see . . . we have an Opel and a Volkswagen. The Volkswagen is smaller.
MARK **Ich nehme den Volkswagen. Ist der Preis mit unbeschränkter Kilometerzahl?** *(UN-be-shrenk-teR) (kee-loh-MAY-teR-tsahl)*	I'll take the Volkswagen. Is the mileage (number of kilometers) included in the price?
ANGESTELLTER **Ja, aber Sie zahlen für das Benzin. Ihr Führerschein und eine Kreditkarte, bitte.** *(ben-TSEEN) (FÜ-reR-shein)*	Yes, but you pay for the gas. Your driver's license and a credit card, please.
MARK **Können Sie mir zeigen, wie die Schaltung und die Lichter funktionieren?** *(TSEI-gen) (SHAL-tung) (funk-tsee-oh-NEE-ren)*	Can you show me how the gear shift and the lights work?
ANGESTELLTER **Natürlich. Hier ist der Schlüssel und die Autopapiere. Ich komme mit Ihnen.** *(na-TŪR-liç) (SHLÜS-el) (OW-toh-pah-pee-reh)*	Of course. Here is the key and the car papers. I am coming with you.
MARK **Das Auto hat automatische Schaltung, nicht wahr?** *(ow-toh-MAH-ti-sheh)*	The car has automatic transmission, right?
ANGESTELLTER **Nein, das Auto hat Gangschaltung.** *(GANG-shal-tung)*	No, the car has manual shift.
MARK **Ach du lieber Himmel, ich kann nur automatische Schaltung fahren!** *(HIM-mel)*	Oh my heavens, I can only drive an automatic!

(VIÇ-ti-ges) (füR) (dayn) (OW-toh-fah-reR)

Wichtiges für den Autofahrer

Essential Phrases for Drivers

(feR-IRT) **Ich habe mich verirrt.**	I am lost.
(ga-RAH-žeh) (NAY-eh) **Gibt es* eine Garage in der Nähe?**	Is there a garage nearby?
Was ist los?	What's the matter?
(ge-rah-deh-OWS) (VEI-teR) **Fahren Sie geradeaus weiter.**	Continue straight ahead.
Fahren Sie hier links, dann rechts.	Turn left here, then right.
(feR-KAYR) (shlim) **Der Verkehr ist schlimm.**	The traffic is bad.
Sie haben recht.	You are right.
(UN-reçt) **Sie haben unrecht.**	You are wrong.
der Schlüssel	key
die Autopapiere	car papers
der Führerschein	driver's license
das Benzin	gasoline
(veit) (NAH-eh) **weit, nahe**	far, near
(dort) (DRÜ-ben) **dort drüben**	over there
an der Ecke von	at the corner of
(NOR-den) (ZÜ-den) (OS-ten) (VES-ten) **der Norden, Süden, Osten, Westen**	north, south, east, west
die Kreditkarte	credit card
die Verkehrsampel	traffic light
bis	until, till

**Es gibt* (literally: "it gives") is the equivalent of "there is" or "there are" in English.

(SHTRAH-sen-shil-deR)
STRASSENSCHILDER
Road Signs

If you're planning to drive while you're abroad, spend some time learning the meanings of these signs.

Dangerous intersection

Danger!

Stop

Speed limit (in km/hr)

Minimum speed

End of limited speed

No entry

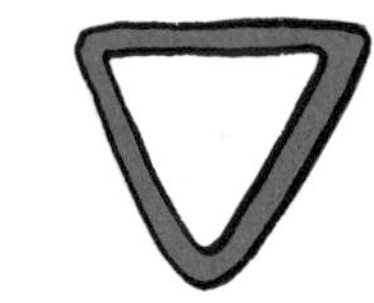
Yield right-of-way

Two-way traffic

Dangerous curve

Entrance to Autobahn

End of Autobahn

Customs

Do not pass

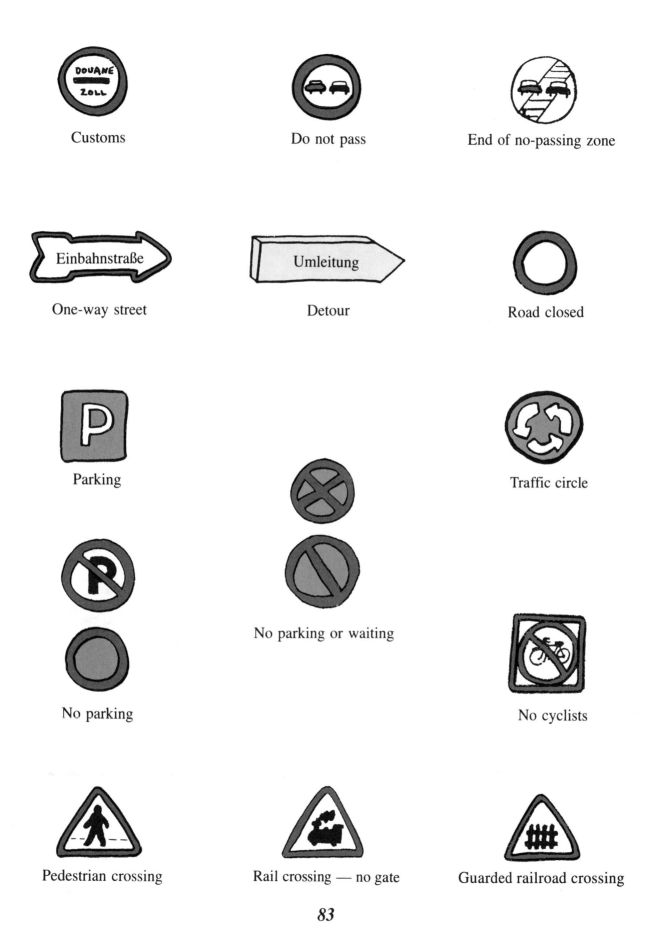

End of no-passing zone

One-way street

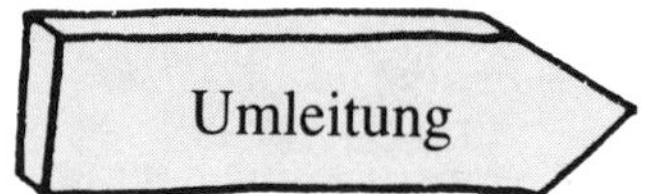

Detour

Road closed

Parking

Traffic circle

No parking or waiting

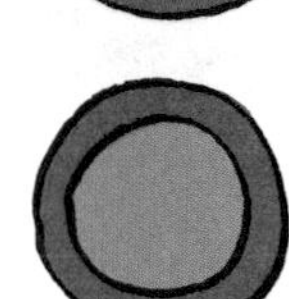

No parking

No cyclists

Pedestrian crossing

Rail crossing — no gate

Guarded railroad crossing

(TANK-shtel-eh)

BEI DER TANKSTELLE

At the Service Station

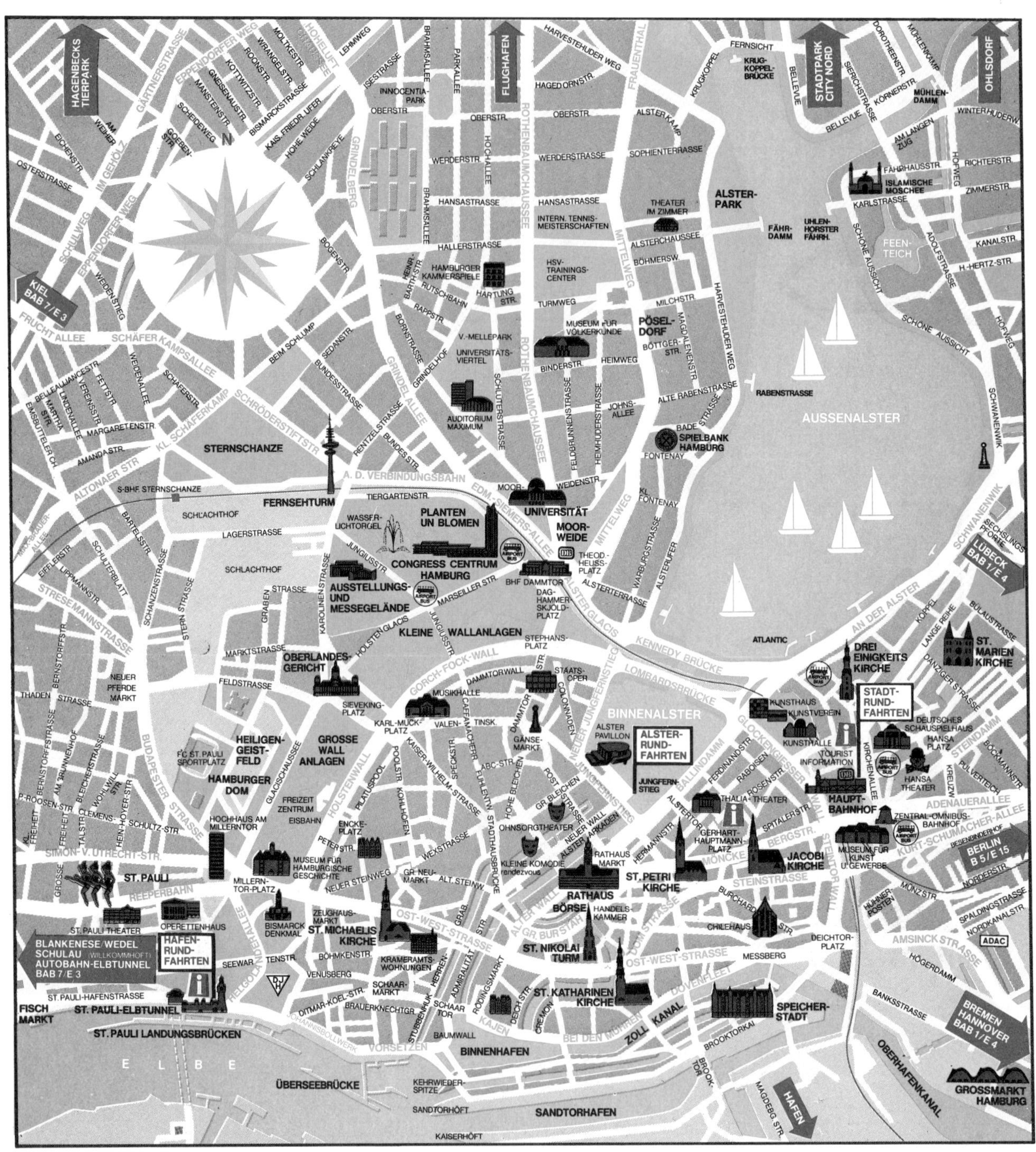

Hamburg *(Courtesy of Hamburg Tourist Office)*

KUNDE customer	*(KUN-deh) (FOL-tan-ken)* **Volltanken, bitte!**	Fill it up, please!
TANKWART attendant	*(TANK-vart) (nor-MAHL) (ZOO-peR) (BLEI-frei)* **Normal oder super? Bleifrei?**	Regular or super? Leadfree?

KUNDE **Normal, bleifrei. Und sehen Sie** *(op) (REI-fen) (ge-NOOK)* **nach, ob die Reifen genug** *(LUFT-druk) (öl)* **Luftdruck haben, auch das Öl und das Wasser.**	Regular, unleaded. And check the air pressure in the tires, the oil and the water too.
TANKWART **Alles ist in Ordnung.** *(be-ZOOCHT)* **Haben Sie Hamburg besucht?**	Everything is okay. Did you visit Hamburg?
KUNDE **Ja, zum ersten Mal.**	Yes, for the first time.
TANKWART **Wie hat Ihnen die Stadt gefallen?**	How did you like the city?
KUNDE *(zankt) (mi-ça-AY-lis)* **Prima. Die St. Michaelis** *(KIR-çeh)* **Kirche—**	Super. St. Michael's Church—
TANKWART *(MI-çel)* **Ah—der große Michel, das** *(VAHR-tsei-çen)* **Wahrzeichen Hamburgs—**	Ah—the great Michel, the symbol of Hamburg—
KUNDE *(RAT-hows) (u-ni-ver-zi-TAYT)* **das Rathaus, die Universität, die Kunsthalle—**	the Town Hall, the University, the Art Museum—
TANKWART *(in-ter-es-ANT)* **Interessant, nicht wahr?**	Interesting, right?
KUNDE *(keel)* **Sehr. Ich fahre nach Kiel. Was ist** *(KÜR-tse-steh) (SHTRE-keh)* **die kürzeste Strecke?**	Very. I'm driving to Kiel. What is the shortest route?
TANKWART *(ge-rah-deh-OWS)* **Von hier geradeaus, bis Sie zur Autobahn kommen. Die geht direkt nach Kiel.**	From here straight ahead until you get to the Autobahn. It goes directly to Kiel.
KUNDE **Ist der Verkehr schlimm?**	Is the traffic bad?
TANKWART **Um diese Zeit gibt es vielleicht** *(feR-KAYRS-shtow-ung-en) (an-ZONS-ten)* **einige Verkehrsstauungen, ansonsten ist die Strecke gut.**	At this time, there may be some traffic jams; otherwise, the road is good.

DAS AUTO

The Car

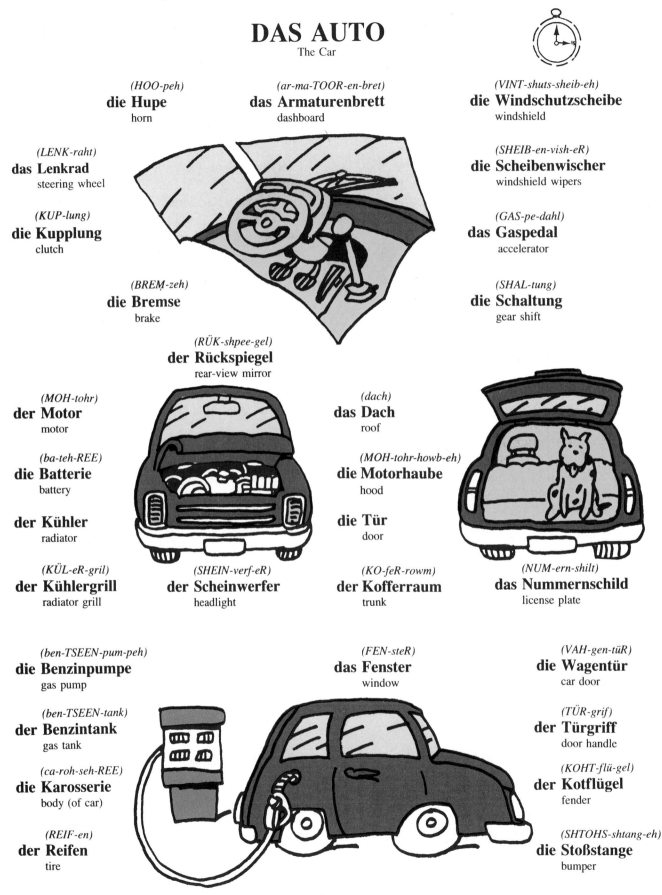

(HOO-peh)
die Hupe
horn

(ar-ma-TOOR-en-bret)
das Armaturenbrett
dashboard

(VINT-shuts-sheib-eh)
die Windschutzscheibe
windshield

(LENK-raht)
das Lenkrad
steering wheel

(KUP-lung)
die Kupplung
clutch

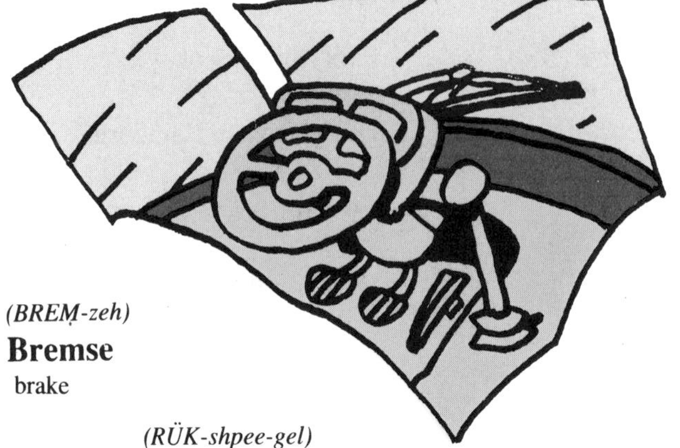

(SHEIB-en-vish-eR)
die Scheibenwischer
windshield wipers

(GAS-pe-dahl)
das Gaspedal
accelerator

(BREM-zeh)
die Bremse
brake

(SHAL-tung)
die Schaltung
gear shift

(RÜK-shpee-gel)
der Rückspiegel
rear-view mirror

(MOH-tohr)
der Motor
motor

(ba-teh-REE)
die Batterie
battery

der Kühler
radiator

(dach)
das Dach
roof

(MOH-tohr-howb-eh)
die Motorhaube
hood

die Tür
door

(KÜL-eR-gril)
der Kühlergrill
radiator grill

(SHEIN-verf-eR)
der Scheinwerfer
headlight

(KO-feR-rowm)
der Kofferraum
trunk

(NUM-ern-shilt)
das Nummernschild
license plate

(ben-TSEEN-pum-peh)
die Benzinpumpe
gas pump

(FEN-steR)
das Fenster
window

(VAH-gen-tüR)
die Wagentür
car door

(ben-TSEEN-tank)
der Benzintank
gas tank

(ca-roh-seh-REE)
die Karosserie
body (of car)

(REIF-en)
der Reifen
tire

(TÜR-grif)
der Türgriff
door handle

(KOHT-flü-gel)
der Kotflügel
fender

(SHTOHS-shtang-eh)
die Stoßstange
bumper

Wichtige Ausdrücke übers Auto

(VIÇ-ti-geh) (OWS-drü-keh) (OW-toh)

Essential Expressions about Your Car

(REI-fen-pan-eh) **Ich habe eine Reifenpanne.**	I have a flat tire.
(shpringt) **Mein Wagen springt nicht an.**	My car does not start.
Meine Bremsen funktionieren nicht.	My brakes don't work.
Ich brauche Benzin.	I need gas.
(öl) **Der Wagen braucht Öl.**	The car needs oil.
(TSÜNT-kert-sen) **Sehen Sie sich die Zündkerzen an.**	Check the sparkplugs.
Waschen Sie den Wagen, bitte.	Wash the car, please.
Eine Straßenkarte, bitte.	A road map, please.
(me-ÇAH-ni-keR) **Ich brauche einen Mechaniker.**	I need a mechanic.
(AP-shlep-vah-gen) **Ich brauche einen Abschleppwagen.**	I need a tow truck.
Der Motor geht aus.	The car stalls.
Das Auto bleibt stehen.	The car doesn't move.
(lek) **Der Kühler hat ein Leck.**	The radiator has a leak.
(KLEE-ma-an-lah-geh) (HEITS-ung) **Die Klimaanlage (Heizung) geht nicht.**	The air-conditioning (heater) doesn't work.
(ka-PUT) **Die Batterie ist kaputt.**	The battery is dead.

Now fill in the names for the following auto parts.

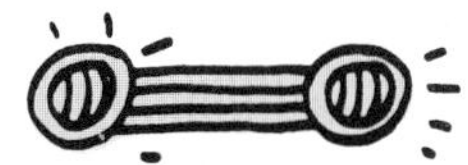

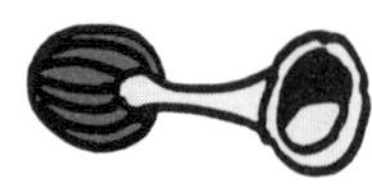

(IM-per-a-teef)

Der Imperativ

The Imperative

In order to have people do things for you, you need to know how to use verbs in a "command" or "imperative" way. In German, the imperative can be formed by using the infinitive of a verb plus "Sie"—for instance, *Essen Sie!* (Eat!), *Lesen (LAY-zen) Sie das Buch!* (Read the book!)

There is also a familiar form of the imperative used among friends and family members. In this form a verb without a personal pronoun is used; the verb is a shortened form of the infinitive. Examples of the familiar imperative are *Antworte bald (balt)!* (Answer soon!), *Fahre mit Vorsicht (FOHR-ziçt)!* (Drive carefully!)

Here are some more examples of the familiar imperative.

For the following type of verb simply chop the ending *-en* off the infinitive to form the familiar imperative:

Stem-ending	Example	English
***komm*en**	**Komm her!**	Come here!
***hol*en**	**Hol das Buch!**	Get the book!
***geh*en**	**Geh ins Haus!**	Go into the house!
***bleib*en**	**Bleib hier!**	Stay here!

If the stem of the verb ends in *-t, -fn* or *-ig* an *-e* is added:

Stem-ending	Example	English
***antwort*en**	**Antworte mir!**	Answer me!
***öffn*en**	**Öffne die Tür!**	Open the door!
***entschuldig*en**	**Entschuldige, bitte!**	Excuse me, please!

Remember the verbs that take an *i* or *ie* in the second person singular? They also change the *e* to *i* or *ie* in the imperative: *Gib! Sprich! Nimm!* As always there are exceptions, such as: *Sei gut, Seien Sie gut* (be good).

(UN-fall)

EIN UNFALL

An Accident

ERSTER FAHRER **Um Himmels** *(HIM-els)* **willen!** *(VIL-en)* **Können Sie nicht vorsichtig** *(FOHR-ziçtiç)* **sein? Können Sie nicht lesen?** *(LAY-zen)* **Können Sie nicht sehen? *Ich* habe Vorfahrt!** *(FOHR-fahRt)*

For heaven's sake! Can't you be careful? Can't you read? Can't you see? *I* have the right-of-way!

ZWEITER FAHRER **Ich weiß. Aber Sie** *(ge-SHVIN-diç-keits-gren-tseh)* **fahren 150. Die Geschwindigkeitsgrenze ist 60.**	I know: But you're driving 150 kilometers per hour. The speed limit is 60 kilometers.
DRITTER FAHRER **Kann ich Ihnen helfen?** *(HEL-fen)*	Can I help you?
ERSTER FAHRER **Ja. Holen Sie den** *(HOH-len)* *(po-li-TSIS-ten)* **Polizisten dort drüben. Er soll sich den** *(SHAH-den) (AN-zay-en)* **Schaden ansehen.**	Yes. Get the policeman over there. Let him look at the damage.
POLIZIST **Was ist los?**	What's the matter?
ERSTER FAHRER **Dieser Idiot** *(i-di-OHT)* **da** *(dah)* **fährt in meinen Wagen rein.** *(rein)* ***Seine* Schuld.** *(shult)*	This idiot runs into my car. *His* fault.
ZWEITER FAHRER **Das ist nicht wahr.** *(vahR)* **Der Kerl** *(kerl)* **fährt wie ein Verrückter.** *(feR-RÜK-teR)* **Er rast.** *(rahst)*	That is not true. The guy drives like a madman. He speeds.
POLIZIST **Niemand** *(NEE-mant)* **ist verletzt?** *(feR-LETST)* **Gut. Ihre Führerscheine, bitte. Informieren** *(in-fohr-MEE-ren)* **Sie Ihre Versicherungsgesellschaften.** *(feR-ZIÇ-e-rungs-ge-zel-shaf-ten)*	Nobody is hurt? Good. Your driver's licenses, please. Inform your insurance companies.
Dort drüben an der Ecke ist eine Garage.	Over there at the corner is a garage.

IN DER GARAGE

At the Garage

ZWEITER FAHRER (to a mechanic at the garage): **Können Sie meinen Wagen rasch** *(rash)* **reparieren?** *(re-pa-REE-ren)*	Can you repair my car quickly?
MECHANIKER *(me-ÇAH-ni-ker)* **Sie haben Glück. Das rechte Hinterrad** *(HIN-teR-raht)* **ist verbogen** *(fer-BOH-gen)* **und der Kotflügel ist eingedrückt.** *(EIN-ge-drükt)* **Das ist alles. Rufen Sie mich morgen nachmittag an.**	You are lucky. The rear right wheel is bent, and the fender is dented. That's all. Telephone me tomorrow afternoon.

(moh-DAHL-ver-ben) *(MÜS-en)* *(KÖN-en)* *(DÜR-fen)*

Modalverben: müssen, können, dürfen

Modal Verbs: must can may

These are three important modal verbs. We use them all the time in German.

For example: *Ich **muß** jetzt gehen.*
I must go now.
*Ich **kann** Deutsch sprechen.*
I can speak German.
*Ich **darf** rauchen.*
I may smoke.

MÜSSEN must	**KÖNNEN** can	**DÜRFEN** may
(mus) **ich muß**	*(kan)* **ich kann**	*(darf)* **ich darf**
(must) **du mußt**	*(kanst)* **du kannst**	*(darfst)* **du darfst**
er / sie / es } muß	**er / sie / es } kann**	**er / sie / es } darf**
wir müssen	**wir können**	**wir dürfen**
(müst) **ihr müßt**	**ihr könnt**	*(dürft)* **ihr dürft**
sie müssen	**sie können**	**sie dürfen**
Sie müssen	**Sie können**	**Sie dürfen**

The modal verbs, sometimes called auxiliaries of mood, are rather easy to learn. You probably noticed that they are used with the infinitive of the verb.

Let's practice them:

1. ____________________ lesen?
   Can't you (plural polite)
2. ____________________ sehen?
   Can't you (plural polite)
3. ____________________ *(ROW-chen)* rauchen.
   I am not allowed to — smoke
4. ____________________ hier bleiben.
   We must
5. ____________________ studieren?
   Do you have to (polite)
6. ____________________ es tun.
   She can

ANSWERS

1. Können Sie nicht **2.** Können Sie nicht **3.** Ich darf nicht **4.** Wir müssen **5.** Müssen Sie **6.** Sie kann

Here's another little exercise.
Put the words into the correct order so they form sentences. Note that you can make a statement of fact (declarative sentence) or a question out of each group of words. It all depends on the word order.

1. gut/er/singen/kann ______________________________
2. kommen/Mark/heute/darf ______________________________
3. du/das/kannst/machen? ______________________________
4. essen/müssen/wir ______________________________

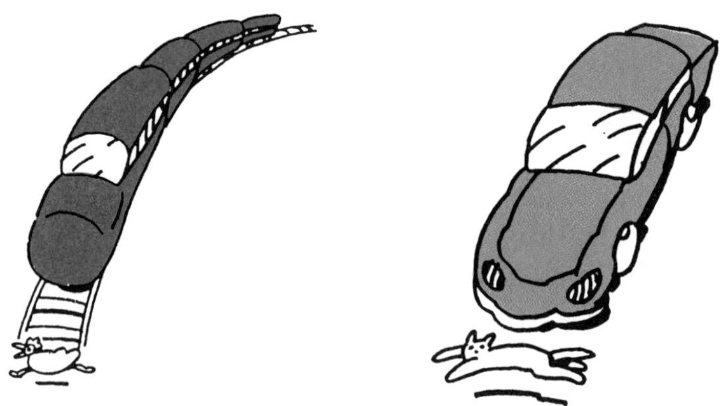

ANSWERS

1. Er kann gut singen. **2.** Darf Mark heute kommen? **3.** Kannst du das machen? **4.** Wir müssen essen.
We are giving two of the answers in the form of declarative sentences, two in the form of questions. All could have been given either way by rearranging the word order. For instance **1.** could have been arranged as *Kann er gut singen?* and **2.** as *Mark darf heute kommen.*

(KEM-ping)
9 Camping
Camping

(OWS-rüs-tung)
AUSRÜSTUNG
Equipment

The following are German words for items you may want to bring along if you go camping—and Germany has many lovely camping spots. You can buy camping gear in most cities as well as in many resort villages.

(tselt)
das Zelt
tent

(SHLAHF-zak)
der Schlafsack
sleeping bag

(KLEI-dungs-shtü-keh)
die Kleidungsstücke
articles of clothing

(PAD-el)
das Paddel
paddle

(DE-keh)
die Decke
blanket

(TASH-en-lam-peh)
die Taschenlampe
flashlight

(TAYR-mos-fla-sheh)
die Thermosflasche
thermos

(korp)
der Korb
basket

(PAD-el-boht)
das Paddelboot
canoe

(SHTEE-fel)
die Stiefel
boots

(AN-gel-roo-teh)
die Angelrute
fishing pole

(DOH-zen)
die Dosen
cans (of food)

(KOCH-ge-shir)
das Kochgeschirr
cooking utensils

(toy-LE-ten-ar-tee-kel)
die Toilettenartikel
toilet articles

(KOF-eR-rah-dee-o)
das Kofferradio
portable radio

(SHTREIÇ-höl-tseR)
die Streichhölzer
matches

(LUFT-ma-tra-tseh)
die Luftmatratze
air mattress

(EI-meR)
der Eimer
bucket

(KOR-ken-tsee-eR)
der Korkenzieher
corkscrew

(SHACH-tel) *(be-HEL-teR)*
die Schachtel, der Behälter
box

(tsum) (KEM-ping-plats)

Zum Campingplatz

To the Campground

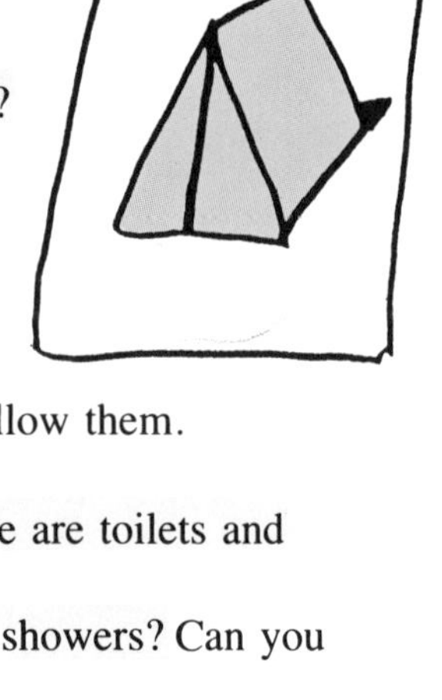

MARK **Entschuldigen Sie. Gibt es einen Campingplatz hier in der Nähe?**

Excuse me. Is there a campground in the vicinity?

JOHANN **Ja, etwa 20 Kilometer von hier. Sehen Sie diese Zeichen** *(TSEI-çen)* **mit dem Zelt? Folgen** *(FOL-gen)* **Sie ihnen.**

Yes, about 20 kilometers from here. Do you see these signs with a tent? Follow them.

MARK **Wissen Sie, ob es dort Toiletten und Trinkwasser** *(TRINK-vas-eR)* **gibt? Und Duschen** *(DOO-shen)***? Kann man dort elektrische** *(e-LEK-tri-sheh)* **Geräte anschließen** *(AN-shlees-sen)***? Und wieviel kostet das?**

Do you know whether there are toilets and drinking water there? And showers? Can you plug in electrical appliances there? And how much does it cost?

JOHANN **Ich weiß nicht. Halten Sie am Campingplatz. Die geben Ihnen gern** *(geRn)* **Auskunft** *(OWS-kunft)***.**

I don't know. Stop at the campground. They'll gladly give you information.

Word Hunt: Can you find the German equivalent of these six terms in this puzzle?

1. tent
2. blanket
3. sleeping bag
4. fishing pole
5. boots
6. cans

D	O	R	Z	N	G	A	S	T	P
O	P	D	E	C	K	E	L	M	R
S	C	H	L	A	F	S	A	C	K
E	G	L	T	K	P	R	U	E	Ü
N	D	B	C	A	L	M	R	S	B
L	A	N	G	E	L	R	U	T	E
M	N	O	S	T	I	E	F	E	L

ANSWERS

Word Hunt. **1.** Zelt **2.** Decke **3.** Schlafsack **4.** Angelrute **5.** Stiefel **6.** Dosen

(LAY-bens-mit-el-ge-sheft)

Im Lebensmittelgeschäft

At the Grocery Store

ANNE	**Guten Morgen. Ich möchte ein halbes** *(HAL-bes)* **Kilo Nudeln** *(NOO-deln)*, **100 Gramm Butter** *(BUT-eR)*, **vier Scheiben Schinken, einen Liter** *(LEE-teR)* **Milch, Salz** *(zalts)*, **und eine Flasche** *(FLA-sheh)* **Wein.**	Good morning. I would like half a kilo of noodles, 100 grams of butter, four slices of ham, a liter of milk, salt, and a bottle of wine.
	Auch eine Schachtel *(SHACH-tel)* **Streichhölzer.**	Also a box of matches.
LADENBESITZER *(LAH-den-be-zits-eR)* Storekeeper	**Zelten** *(TSEL-ten)* **Sie hier? Kommen Sie jedes Jahr hierher** *(heeR-HAYR)*?	Are you camping here? Do you come here every year?
ANNE	**Ja, aber nicht nächstes Jahr. Nächstes Jahr reise ich nach Norwegen. Wieviel kosten die Äpfel?**	Yes, but not next year. Next year I will travel to Norway. How much are the apples?
LADENBESITZER	**Achtzig Pfennig per Stück.**	Eighty pfennings apiece.
ANNE	**Soviel? Ich nehme einen.**	So much? I'll take one.
LADENBESITZER	**Ja, die Äpfel sind teuer** *(TOY-eR)*. **Zehn Eier kosten zwei Mark.**	Yes, the apples are expensive. Ten eggs cost two marks.
ANNE	**Zwei Mark für zehn Eier? Sind die nicht zu klein?**	Two marks for ten eggs? Aren't they too small?
LADENBESITZER	**Ja; der Bauer** *(BOW-eR)*, **der sie mir bringt, nimmt sie immer zu früh aus dem Nest heraus.**	Yes; the farmer who brings them always takes them out of the nest too early.

Can you remember these basics? Try writing the following expressions in German.

1. I need a box of matches. ______________________________
2. I know. ______________________________
3. I don't know. ______________________________
4. Is there a camping ground near here? ______________________________
5. Is there a service station near here? ______________________________
6. Is there a hotel near here? ______________________________
7. Excuse me. ______________________________

(mayR) (VIÇ-ti-geh)

Mehr wichtige Verben

More Important Verbs

INFINITIVE	EXAMPLE	
(LAY-gen) **legen**—to put, lay	**Ich lege es auf den Tisch.**	I put it on the table.
sich legen—to lie down	**Ich lege mich aufs Sofa.**	I lie down on the sofa.
(LEE-gen) **liegen**—to lie	**Sie liegt im Bett.**	She lies (is lying) in bed.
(ZIT-sen) **sitzen**—to sit	**Warum sitzt du hier?**	Why are you sitting here?
sich setzen—to sit down	**Setz dich!**	Sit down!
(SHTAY-en) **stehen**—to stand	**Er steht im Zimmer.**	He is standing in the room.

Now let's try to use the new verbs in sentences. Fill in the blanks below.

1. Sie ______________ (lies) auf dem Sofa.
2. Er ______________ (stands) vor dem Spiegel.
3. Bitte ______________ (sit down (formal))!
4. Wir ______________ (sit down).
5. Er ______________ (puts) das Buch auf den Stuhl.
6. ______________ (stand there! (familiar))!

ANSWERS

Can you remember?
1. Ich brauche eine Schachtel Streichhölzer. **2.** Ich weiß. **3.** Ich weiß nicht. **4.** Gibt es einen Campingplatz hier in der Nähe? **5.** Gibt es eine Tankstelle hier in der Nähe? **6.** Gibt es ein Hotel hier in der Nähe? **7.** Entschuldigen Sie.

Verbs.
1. liegt **2.** steht **3.** setzen Sie sich. **4.** setzen uns **5.** legt **6.** Steh dort

Wie sagt man . . .
How do you say . . .

Here are some everyday expressions.

(kalt)
Mir ist kalt.
I am cold.

(heis)
Ihr ist heiß.
She is hot.

(FÜRÇ-ten)
Sie fürchten sich.
They are afraid.

(zoh-unt-zoh) *(SHLAYF-riç)*
Herr So-und-so ist schläfrig.
Mr. So-and-so is sleepy.

(shaymt)
Frau So-und-so schämt sich.
Mrs. So-and-so is ashamed.

Peter braucht etwas Brot.
Peter needs some bread.

Let's try an exercise based on the camping vocabulary you learned in this unit. Write in the proper words from the ones listed here:

Stiefel, Zelt, Schlafsack, Korkenzieher, Streichhölzer, Korb, Kofferradio, Angelrute

1. Wir brauchen einen ________________ für die Weinflasche.
2. Er fischt mit der ________________.
3. Wir alle liegen unter einem ________________.
4. Das Brot ist in einem ________________.
5. Jeder schläft in einem ________________.
6. Zum Feueranmachen brauchen wir ________________.
7. An den Füßen haben wir gute ________________.
8. Aus unserem ________________ kommt schöne Musik.

ANSWERS

1. Korkenzieher **2.** Angelrute **3.** Zelt **4.** Korb **5.** Schlafsack **6.** Streichhölzer **7.** Stiefel **8.** Kofferradio

This is a similar fill-in-the-blank exercise. Now use the words:

kalt, heiß, schläfrig

1. Mir ist ____________________. Ich brauche einen Pullover.
2. Ihm ist ____________________. Er liegt in der Sonne. *(ZON-eh)* sun
3. Ihr ist ____________________. Sie braucht keinen Pullover.
4. Sie ist ____________________. Sie geht schlafen.

Let's practice some of our irregular verbs again. Fill in the proper German forms.

Example: I am American.—Ich bin Amerikaner.

1. You (polite form) are American.—Sie sind Amerikaner.

   He ____________________ You (familiar, singular) ____________________

   She ____________________ (watch this!) They ____________________

   We ____________________

2. I do not know.—Ich weiß nicht.

   You (polite form) ____________________ You (familiar, plural) ____________________

   We ____________________ He ____________________

3. I can go (I am able to go).—Ich kann gehen.

   He ____________________ You (polite) ____________________

   We ____________________ You (familiar, singular) ____________________

4. Ich habe ein Auto.—I have a car.

   You (familiar, singular) ____________________ We ____________________

   He ____________________ You (polite) ____________________

ANSWERS

kalt/heiß/schläfrig

1. kalt **2.** heiß **3.** heiß **4.** schläfrig

Irregular verbs.

1. Er ist Amerikaner. Sie ist Amerikanerin (note the feminine "-in" ending). Wir sind Amerikaner. Du bist Amerikaner. Sie sind Amerikaner. **2.** Sie wissen nicht. Wir wissen nicht. Ihr wißt nicht. Er weiß nicht. **3.** Er kann gehen. Wir können gehen. Sie können gehen. Du kannst gehen. **4.** Du hast ein Auto. Er hat ein Auto. Wir haben ein Auto. Sie haben ein Auto.

10 Das Wetter / Die Jahreszeiten

(VET-eR) (YAH-res-tsei-ten)

Weather / Seasons

Tage, Wochen, Monate

(TAH-geh) (VO-chen) (MOH-nah-teh)

Days, Weeks, Months

Did you notice that the German names for the months are almost the same as the English names? There also are similarities in the names of the seasons and in expressions about the weather.

(FRÜ-ling) **Es ist Frühling.**	It's spring.
(kül) **Es ist kühl.**	It's cool.
(ZON-iç) **Es ist sonnig.**	It's sunny.
(ZOM-eR) **Es ist Sommer.**	It's summer.
Es ist heiß.	It's hot.
Es ist ein schöner Tag.	It's a beautiful day.
(foyçt) **Es ist feucht.**	It's humid.
(shvül) **Es ist schwül.**	It's muggy.
(SHTÜR-mish) **Es ist stürmisch.**	It's stormy.
(RAY-gne-rish) **Es ist regnerisch.**	It's rainy.
(DO-nert) **Es donnert** *(blitst)* **und blitzt.**	There's thunder and lightning.
(herpst) **Es ist Herbst.**	It's fall.
(geest) *(SHTRÖ-men)* **Es gießt in Strömen.**	It's raining cats and dogs.
(VIN-diç) **Es ist windig.**	It's windy.
(NAYB-liç) **Es ist neblig.**	It's foggy.
(VIN-teR) **Es ist Winter.**	It's winter.
(kalt) **Es ist kalt.**	It's cold.
(BAY-ren-kel-teh) **Es ist eine Bärenkälte.**	It's fiercely cold.
(schneit) **Es schneit.**	It's snowing.

WIE IST DAS WETTER?

How Is the Weather?

Das Wetter ist schön. The weather is beautiful.

Das Wetter ist gut. The weather is good.

(HER-liç)
Das Wetter ist herrlich. The weather is superb.

(GROHS-ar-tiç)
Das Wetter ist großartig. The weather is splendid.

(PREÇ-tiç)
Das Wetter ist prächtig. The weather is magnificent.

Das Wetter ist kalt. The weather is cold.

Das Wetter ist warm. The weather is warm.

(shleçt)
Das Wetter ist schlecht. The weather is bad.

(FURÇT-baR)
Das Wetter ist furchtbar. The weather is awful.

(SHREK-liç)
Das Wetter ist schrecklich. The weather is horrible.

(ad-yek-TEE-veh)
Adjektive

Adjectives

An adjective is a word used to modify a noun or pronoun. You've already been introduced to many adjectives in this book. Here are a few more. Remember to read them out loud.

(DUN-kel)
dunkel dark — **Das Zimmer ist dunkel.** The room is dark.

(hel)
hell light — **Das Zimmer ist hell.** The room is light.

(AN-ge-naym)
angenehm pleasant — **Das Wetter ist angenehm.** The weather is pleasant.

(hüpsh)
hübsch pretty — **Das Mädchen ist hübsch.** The girl is pretty.

(ZOW-beR)
sauber clean — **Die Hand ist sauber.** The hand is clean.

(HES-liç) **häßlich**	ugly	**Der Mann ist häßlich.**	The man is ugly.
(SHMU-tsiç) **schmutzig**	dirty	**Der Wagen ist schmutzig.**	The car is dirty.
(OF-en) **offen**	open	**Die Tür ist offen.**	The door is open.
(ge-SHLO-sen) **geschlossen**	closed	**Die Tür ist geschlossen.**	The door is closed.
(MÜ-deh) **müde**	tired	**Ich bin müde.**	I am tired.
(tsoo-FREE-den) **zufrieden**	satisfied	**Er ist zufrieden.**	He is satisfied.
(TSOR-niç) **zornig**	furious	**Sie ist zornig.**	She is furious.
(alt) **alt**	old	**Er ist alt.**	He is old.
(yung) **jung**	young	**Das Kind ist jung.**	The child is young.

(be-KVAYM)
groß, klein, laut, bequem
big, little, noisy, comfortable

Mein Zimmer ist groß, klein, laut, bequem

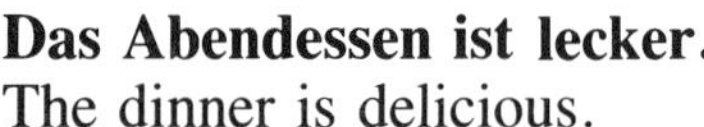

(LEK-eR) **lecker**	delicious	**Das Abendessen ist lecker.** The dinner is delicious.
(be-REIT) **bereit**	ready	**Das Abendessen ist bereit.** Dinner is ready.
(REIÇ-liç) **reichlich**	ample	**Das Abendessen ist reichlich.** The dinner is ample.
(TAH-del-lohs) **tadellos**	perfect	**Das Abendessen ist tadellos.** The dinner is perfect.
(leiçt) **leicht**	light	**Das Abendessen ist leicht.** The dinner is light.

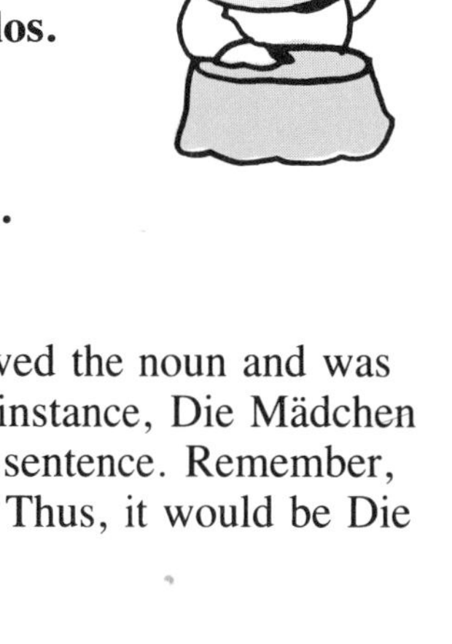

You probably noticed that in every example above the adjective followed the noun and was preceded by *ist*. We could also have formed the plural by saying, for instance, Die Mädchen *sind* hübsch. The adjective stays the same in the plural in this type of sentence. Remember, however, that if the adjective precedes the noun it must agree with it. Thus, it would be Die hübschen Mädchen.

Here's a short dialogue set in a hotel room:

ANN	**Wieviel Uhr ist es?**	What time is it?
SUSAN	**Sieben Uhr dreißig.**	7:30.
ANN	*(DON-eR-vet-eR)* **Donnerwetter!** *(shpayt)* **Schon so spät?** *(SHÖ-neR)* **Ist es ein schöner Tag?**	My gosh! (*lit.* thunderstorm) So late already? Is it a beautiful day?
SUSAN	**Herrlich! Und der** *(ZON-en-owf-gang)* **Sonnenaufgang! Der Himmel ist** *(VOL-ken-frei)* **wolkenfrei. Was hast du dort?**	Superb! And that sunrise! The sky is cloudless. What do you have there?
ANN	**Die** *(VET-eR-fohR-ows-za-geh)* **Wettervoraussage: Sonnig den** *(GAN-tsen)* **ganzen Tag.**	The weather forecast: Sunny all day.
SUSAN	**Kein** *(RAY-gen)* **Regen?**	No rain?
ANN	*(fee-LEIÇT)* **Vielleicht am** *(AH-bent)* **Abend.**	Maybe in the evening.
SUSAN	**Ich steh auf; ich bin sehr** *(HUN-griç)* **hungrig.**	I'm getting up; I am very hungry.

Die Wettervoraussage

Weather Forecast

(ZON-eh) SONNE sun

(RAY-gen) REGEN rain

(ge-VIT-er) GEWITTER thunderstorms

(SHOW-er) SCHAUER showers

(NAY-bel) NEBEL fog

(shnay) SCHNEE snow

(HOHCH-druk-ge-beet)
H = Hochdruckgebiet
High pressure area

(TEEF-druk-ge-beet)
T = Tiefdruckgebiet
Low pressure area

(ven) (HOY-teh) (DEENS-tahk)

WENN HEUTE DIENSTAG IST, DANN . . .

If Today Is Tuesday, Then . . .

Let's learn the days of the week.

(MOHN-tahk) **Am *Montag* besuche ich meine Mutter.**	On Monday I visit my mother.
(DEENS-tahk) **Am *Dienstag* gehe ich ins Kino.**	On Tuesday I go to the movies.
(MIT-voch) **Am *Mittwoch* esse ich Wiener Schnitzel.**	On Wednesday I eat Wiener schnitzel.
(DO-ners-tahk) (SHPEE-leh) **Am *Donnerstag* spiele ich Bridge.**	On Thursday I play bridge.
(FREI-tahk) **Am *Freitag* esse ich Fisch.**	On Friday I eat fish.
(BLEI-beh) **Am Freitag dem dreizehnten bleibe ich**	On Friday the 13th I stay in bed
(AH-beR-gloy-bish) **im Bett (ich bin abergläubisch).**	(I am superstitious).
(ZAMS-tahk) (ZON-ah-bent) **Am *Samstag* (oder *Sonnabend*)**	On Saturday I go dancing.
(TANT-sen) **gehe ich tanzen.**	
(MÜ-deh) **Am *Sonntag* bin ich müde vom Samstag.**	On Sunday I am tired from Saturday.

Now let's learn the names of the months in German. This should be easy. There are many similarities with English.

(YA-noo-aR) *(ge-VÖN-liç)*
Im *Januar* ist es gewöhnlich sehr kalt.
In January it usually is very cold.

(FAY-broo-ar) *(freert)* *(KUR-tser)*
Im *Februar* friert man auch, aber es ist ein kurzer Monat.
In February one freezes also, but it is a short month.

(AN-ge-pliç) *(FRÜ-ling)*
Im *März* beginnt angeblich der Frühling.
In March spring allegedly begins.

(ge-BURTS-tahk)
Ich habe am ersten (1.) *März* Geburtstag.
March 1 is my birthday.

(ah-PRIL) *(BINT-fay-den)*
Im *April* regnet es Bindfäden.
In April it rains cats and dogs.

(mei) *(HEI-rah-ten)*
Im *Mai* soll man nicht heiraten.
In May one should not marry.

(YOO-nee) *(HOCH-tsei-ten)*
Im *Juni* sind die meisten Hochzeiten.
In June most weddings are held.

(YOO-lee) *(VAHN-zin-iç)*
Im *Juli* ist es wahnsinnig heiß.
In July it is insanely hot.

(ow-GUST) *(OOR-lowp)*
Im *August* fährt man auf Urlaub.
In August one goes on vacation.

(zep-TEM-beR) *(TROW-riç)* *(fohr-Ü-beR)*
Im *September* ist man traurig, daß der Sommer vorüber ist.
In September one is sad that summer is over.

(ok-TOH-beR) *(glük)* *(sheint)*
Im *Oktober* hat man Glück, wenn die Sonne scheint.
In October one is lucky if the sun is shining.

(noh-VEM-beR)
Im *November* ist es neblig und naß.
In November it is foggy and wet.

(day-TSEM-beR)
Im *Dezember* gibt man eine Menge Geld aus.
In December one spends a lot of money.

11 Flugzeuge

(FLOOK-tsoy-geh)

Airplanes

See if you can find the following in this picture.

(FLOOK-kar-ten-shal-teR) **der Flugkartenschalter**	ticket counter
die Uhr	clock
(ROL-trep-eh) **die Rolltreppe**	escalator
(FLEES-bant) **das Fließband**	conveyor belt
(TSOL-be-am-teh) **der Zollbeamte**	customs inspector
(PAS-kon-tro-leh) **die Paßkontrolle**	passport control
das Gepäck	luggage
(pee-LOHT) **der Pilot**	pilot
(KOH-pee-loht) **der Kopilot**	copilot
(FLOOK-be-glei-teR-in) **die Flugbegleiterin**	flight attendant (fem.)
(kon-TROL-turm) **der Kontrollturm**	control tower
(FLOOK-shteik) **der Flugsteig**	gate

(FLOOK-tsoyk)

DAS FLUGZEUG

The Plane

Can you find these items in the picture?

(zits) **der Sitz**	the seat	*(pa-sa-ZEER)* **der Passagier**	passenger
(ZIÇ-eR-heits-gurt) **der Sicherheitsgurt**	seat belt	*(SHTART-bahn)* **die Startbahn**	runway
(ka-BEE-neh) **die Kabine**	cabin	*(be-ZAT-sung)* **die Besatzung**	crew
(rumpf) **der Rumpf**	fuselage	*(ta-BLET)* **das Tablett**	tray
(NOHT-ows-gang) **der Notausgang**	emergency exit	*(FEN-steR)* **das Fenster**	window

Now watch how the vocabulary on flying is used in the following dialogue.

PILOT **Wir fliegen in ein paar Minuten von Boston ab. Bitte machen Sie Ihren Sicherheitsgurt fest.**	We take off from Boston in a few minutes. Please fasten your seat belt.

ERSTER PASSAGIER *(pa-sa-ŽEER)* **Ist es das erste Mal, daß Sie Deutschland besuchen?**	Is this the first time you are visiting Germany?
ZWEITER PASSAGIER **Ja. Und es ist auch das erste Mal, daß ich über den Atlantik** *(at-LAN-tik)* **fliege.**	Yes. And it is also the first time I fly across the Atlantic Ocean.
PILOT **Wir werden um vierzehn Uhr dreißig in Frankfurt landen. Wir fliegen in einer Höhe** *(HÖ-eh)* **von 10 000 Meter. Das Wetter in Frankfurt ist wolkig** *(VOL-kiç)* **und regnerisch** *(RAYG-neR-ish)* **und die Temperatur** *(tem-pe-rah-TOOR)* **ist 25 Grad** *(graht)* **Celsius** *(TSEL-zee-us)*.	We will land in Frankfurt at 14.30 (2:30 p.m.) We are flying at an altitude of 10,000 meters. The weather at Frankfurt is cloudy and rainy, and the temperature is 25 degrees Celsius (77° Fahrenheit).
ERSTER PASSAGIER **Fräulein** *(FROY-lein)*, **servieren** *(zeR-VEER-en)* **Sie uns das Abendessen** *(AH-bent-es-en)*?	Miss, are you going to serve us dinner?
FLUGBEGLEITERIN **Ich bringe es Ihnen in ein paar Minuten.**	I will bring it to you in a couple of minutes.
ZWEITER PASSAGIER **Wunderbar!** *(VUN-der-baR)* **Im Flugzeug esse ich sehr gern, es vertreibt** *(feR-TREIPT)* **die Zeit.**	Great! I love eating on planes. It makes the time go faster.

(gra-MAH-tik)

Etwas Grammatik

Some Grammar

We have talked about pronouns before. Now let's focus on pronouns in the accusative case.

DIRECT OBJECT PRONOUNS

mich	me	**uns**	us
dich	you (familiar)	**euch**	you
ihn	him, it		
sie	her, it	**sie**	them
es	it		
	Sie	you (polite)	

The personal pronouns are in the accusative case when they are the direct objects of verbs.

What is a direct object?

Take a sentence like:

Paul	loves	Pauline.
Paul	liebt	Pauline.
subject	*verb*	*direct object*

Whom does Paul love: Pauline.
Pauline obviously is the object, the *direct object* of his affection.

Now let's go one step further. Instead of the name, the noun *Pauline,* you can use a form that takes its place, a pronoun. In this particular case it would be—you guessed it—*her,* in German, *sie:*

Paul	loves	her.
Paul	liebt	sie.
subject	*verb*	*direct object*

Nothing much has changed, except that we have replaced the direct object noun by a direct object pronoun.

Let's practice this:

1. Karl braucht ______ (him).
2. Er ißt ______ (it (das Brot)).
3. Anton sieht ______ (you (familiar)).
4. Susan besucht ______ (me).
5. Siehst du ______ (them)?

Of course, the direct object can be either a person or a thing. Let's replace some more nouns with direct-object pronouns. Number 6 is done for you.

6. Er liest es (das Buch).
7. Er sieht ______ (you (polite)).
8. Ich brauche ______ (you (my son)).
9. Er liebt ______ (you (familiar)).
10. Er hat ______ (den Schlüssel).
11. Sie kauft ______ (die Blumen).

ANSWERS

Practice. **1.** ihn **2.** es **3.** dich **4.** mich **5.** sie **7.** Sie **8.** dich **9.** dich **10.** ihn **11.** sie

ENTERTAINMENT

(un-teR-HAL-tung)
Unterhaltung

12 *(tay-AH-teR)* Theater / *(KEE-noh)* Kino / *(FEI-eR-tahg-eh)* Feiertage

Theater Movies Holidays

THEATER

Theater

John and Mary are a middle-aged couple from Omaha, Nebraska, who are making their first trip to Germany. They like the theater. The place is Munich on the second day of their stay. Being of German descent, they both speak German quite well. "Not one word of English during our vacation," they decide.

(In the hotel:)

JOHN **Möchtest du heute abend ins Theater** *(GERT-neR)* **gehen? Im Theater am Gärtnerplatz** *(LUS-tig-eh) (VIT-veh)* **spielt man *Die lustige Witwe*** *(frants) (LAY-har)* **von Franz Lehar.**	Would you like to go to the theatre tonight? In the theatre on Gärtnerplatz they are playing *The Merry Widow* by Franz Lehar.
MARY *(kayz)* **Diesen alten Käs?**	That old warhorse?
JOHN *(me-loh-DEE-en)* **Ja, aber die Melodien sind sehr** *(tekst) (dum)* **schön. Und der Text ist so dumm,** *(ROL-eh)* **es spielt keine Rolle, wenn man ihn nicht versteht. Ich möchte auch *Siegfried* hören.**	Yes, but the melodies are very beautiful. And the words are so dumb, it doesn't matter if you don't understand. I would like to hear *Siegfried*, also.
MARY *(VAHG-neR)* **Die Wagner-Oper?**	The Wagner opera?

JOHN **Ja.**

Yes.

MARY **Fünf Stunden dort sitzen? Mir ist** *(LANG-vei-liç)* **das zu langweilig. Ich gehe inzwischen** *(in-TSVISH-en)* **zu Tante Sophie,** *(ZOH-fee)* **die du eh nicht magst.** *(mahkst)* **Dann sind wir beide** *(BEID-eh)* **glücklich.**

To sit there for five hours? That's too boring for me. I'll go in the meantime to Aunt Sophie, whom you don't like anyway. Then both of us are happy.

JOHN **Gute Idee!** *(KOW-feh)* **Wo kaufe ich die Karten?** *(KAR-ten)*

Good idea. Where do I buy the tickets?

MARY **Der Kartenverkauf ist unten** *(UN-ten)* **im Hotel.** *(hoh-TEL)* **Also bis später. Ich muß zum Friseur.** *(fri-ZÖR)*

The ticket office is downstairs in the hotel. See you later. I must go to the hairdresser.

JOHN **Wiedersehen.**

See you.

Notice how similar these words are in English and German:

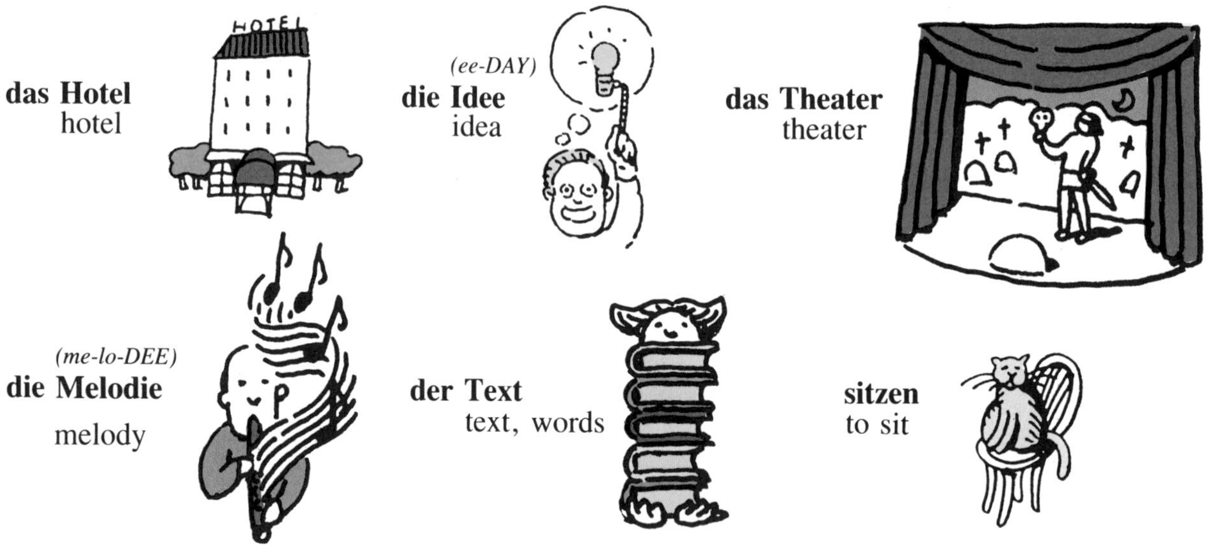

das Hotel hotel

die Idee *(ee-DAY)* idea

das Theater theater

die Melodie *(me-lo-DEE)* melody

der Text text, words

sitzen to sit

(veR-GES-en)

Bitte nicht vergessen . . .

Please Don't Forget . . .

möchtest du gern, möchten Sie gern — would you like to

Diesen alten Käs? — Here **Käs(e)** (cheese) means old warhorse or old chestnut; it has nothing to do with cheese.

Es (das) spielt keine Rolle. **Es (das) macht nichts.**	It doesn't matter.
Ich muß zum Friseur (gehen).	I must go to the hairdresser.

Willst du *mir* das Geld geben?

Will You Give the Money *to Me*?

In the previous unit you learned how to say "me, him, them," etc. Now you will learn how to say "to me, to him, to them," etc. These are called "indirect object pronouns."

INDIRECT OBJECT PRONOUNS

mir	to me	**uns**	to us
dir	to you (familiar)	**euch**	to you (familiar)
ihm	to him, it		
ihr	to her, it	**ihnen**	to them

Ihnen to you (polite)

In German the indirect object precedes the direct object in a sentence.

	Indirect object	Direct object
Mary gives **Mary gibt**	(to) the boy **dem Jungen**	a book. **ein Buch.**
He gives **Er gibt**	to him **ihm**	the money. **das Geld.**
I send **Ich sende**	(to) my mother **meiner Mutter**	flowers. **Blumen.**

DAS KINO

The Movies

MARY	**Ein Kino ist links um die Ecke.**	A movie theater is to the left around the corner.
	Möchtest du einen Film sehen?	Would you like to see a film?
JOHN	**Was läuft?** *(loyft)*	What is playing?
MARY	**Ein deutscher Film.**	A German film.
JOHN	**Mit Untertiteln?**	With subtitles?
MARY	**In Deutschland? Nein.**	In Germany? No.
JOHN	**Glaubst du, wir verstehen den Film?**	Do you believe we'll understand the picture?
MARY	**Ich glaube schon.**	I think so.
JOHN	**Ich kaufe Bonbons.** *(bong-BONGS)*	I'll buy candy.

(two hours later)

MARY	**Ich bin froh, es ist zu Ende.**	I am glad it is over. Do you know something?
	Weißt du was? Auch die Deutschen machen langweilige Filme. *(LANG-veil-i-geh)*	The Germans, too, make boring pictures.
JOHN	**Und dafür müssen wir 8000 Kilometer herfliegen.**	And for that we have to fly 8000 kilometers.

Bitte nicht vergessen . . .

Please Don't Forget . . .

links um die Ecke	to the left around the corner
Ich glaube schon.	I think so.

Draw lines between the matching English and German words or expressions.

1. zu Ende	a. subtitles
2. Ecke	b. glad
3. kaufen	c. over
4. Untertitel	d. candy
5. froh	e. corner
6. Bonbons	f. to buy

True or false?

7. ________ John und Mary möchten ins Theater gehen.

8. ________ *Siegfried* dauert zwei Stunden.

9. ________ Mary muß zum Friseur.

10. ________ Sie sehen einen amerikanischen Film.

11. ________ Mary und John gehen ins Kino.

12. ________ Der Film hat Untertitel.

(FEI-eR-tah-geh)

FEIERTAGE

Holidays

(in-te-re-SANT)

JOHN **Es ist interessant, die deutschen Feiertage mit den amerikanischen zu vergleichen.** *(feR-GLEI-çen)* — It is interesting to compare the German holidays with the American ones.

Also der Neujahrstag *(NOY-yahRs-tahk)* **ist natürlich international.** — Well, New Year's Day, of course, is international.

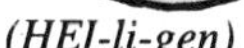

Dann kommt der 6. Januar, die Heiligen *(HEI-li-gen)* **Drei Könige.** *(KÖ-ni-geh)* — Next comes January 6, Epiphany.

ANSWERS

Matching. **1.** c **2.** e **3.** f **4.** a **5.** b **6.** d
True/False. **7.** T **8.** F **9.** T **10.** F **11.** T **12.** F

MARY	*(OS-tern)* **Ostern feiern sie zwei Tage lang, Sonntag und Montag.**	They celebrate Easter for two days, Sunday and Monday.
	(PFING-sten) **Auch Pfingsten.**	Pentecost, too.
JOHN	**Im Juli und August ist fast gar** *(gahR)* **nichts los.**	In July and August there is almost nothing going on.
MARY	**Um diese Zeit gehen die Deutschen wahrscheinlich** *(vahR-SHEIN-liç)* **auf Urlaub** *(OOR-lowp)*.	At that time Germans probably go on vacation.
JOHN	**Und dann nichts bis November.**	And then nothing till November.
MARY	**Die armen Deutschen! Wie können sie das so lange aushalten?** *(OWS-halt-en)*	The poor Germans! How can they stand it that long?
JOHN	**Am 1. November ist Allerheiligen,** *(AL-eR-HEI-li-gen)* **und dann . . .**	On November 1 is All Saints' Day, and then . . .
MARY	**. . . kommt Weihnachten.** *(VEI-naç-ten)*	comes Christmas.
JOHN	**Wieder** *(VEE-deR)* **zwei Tage, am 25. und 26. Dezember.**	Two days again, on December 25 and 26.
MARY	**Und am 31. Dezember, Silvester.** *(zil-VES-teR)* **Die Deutschen feiern wie die Amerikaner—bis tief in die Nacht hinein.**	And on December 31, New Year's Eve. The Germans celebrate like Americans—far into the night.

Let's see how much you remember from the dialogues. Fill in the correct German word.

1. Inzwischen besucht Mary ihre __________. (Aunt Sophie)
2. Das Kino ist links um die __________. (corner)
3. Sie sehen einen __________. (German film)
4. John kauft __________. (candy)
5. __________ (Christmas) ist am 25. und 26. Dezember.

ANSWERS

Dialogue. **1.** Tante Sophie **2.** Ecke **3.** deutschen Film **4.** Bonbons **5.** Weihnachten

(RAYT-sel)

Ein Rätsel

A Puzzle

Complete the German words.

1. again
2. indefinite article
3. interesting
4. half
5. a holiday
6. another holiday
7. temperature scale
8. hand
9. theater
10. first
11. a month

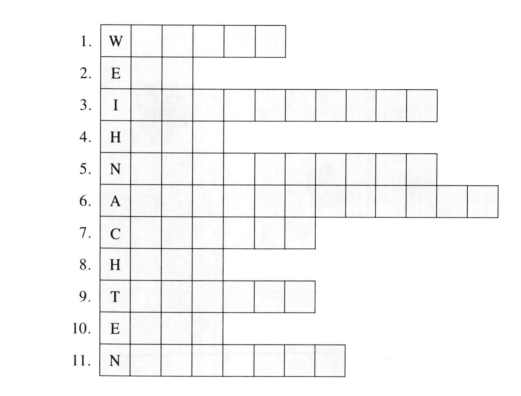

1.	W												
2.	E												
3.	I												
4.	H												
5.	N												
6.	A												
7.	C												
8.	H												
9.	T												
10.	E												
11.	N												

ANSWERS

Puzzle.
1. wieder **2.** ein **3.** interessant **4.** halb **5.** Neujahrstag **6.** Allerheiligen **7.** Celsius **8.** Hand **9.** Theater **10.** Erst **11.** November

13 der Sport

(shport)
Sports

WANDERN UND JOGGING

(VAN-dern) *(DJOG-ging)*
Hiking and Jogging

REPORTER **Herr Dr. Steiner?**	Dr. Steiner?
STEINER **Ja, das bin ich.**	Yes, that's me.
REPORTER **Ich bin Karl Frank, Reporter vom *Morgen am Abend* aus Cincinnati, Ohio.**	I am Karl Frank, a reporter of *Morgen am Abend* from Cincinnati, Ohio.
STEINER **Sie wollen ein Interview?**	You want an interview?
REPORTER **Genau.**	Exactly.
STEINER **Und worüber, wenn ich bitten darf?**	And what about, if I may ask?
REPORTER **Als Präsident des Deutschen Amateursportverbandes sind Sie bestimmt über Jogging, Wandern, Radfahren und Schwimmen sehr gut informiert.**	As the president of the German Amateur Sports League you are surely very well informed about jogging, hiking, bicycle riding, and swimming.
STEINER **Sie schmeicheln mir.** *(SHMEI-çeln)*	You flatter me.

REPORTER **Ich möchte darüber einen Artikel**
(ZAM-leh) (mah-tay-ree-AL)
schreiben und sammle Material.

I would like to write an article about these things and I am collecting material.

(SHEE-sen)
STEINER **Schießen Sie los!**

Shoot!

REPORTER **Zunächst über das Jogging.**

First about jogging.

STEINER **Ja, das ist hier sehr populär. Wie vieles andere, kommt das natürlich auch**
(oy-ROH-pa)
aus Amerika und jetzt ist ganz Europa
(ver-RÜKT)
verrückt danach.
(zoh-GAHR)
Sogar das *Wort*
(im-por-TEE-ren)
importieren wir.
(loyft)
Man läuft nicht mehr,
(djogt)
man joggt.

Yes, that's very popular. Like many other things, this too, naturally, comes from America, and now all of Europe is crazy about it.

We even import the word.

One doesn't run anymore,

one jogs.

REPORTER **Sie auch, Herr Doktor?**

You, too, sir?

(klahr) (ge-ZUN-deR)
STEINER **Klar. Jogging ist ein gesunder und**
(BI-li-geR)
billiger Sport. Alles, was Sie da kaufen müssen, ist ein Sweatshirt und ein paar bequeme Joggingschuhe.

You bet. Jogging is a healthy and inexpensive sport. All you have to buy is a sweat shirt and a pair of comfortable jogging shoes.

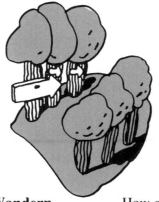

REPORTER **Wie steht's mit dem Wandern, Herr Doktor?**

How about hiking, sir?

STEINER **Ein herrlicher Sport.**

Und hier in Deutschland
(be-DOY-tung)
von großer Bedeutung.

Alle unsere Wanderwege
(mar-KEERT)
sind markiert; es ist

unmöglich, sich zu verirren.

A marvelous sport, and here in Germany of great importance. All our trails are marked; it's impossible to lose one's way.

REPORTER **Was brauche ich für den Sport?**

What do I need for the sport?

(RUK-zak)
STEINER **Einen Rucksack und ein Paar**
(KREF-ti-geh)
kräftige Beine mit

guten Wanderschuhen.

A backpack and a strong pair of legs with good hiking shoes.

(AYR-gei-tsiç)
Wenn Sie ehrgeizig sind, vielleicht
(KOCH-ge-shir)
Schlafsack, Kochgeschirr
(FELT-fla-sheh)
und Feldflasche.

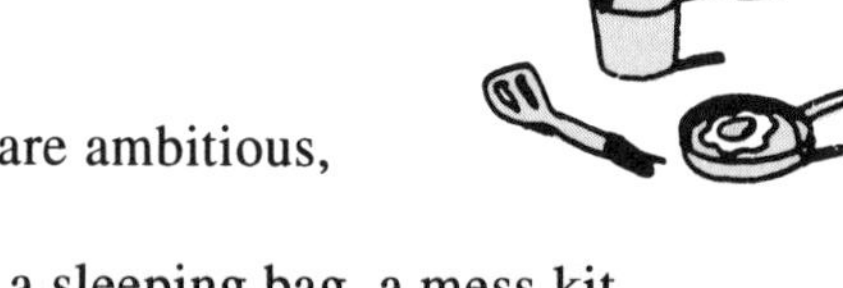

If you are ambitious, maybe a sleeping bag, a mess kit, and a canteen.

Bitte nicht vergessen . . .

Please Don't Forget . . .

Worüber wollen Sie sprechen?	What do you want to talk about?
Worum handelt es sich?	What is it about?
Wozu brauchen Sie das?	To what purpose (why) do you need this?

Please note:

Wir *importieren* ein Wort.	We *import* a word.

Verbs that end in **-ieren** are stressed on the next to last syllable and are regular weak verbs. They don't change their vowels.

You have no doubt noticed that there are now a great number of American words being used as German words. Examples of such foreign words *(Fremdwörter)* *(FREMT-vör-teR)* are *Jogging* and *Sweatshirt*.

Let's learn a new verb.

SAMMELN (TO COLLECT)

ich samm*le*	I collect, am collecting
du samm*elst*	you collect, are collecting
er, sie, es samm*elt*	he, she, it collects, is collecting
wir samm*eln*	we collect, are collecting
ihr samm*elt*	you collect, are collecting
sie samm*eln*	they collect, are collecting
Sie samm*eln*	You (polite) collect, are collecting

(RAT-fah-ren) *(SHVI-men)*

RADFAHREN UND SCHWIMMEN

Bicycling and Swimming

REPORTER **Was halten Sie vom Radfahren, Herr Doktor?**	What do you think of bicycle riding, sir?

STEINER	*(BLÖD-eR)* *(UN-tsoo-leng-liç-es)* **Ein blöder Sport, ein unzulängliches**	A stupid sport, an unsatisfactory means of
	(trans-PORT-mit-el) *(tsahm)* **Transportmittel. Ist doch viel zu zahm.**	transportation. It's much too tame.
	(ge-SHVIN-diç-keit) **Keine Geschwindigkeit, nichts.**	No speed, nothing.
	(bayrk-OWF) **Wenn's bergauf geht,**	Uphill you have
	(ding) **muß man das Ding schieben.**	to push the thing.
	(SHTREN-gen) *(RAY-geln)* **Und diese strengen Regeln!**	And these strict rules!
	(FOR-deR) *(RÜK-liçt)* **Müssen Sie Vorder- und Rücklicht in**	Do you need front and back lights in
	Amerika haben?	America?
REPORTER	**Nein.**	No.

REPORTER	**Was halten Sie vom Schwimmen?**	What do you think of swimming?
STEINER	*(be-GEIS-tert)* **Ich bin begeistert davon.**	I am enthusiastic about it.
	(artst) **Mein Arzt sagt mir,**	My doctor tells me
	(BES-teh) **das ist der beste und der**	it is the best and the healthiest
	(ge-ZÜND-es-teh) **gesündeste Sport, den es gibt.**	sport there is.
	(MI-ni-mum) **Auch hier investieren Sie ein Minimum:**	Here, too, you invest a minimum:
	(BAH-deh-hoh-zeh) *(BAH-deh-an-tsook)* **Eine Badehose oder einen Badeanzug—**	bathing trunks or bathing suit—
REPORTER	*(ay-ven-too-EL)* *(bi-KEE-nee)* **eventuell einen Bikini—**	perhaps a bikini—

STEINER **Das ist alles. Vielleicht eine** *(TOW-cheR-bri-leh)* **Taucherbrille—**

That's all. Maybe diving-goggles—

REPORTER **Wie fängt ein Neuling** *(fenkt) (NOY-ling)* **hier mit dem Schwimmen an?**

How does a beginner start swimming here?

STEINER **Mit dem Brustschwimmen.** *(BRUST-shvim-en)*

With the breast stroke.

Dann kommt das Kraulen *(KROWL-en)*

Then comes the crawl

und das Rückenschwimmen. *(RÜK-en-shvim-en)*

and the back stroke.

REPORTER **Haben Sie regelmäßige** *(RAY-gel-may-si-geh)* **Prüfungen?** *(PRÜ-fun-gen)*

Do you have regular tests?

STEINER **Absolut.** *(ap-sȯh-LOOT)* **Wenn einer die Prüfung fürs Freischwimmen besteht,** *(be-SHTAYT)* **kann er sich ein kleines Abzeichen** *(AP-tsei-çen)* **stolz** *(shtolts)* **auf die Badehose nähen.** *(NAY-en)*

Absolutely. If someone passes the free-swimming test, he can proudly sew a little badge on his bathing trunks.

REPORTER **Herr Doktor, ich danke Ihnen für das Gespräch.** *(ge-SHPRAYÇ)*

Sir, I thank you for the interview.

Bitte nicht vergessen . . .

Please Don't Forget . . .

Watch the word **eventuell** and how you use it. In German it means *possibly* or *perhaps*. The English word *eventual* means *ultimate, final*.

Gewiß, **bestimmt**, **freilich**, **natürlich**, **selbstverständlich**, **absolut**, **klar**—they all mean more or less the same thing, the equivalent of *sure*, *certainly*, *naturally*, *of course*, *you bet*, *yes indeed*.

Note that the stress in most of these words is on a syllable other than the first.

Also, notice that in Germany persons who have earned a doctorate (Ph.D.) are addressed as "Herr Doktor," not just "Herr." Titles are very important in Germany, and a person would feel hurt, even insulted, if this "Doktor" were left out.

1. Was ist das? Das ist ein ____________________

2. Was ist das? Das ist eine ____________________

3. Was ist das? Das ist ____________________

4. Was ist das? Das ist ____________________

5. Was ist das? Das ist ____________________

Answers

Pictures.
1. Radfahrer **2.** Taucherbrille **3.** Brustschwimmen **4.** Kraulen **5.** Rückenschwimmen

Draw lines between the matching English words or expressions:

1.	Wochenblatt	A.	crazy
2.	zunächst	B.	actually
3.	verrückt	C.	comfortable
4.	fliegen	D.	weekly
5.	eigentlich	E.	first of all
6.	Prüfung	F.	glasses (goggles)
7.	bequem	G.	test
8.	Schlafsack	H.	to fly
9.	schieben	I.	sleeping bag
10.	Brille	J.	to push

ANSWERS

Matching.
1. D **2.** E **3.** A **4.** H **5.** B **6.** G **7.** C **8.** I **9.** J **10.** F

ORDERING FOOD

(ES-en) (be-SHTEL-en)
Essen bestellen

14 Mahlzeiten / Speisen

(MAHL-tsei-ten) (SHPEI-zen)
Meals / Food

Was man sagt, wenn man etwas *gern mag*

(gern) (mahk)

What to Say When You *Like* Something

Verb + GERN	
Ich esse gern.	I like to eat.
Ich esse nicht gern.	I do not like to eat.

I like ice cream.

Ich esse gern Eis.

I don't like vegetables.

Ich esse nicht gern Gemüse.

Gern, being an adverb, always modifies a verb:
Ich esse gern. Or: **Ich esse nicht gern.**

If the object of "to like" is a person, we use **haben**:

Ich habe meine Schwester gern. **Ich habe Klaus gern.** *(klows)* **Ich habe die Räuber nicht gern.** *(ROY-beR)* robbers

As you can see, the object (Schwester, Klaus, die Räuber) always stands between the verb **habe** and the adverb **gern** (or **nicht gern**). The negative **nicht** always precedes the **gern**.

If the object of "to like" is a thing, we use **mögen**: *(MŐ-gen)*

Ich mag gern Eis. **Ich mag nicht gern Gemüse.**

You probably noticed that the object follows the verb **mag** and the adverb **gern**; it can also stand between them.

To convey the idea of preferring something, we frequently use the comparative form of **gern**, which is *(LEE-beR)* **lieber**:

I prefer to eat at eight.	Ich esse lieber um acht.
I prefer tomato juice.	Ich **mag** *(toh-MAH-ten-zaft)* Tomatensaft lieber.
I prefer to drink tea.	Ich trinke lieber *(tay)* Tee.
I like coffee most.	Ich **mag** Kaffee *(am LEEP-sten)* *am liebsten*.

ESSEN
Eating

ESSEN to eat					
ich	**esse**	I eat, am eating	**wir**	**essen**	we eat, are eating
du	*(ist)* **ißt**	you eat, are eating	**ihr**	**eßt**	you eat, are eating
er, sie, es	**ißt**	he, she, it eats, is eating	**sie**	**essen**	they eat, are eating
	Sie	**essen**	You (polite) eat, are eating		

FRÜHSTÜCK
Breakfast

Frühstück essen
Eating breakfast

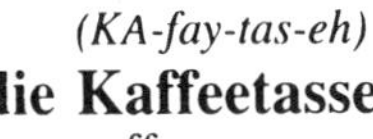

(KA-fay-tas-eh)
die Kaffeetasse
coffee cup

der Kaffee
coffee

(ZAH-neh)
mit Sahne
with cream

(TAY-ta-seh)
die Teetasse
tea cup

(TAY-boy-tel)
der Teebeutel
tea bag

PAUL	**Um wieviel Uhr ißt du gern Frühstück?**	At what time do you like to eat breakfast?
ANNA	**Ich esse Frühstück gern um acht.**	I like to eat breakfast at eight.
PAUL	**Ich esse Frühstück lieber um 7.45.**	I prefer to eat breakfast at 7:45.
ANNA	**Magst du lieber Kaffee mit** *(ZAH-neh)* **Sahne oder** *(SHVAR-tsen)* **schwarzen Kaffee?**	Do you prefer coffee with cream or black coffee?

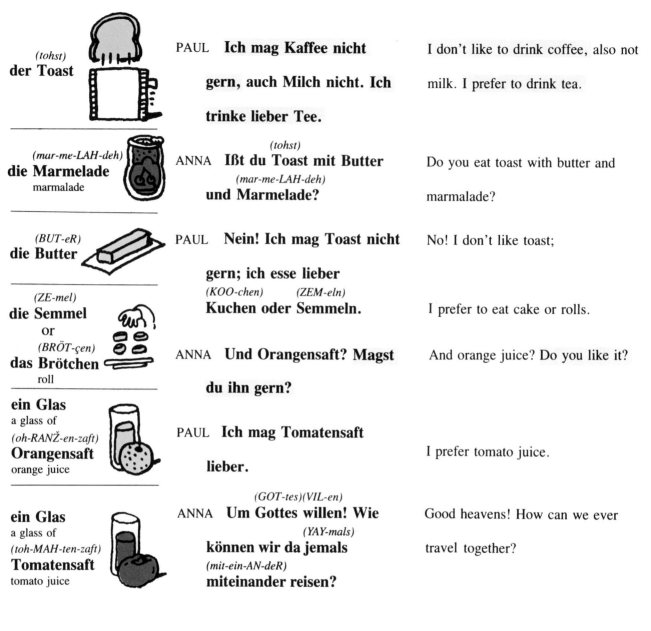

(tohst)
der Toast

PAUL **Ich mag Kaffee nicht gern, auch Milch nicht. Ich trinke lieber Tee.**

I don't like to drink coffee, also not milk. I prefer to drink tea.

(mar-me-LAH-deh)
die Marmelade
marmalade

ANNA *(tohst)* *(mar-me-LAH-deh)*
Ißt du Toast mit Butter und Marmelade?

Do you eat toast with butter and marmalade?

(BUT-eR)
die Butter

PAUL **Nein! Ich mag Toast nicht gern; ich esse lieber**
(KOO-chen) *(ZEM-eln)*
Kuchen oder Semmeln.

No! I don't like toast;
I prefer to eat cake or rolls.

(ZE-mel)
die Semmel
or
(BRÖT-çen)
das Brötchen
roll

ANNA **Und Orangensaft? Magst du ihn gern?**

And orange juice? Do you like it?

ein Glas
a glass of
(oh-RANŽ-en-zaft)
Orangensaft
orange juice

PAUL **Ich mag Tomatensaft lieber.**

I prefer tomato juice.

ein Glas
a glass of
(toh-MAH-ten-zaft)
Tomatensaft
tomato juice

ANNA *(GOT-tes)(VIL-en)*
Um Gottes willen! Wie
(YAY-mals)
können wir da jemals
(mit-ein-AN-deR)
miteinander reisen?

Good heavens! How can we ever travel together?

Try to complete the following sentences:

1. I like to swim. — Ich schwimme ____________.
2. I don't like to dance. — Ich tanze ________ ________.
3. I like Michael. — Ich ________ *(MIÇ-ah-ayl)* Michael ________.
4. I don't like my auto. — Ich ________ ________ ________ mein Auto.

ANSWERS

1. gern **2.** nicht gern **3.** habe, gern **4.** mag nicht gern

Let's practice *gern* and *lieber*. See how much of the conversation you remember by filling in the blanks with the missing word. Then read the sentence aloud.

1. Anna sagt: Ich esse Frühstück ________________ um acht.
2. Paul sagt: Ich esse Frühstück ________________ um 7.45.
   preferably
3. Paul sagt: Ich mag Kaffee ________________ ________________.
4. Paul trinkt ________________ Tee.
   preferably
5. Paul mag Toast ________________ ________________.
6. Er ißt ________________ Kuchen oder Semmeln.

Fill in the blanks as indicated. Be sure to say the words aloud.

(HEIS-eh) (ge-TREN-keh)
7. 2 heiße Getränke ________________, ________________

(FRUCHT-zef-teh)
8. 2 Fruchtsäfte (juices) ________________, ________________

(ZACH-en)
9. 2 Sachen von der Bäckerei ________________, ________________
   items
10. Was ist auf dem Toast oder der Semmel? ________________ und ________________

Using the pictures and the words and phrases from Anna and Paul's conversation, try answering these questions:

1. Wann essen Sie Frühstück? ________________________________

(MÖ-gen)
2. Was mögen Sie lieber, Kaffee mit Sahne, schwarzen Kaffee oder Tee?

   ____

3. Mögen Sie Orangensaft oder Tomatensaft?

   ____

4. Was ist auf Ihrem Toast? ________________________________

ANSWERS

1. gern **2.** lieber **3.** nicht gern **4.** lieber **5.** nicht gern **6.** lieber **7.** Tee, Kaffee **8.** Tomatensaft, Orangensaft **9.** Kuchen, Semmeln **10.** Butter, Marmelade

(tish)
DER TISCH
The Table

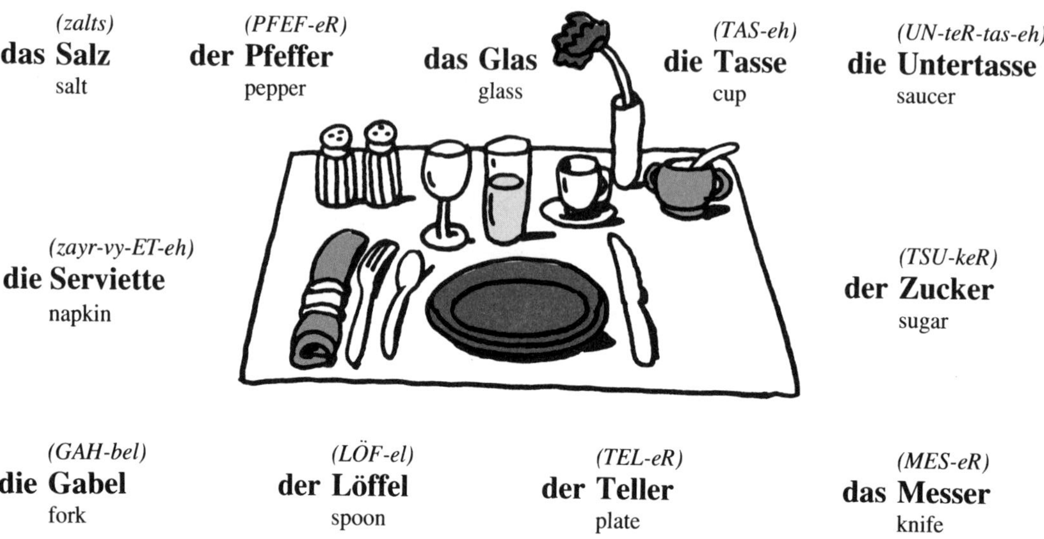

Here's a little fun. And a little learning. Draw a line from each item in Column 1 to the item in Column 2 you associate it with.

1. Gabel	A. Fruchtsaft
2. Frühstück	B. Serviette
3. Tasse	C. Tee
4. Orangensaft	D. Toast und Kaffee
5. den Mund abwischen *(AP-vi-shen)* to wipe	E. Pfeffer
6. Glas	F. Messer
7. Salz	G. Tomatensaft

ANSWERS

Matching 1. F 2. D 3. C 4. A 5. B 6. G 7. E

(HOWPT-mahl-tseit)
DIE HAUPTMAHLZEIT
The Main Meal

(MI-tag-es-en)
DAS MITTAGESSEN
The Noon Meal

An ample Sunday meal:

(krowt) **das Kraut** cabbage

(KNÖ-del) **der Knödel** dumpling

(fish) **der Fisch**

(NACH-tish) **der Nachtisch** dessert

(KU-chen) **der Kuchen** cake

(TOR-teh) **die Torte** pie

(ZU-peh) **die Suppe** soup

(ge-MÜ-zeh) **das Gemüse** vegetable

(kaR-TOF-eln) **die Kartoffeln** potatoes

(fleish) **das Fleisch** meat

(SHVEI-neh-brah-ten) **der Schweinebraten** roast pork

Depending on the region, you drink beer or wine with your meal. Coffee is hardly ever served with it. *Vorspeisen* *(FOHR-shpei-zen)* (appetizers) are available in enormous variety in Germany and Austria. The main meal of the day often begins with soup.

1. Was trinken Sie gewöhnlich *(ge-VÖN-liç)* (usually) aus einem Glas?

____

2. Was schneiden Sie gewöhnlich mit einem Messer?

____

3. Was trinken Sie gewöhnlich aus einer Tasse?

____

4. Was für Gänge *(GEN-geh)* (courses) kommen vor dem Hauptgang *(HOWPT-gang)* (main course)?

____

5. Was ist der letzte Gang? _______________________

ANSWERS

1. das Bier **2.** das Fleisch **3.** den Kaffee **4.** die Vorspeisen, die Suppe **5.** der Nachtisch

Try answering these questions about the meal:

1. Was ist der erste Gang der Mahlzeit? ______________________________

   (VEL-çen)
2. Welchen Gang haben Sie am liebsten? ______________________________

   which

   (FOR-tsee-hen)
3. Ziehen Sie Fisch oder Fleisch vor (vorziehen)?

   to prefer

   ____

   (FROYN-deh)
4. Was haben Ihre Freunde gern?

   friends

   ____

MAHLZEITEN IN DEUTSCHLAND UND ÖSTERREICH

Meals in Germany and Austria

Meals in Germany and Austria are taken at about the same time as in America. But while lunch in the United States usually is of no great consequence, lunch *(das Mittagessen)* *(MI-tag-es-en)* in Germany and Austria is the major meal of the day. The evening meal *(das Abendessen)* *(AH-bent-es-en)* is of lesser importance. It is more like a light supper or like the American lunch, often consisting mainly of bread, cold cuts, and cheeses with perhaps a salad or dessert as well. It is sometimes called *Abendbrot* *(AH-bent-broht)* ("evening bread"), and this name accurately reflects the nature of the meal.

There also are in-between meals, especially in southern German-speaking areas. For instance, *Gabelfrühstück,* *(GAH-bel-frū-shtük)* served at about ten in the morning, is a warm meal, maybe goulash and beer. In Austria, *Jause*, *(YOW-zeh)* served at about four in the afternoon, is a snack consisting of coffee and cake. In Germany this is called *Kaffeetrinken*.

ANSWERS

1. Vorspeise *or* Suppe **2.** Vorspeise, Suppe, Hauptgang, *or* Nachtisch **3.** Ich ziehe — vor. **4.** Meine Freunde haben — gern.

Let's try some exercises about meals.

What are the names of the morning, noon, and evening meals?

das ____________________, das ____________________, das ____________________.

Can you show the correctness of these statements by writing TRUE or FALSE after them?

1. In Deutschland servieren sie die Hauptmahlzeit um 9 Uhr abends. ____________________

2. Wenn ich hungrig bin, trinke ich Wasser. ____________________

3. Wenn ich durstig bin, esse ich ein Schinkenbrot (*SHIN-ken-broht*) (ham sandwich). ____________________

4. Es ist möglich, einen Imbiß (*IM-bis*) (snack) zwischen der Hauptmahlzeit und dem Abendessen zu essen.

   ____

5. Es gibt eine leichte Mahlzeit zwischen dem Frühstück und der Hauptmahlzeit. ____________________

See if you can supply the missing letter(s) in the following sentences.

1. Ich esse ge___n Toa___t mit Marm___lad___ und Bu___ ___er.

2. Paul i___t li___ber Kuchen.

3. Sie___ ___ink___ gern Kaf___e___.

4. Sie ser___ie___t das Fr___ ___st___ck um si___ben.

5. Wir es___en am A___end um s___chs.

Try answering these questions:

1. Was tun Sie, wenn Sie hungrig sind?

   ____

2. Was tun Sie, wenn Sie durstig sind?

   ____

ANSWERS

Meals. Frühstück, Mittagessen, Abendessen

True/false. **1.** F **2.** F **3.** F **4.** T **5.** T

Missing letters. **1.** gern, Toast, Marmelade, Butter **2.** ißt lieber **3.** trinkt, Kaffee **4.** serviert, Frühstück, sieben **5.** essen, Abend, sechs

Questions. **1.** Ich esse. **2.** Ich trinke.

Can you find the hidden words? There are 5 of them, not counting the example. The words are very similar to the English ones.

S	A	L	A	T	G	G	O	G	E	L
N	W	O	C	E	N	L	M	N	P	U
M	A	R	M	E	L	A	D	E	N	F
P	S	O	I	S	F	S	U	P	P	E
L	S	E	L	T	O	M	G	X	N	A
A	E	N	C	B	R	O	M	L	S	E
O	R	E	H	N	S	O	P	Z	L	A

(GAY-ben) (NAY-men)

Geben und Nehmen

to give to take

These are two important and quite common verbs worth repeating and remembering.

Let's practice them:

Ich gebe **dir ein Buch.**	I give you a book.
Du gibst **mir die Zeitung.**	You give me the newspaper.
Er (sie, es) gibt **mir ein Glas.**	He (she, it) gives me a glass.
Wir geben **ihr Blumen.**	We give her flowers.
Ihr gebt **uns den Schlüssel.**	You give us the key.
Sie geben **uns das Messer.**	They give us the knife.
Geben Sie **uns die Speisekarte!**	Give us the menu.
Was für einen Salat *gibt es*?	What kind of salad is there?

Ich nehme **gefüllte Eier.**	I'll take deviled eggs.
Du nimmst **lieber Fisch.**	You prefer fish.
Er (sie, es) nimmt **Fleisch.**	He (she, it) takes meat.
Wir nehmen **Suppe.**	We take soup.
Ihr nehmt **Kartoffeln.**	You take potatoes.
Sie nehmen **Salat.**	They take salad.
Nehmen Sie **Backhuhn!**	Take fried chicken.

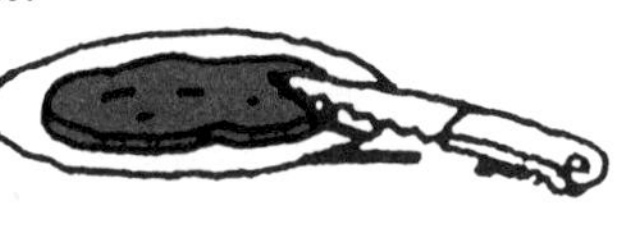

ANSWERS

Hidden words. Salat, Wasser, Marmelade, Tee, Milch

15

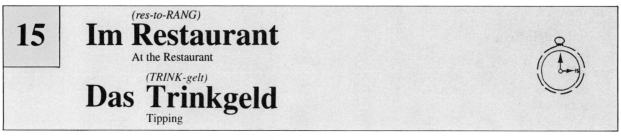

(res-to-RANG)
Im Restaurant
At the Restaurant

(TRINK-gelt)
Das Trinkgeld
Tipping

(SHPEI-zeh-kaR-teh)
Die Speisekarte bitte!
The menu, please

After carefully perusing the voluminous menu laid before them by the waiter, Karl and Josef decide to make their choice from the following items:

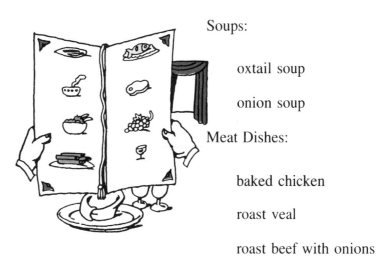

Vorspeisen:	Appetizers:
(laks) **Norwegischer Lachs mit Toast**	Norwegian salmon with toast
(ge-FÜL-teh) (EI-eR) **Gefüllte Eier**	deviled eggs
Suppen:	Soups:
(OK-sen-shvants) **Ochsenschwanzsuppe**	oxtail soup
(TSVEE-bel-zu-peh) **Zwiebelsuppe**	onion soup
Fleischspeisen:	Meat Dishes:
(BAK-hoon) **Backhuhn**	baked chicken
(KALPS-brah-ten) **Kalbsbraten**	roast veal
(TSVEE-bel-rost-brah-ten) **Zwiebelrostbraten**	roast beef with onions

Gemüse:	Vegetables:
Salzkartoffeln	boiled potatoes
(reis) **Reis**	rice
(SHPAR-gel) **Spargel**	asparagus
Salate:	Salads:
(GUR-ken) **Gurken mit Tomaten**	cucumbers with tomatoes
Kohlsalat	cole slaw
Nachtisch:	Dessert:
Käsekuchen	cheese cake
(ZA-cheR-tor-teh) **Sachertorte**	Sacher torte
Getränke:	Beverages:
(PILS-neR) **Pilsner Bier**	Pilsen beer
(REIN-vein) **Rheinwein**	Rhine wine

On a separate page they find also "Specialties of the House," among which they have a hard time choosing.

(FISH-ge-riç-teh)
Fischgerichte:
fish dishes

(pa-NEER-teR) (KAR-pfen) **panierter Karpfen**	breaded carp
(fo-REL-eh) **Forelle**	trout
(SHOL-eh) **Scholle**	flounder

Finally they are ready to order. The waiter approaches the table.

(BAK-hoon)
das Backhuhn
baked chicken

KELLNER **Möchten Sie bestellen,** *(be-SHTEL-en)*	Would you like to order, gentlemen?
meine Herren? Das Backhuhn kann ich bestens empfehlen. *(emp-FAY-len)*	I highly recommend the baked chicken.

JOSEF **Wie sind Ihre gefüllten Eier?**

KELLNER **Ausgezeichnet, mein Herr.** *(OWS-ge-tseiç-net)*

JOSEF **Also gefüllte Eier und dann Ochsenschwanzsuppe. Und für mich ein halbes Backhuhn. Bestellst du lieber Fisch, Karl?**

KARL **Ja. Wie ist die Forelle?**

KELLNER **Unsere Spezialität.** *(shpe-tsee-a-lee-TAYT)*

KARL **Also gut. Forelle für mich. Mit Salzkartoffeln.**

JOSEF **Was für einen Salat gibt es?**

KELLNER **Gurken mit Tomaten.**

JOSEF **Gut.**

KELLNER **Der andere Herr nimmt auch einen?**

KARL **Ja. Zwei Salate.**

KELLNER **Und zum Nachtisch?**

JOSEF **Geben Sie uns noch einmal die Speisekarte.**

(Er nimmt sie und liest.)

Möchtest du Sachertorte, Karl? *(ZACH-eR-tor-teh)*

(ge-FÜL-teh EI-eR)
gefüllte Eier
deviled eggs

(ZU-peh)
die Suppe
soup

die Forelle
trout

(zalts) *(PFEF-eR)*
Salz und Pfeffer
salt and pepper

(zah-LAT)
der Salat
salad

(SHVARTS-broht)
das Schwarzbrot
dark bread

(KAY-zeh)
der Käse
cheese

(VEIN-trow-ben)
die Weintrauben
grapes

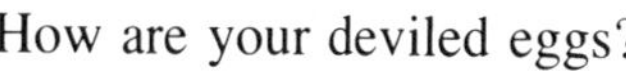

How are your deviled eggs?

Excellent, sir.

So, deviled eggs and then oxtail soup. And, for me, half a baked chicken. Do you prefer to order fish, Karl?

Yes. How is the trout?

Our specialty.

Good! Trout for me. With boiled potatoes.

What kind of salad do you have?

Cucumbers and tomatoes.

Good.

Does the other gentleman also want one?

Yes. Two salads.

And for dessert?

Give us the menu again.

(He takes it and reads.)

Would you like Sachertorte, Karl?

KARL **Gute Idee. Sachertorte mit** *(SHLAK-zah-neh)* **Schlagsahne.** — Good idea. Sachertorte with whipped cream.

(vein) **der Wein** wine

JOSEF **Also Sachertorte mit Schlagsahne.** — So, Sachertorte with whipped cream.

KARL **Zum Fisch einen guten Rheinwein.** — With fish a good Rhine wine.

(beeR) **das Bier** beer

JOSEF **Und für mich ein großes Glas Bier.** — And for me a large glass of beer.

Let's look at an important reflexive verb.

(FÜ-len)
WIE FÜHLEN SIE SICH?
How Do You Feel?

SICH FÜHLEN

Ich fühle mich (nicht) wohl	I (don't) feel well
Du fühlst dich (nicht) wohl	You (don't) feel well
Er, sie, es fühlt sich (nicht) wohl	He, she (doesn't) feel well
Wir fühlen uns (nicht) wohl	We (don't) feel well
Ihr fühlt euch (nicht) wohl	You (don't) feel well
Sie fühlen sich (nicht) wohl	They (don't) feel well
Sie fühlen sich (nicht) wohl	You (don't) feel well (polite)

Damen
Women

Herren
Men

Here are a few exercises based on what we've learned about eating in a restaurant. You're well into your new language, so the exercises should be easy. Like a piece of cake.

Place the numbers of the courses in front of the dishes and drinks to show in which course(s) each is typically served.

1. Vorspeisen 2. Suppe 3. Salat
4. Fisch 5. Fleisch 6. Nachtisch

a. ______ Gurken mit Tomaten
b. ______ Backhuhn
c. ______ Bier
d. ______ Sachertorte
e. ______ Rheinwein
f. ______ Reis
g. ______ Salzkartoffeln
h. ______ gefüllte Eier
i. ______ Brötchen
j. ______ Zwiebelsuppe
k. ______ Gemüse.

Now try to fill in the blanks with the German version of the English words in parentheses.

1. ________________ (The waiter) gibt Josef die Speisekarte.
2. ________________ (He gives him) die Speisekarte.
3. ________________ (He takes) die Speisekarte.
4. Der Kellner empfiehlt ________________ (baked chicken).
5. Karl (prefers) ________________ Forelle ________________.
6. Er trinkt eine ________________ (bottle) Rheinwein.

Wie sagt man das Folgende (*FOL-gen-deh*; following) auf Deutsch?

1. Where are the restrooms? ________________
2. Please bring . . . to me. ________________

ANSWERS

Courses. **a.** 3 **b.** 5 **c.** 5 **d.** 6 **e.** 4 **f.** 4,5 **g.** 4,5 **h.** 1 **i.** 1,4,5 **j.** 2 **k.** 4,5

Fill-ins. **1.** Der Kellner **2.** Er gibt ihm **3.** Er nimmt **4.** Backhuhn **5.** zieht, vor **6.** Flasche

Auf Deutsch. **1.** Wo sind die Toiletten? **2.** Bitte bringen Sie mir . . . .

VORSPEISEN

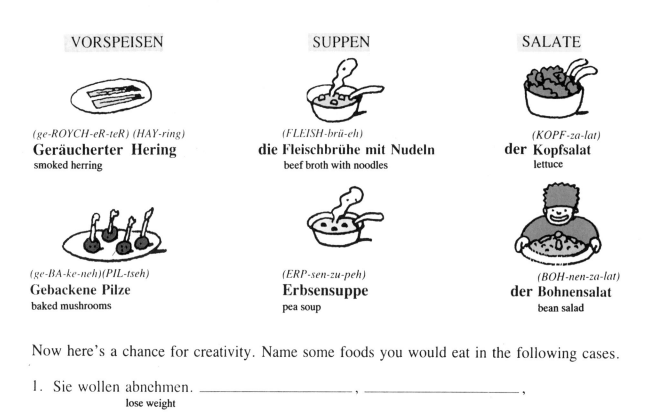

(ge-ROYCH-eR-teR) (HAY-ring)
Geräucherter Hering
smoked herring

(ge-BA-ke-neh)(PIL-tseh)
Gebackene Pilze
baked mushrooms

SUPPEN

(FLEISH-brü-eh)
die Fleischbrühe mit Nudeln
beef broth with noodles

(ERP-sen-zu-peh)
Erbsensuppe
pea soup

SALATE

(KOPF-za-lat)
der Kopfsalat
lettuce

(BOH-nen-za-lat)
der Bohnensalat
bean salad

Now here's a chance for creativity. Name some foods you would eat in the following cases.

1. Sie wollen abnehmen. ____________________, ____________________,
   lose weight
   ____

2. Sie wollen zunehmen. ____________________, ____________________,
   gain weight
   ____

(vits)
EIN WITZ
A joke

KELLNER Tee oder Kaffee?

GAST Kaffee ohne Sahne.

KELLNER Sie müssen ihn ohne Milch nehmen. Wir haben keine Sahne.

Many restaurants and lunch counters serve a daily special that is quite inexpensive. It is especially good for tourists who wish to economize. Nowadays the North American influence is seen in fast-food restaurants and in the food they serve. If you have a yen for a hamburger, you can find it in Germany and Austria. But you may prefer to try out the food of the country. If you feel like having a soft drink of a North American brand, it is possible to find it at any café or restaurant. You can stay there a long time, and you don't have to drink up in a hurry. When you pay the bill, ask whether the service **(Bedienung)** is included. If not, leave a tip of 10%–15% for the waiter or waitress. In restaurants, service is usually included, but you should still leave a small tip, rounding the bill off to the nearest mark.

ANSWERS

Things to eat. 1. Fisch, Gemüse, Salat **2.** Backhuhn, Kartoffeln, Torte

(ge-MÜ-zeh)
GEMÜSE

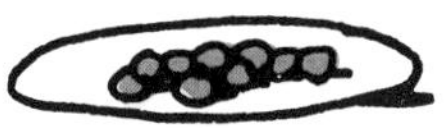

(ERP-sen)
die Erbsen
peas

(BLOO-men-kohl)
der Blumenkohl
cauliflower

FISCH

(HE-ring)
der Hering
herring

(heçt)
der Hecht
pike

NACHTISCH

(AP-fel-shtroo-del)
der Apfelstrudel
apple strudel

(VINT-boy-tel)
der Windbeutel
cream puff, éclair

FLEISCH

(RINT-fleish)
das Rindfleisch
beef

(LAM-fleish)
das Lammfleisch
lamb

GETRÄNKE

(mi-ne-RAHL-vas-eR)
das Mineralwasser
mineral water

(VEIN-brant)
der Weinbrand
brandy

True or False?

1. Karl und Josef bestellen norwegischen Lachs. __________
2. Dann haben sie Ochsenschwanzsuppe. __________
3. Karl hat Forelle nicht gern. __________
4. Josef sagt: ,,Kartoffeln machen dick *(dik)* fat. Ich habe Reis lieber.'' __________
5. Zum Nachtisch essen sie Sachertorte. __________
6. Sie trinken französischen Wein lieber als Rheinwein. __________

Answer the following questions based on your personal preferences.

1. Was essen Sie morgen als Hauptmahlzeit?
2. Und zum for the Frühstück?
3. Und zum Abendessen?

ANSWERS

True-False. 1. F **2.** T **3.** F **4.** F **5.** T **6.** F

Try putting the words together in the right order so they make sense:

1. empfehlen, kann, das, bestens, ich, Backhuhn

 ____

2. bestellen, meine, Sie, möchten, Herren?

 ____

3. Salat, was, es, gibt, einen, für?

 ____

4. für, Glas, und, ein, Bier, mich, großes

 ____

(GOO-ten) *(a-pe-TEET)* *(MAHL-tseit)*

Guten Appetit! Mahlzeit!

Enjoy Your Meal!

Congratulations. We hear you have just been named Chef of the Year. All of your friends are coming over tonight for a very special dinner which you are preparing to celebrate the occasion. Draw up a menu, course by course, of what you plan to serve.

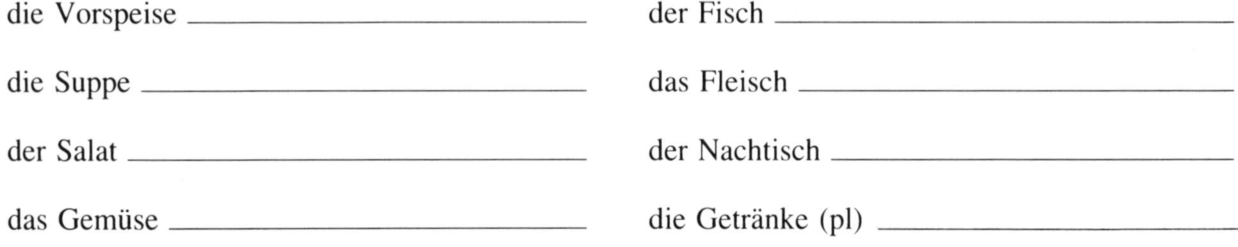

die Vorspeise ____________________ der Fisch ____________________

die Suppe ____________________ das Fleisch ____________________

der Salat ____________________ der Nachtisch ____________________

das Gemüse ____________________ die Getränke (pl) ____________________

ANSWERS

1. Ich kann das Backhuhn bestens empfehlen. **2.** Möchten Sie bestellen, meine Herren? **3.** Was für einen Salat gibt es? **4.** Und ein großes Glas Bier für mich.

HOW'RE WE DOING?

Na, wie geht's?

You're more than halfway through.
You've come a long way — you've learned a lot.

It's a good idea to go through the first part of the book again, reviewing the vocabulary and rereading the dialogues. If you're confused about a point, study it closely—you'll catch on soon enough!

After you've reviewed the material, try to complete the following quiz. It'll probably be easy. If you have any difficulty, reread the appropriate section of the book.

(feel) (glük) *(shpahs)*
Viel Glück—und viel Spaß!
Good luck lots of fun

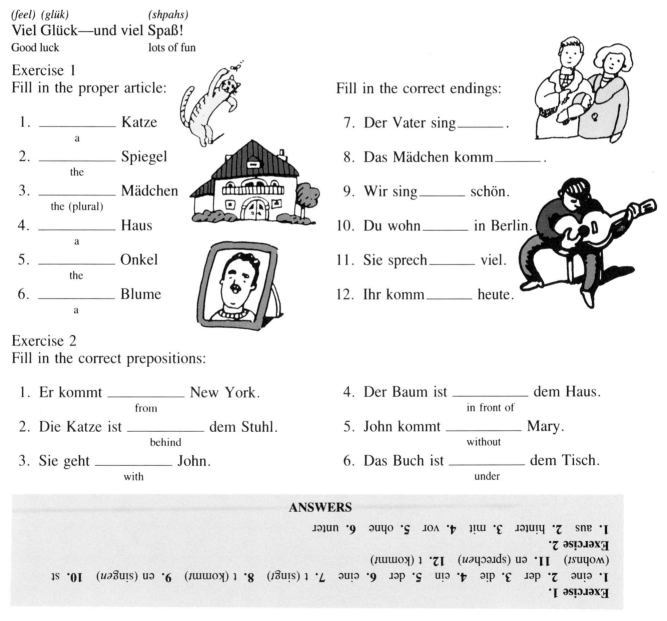

Exercise 1
Fill in the proper article:

1. _________ Katze (a)
2. _________ Spiegel (the)
3. _________ Mädchen (the (plural))
4. _________ Haus (a)
5. _________ Onkel (the)
6. _________ Blume (a)

Fill in the correct endings:

7. Der Vater sing_____.
8. Das Mädchen komm_____.
9. Wir sing_____ schön.
10. Du wohn_____ in Berlin.
11. Sie sprech_____ viel.
12. Ihr komm_____ heute.

Exercise 2
Fill in the correct prepositions:

1. Er kommt _________ New York. (from)
2. Die Katze ist _________ dem Stuhl. (behind)
3. Sie geht _________ John. (with)
4. Der Baum ist _________ dem Haus. (in front of)
5. John kommt _________ Mary. (without)
6. Das Buch ist _________ dem Tisch. (under)

ANSWERS

Exercise 1.
1. eine **2.** der **3.** die **4.** ein **5.** der **6.** eine **7.** t (sing*t*) **8.** t (komm*t*) **9.** en (sing*en*) **10.** st (wohn*st*) **11.** en (sprech*en*) **12.** t (komm*t*)

Exercise 2.
1. aus **2.** hinter **3.** mit **4.** vor **5.** ohne **6.** unter

Exercise 2
Fill in the verbs with the correct endings:

7. Ich __________ nicht.
   speak
8. Du __________ gut.
   see
9. Sie __________ nicht.
   speak (polite form)
10. Er __________ das Mädchen.
    see
11. Du __________ schnell.
    speak
12. Sie __________ den Mann.
    sees

Exercise 3
Fill in the proper words (in two possible ways):

1. __________ or __________ Katze
   this
2. __________ or __________ Vater
   this
3. __________ or __________ Mädchen
   this
4. __________ or __________ Häuser
   these
5. __________ or __________ Füße
   these
6. __________ or __________ Blumen
   these

Fill in the verbs with the correct endings:

7. Er __________ zwanzig Mark.
   takes
8. Du __________ acht Stunden.
   sleep
9. Sie __________ nach Wien.
   travels
10. Das __________ zu viel.
    costs
11. Er __________ das Auto.
    washes
12. Wir __________ das Buch.
    take

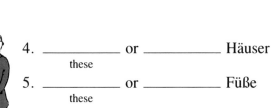

Exercise 4
Fill in the proper words:

1. Sie müssen hier __________. (to get off)
2. Er __________ hier __________. (to get on)
3. Der Bus __________ hier __________. (to stop)
4. Wir __________ hier __________. (to transfer)
5. Eine __________, bitte.
   ticket
6. Das ist die __________.
   stop

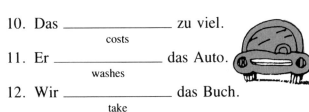

ANSWERS

Exercise 2.
7. spreche **8.** siehst **9.** sprechen **10.** sieht **11.** sprichst **12.** sieht

Exercise 3.
1. diese, die **2.** dieser, der **3.** dieses, das **4.** diese, die **5.** diese, die **6.** diese, die **7.** nimmt
8. schläfst **9.** fährt **10.** kostet **11.** wäscht **12.** nehmen

Exercise 4.
1. aussteigen **2.** steigt, ein **3.** bleibt, stehen **4.** steigen, um **5.** Fahrkarte **6.** Haltestelle

Exercise 4
Fill in the correct verb form of *sein* and of *haben*:

7. Er ____________ ein Junge. (sein)
8. Du ____________ ein Mädchen. (sein)
9. Wir ____________ Frauen. (sein)
10. Sie ____________ ein Mann. (polite, sein)
11. Du ____________ ein Buch. (haben)
12. Er ____________ eine Katze. (haben)

Exercise 5
Try these contractions:

1. Er kommt ____beim____ Haus an.
   bei dem
2. Die Katze springt ____________ Sofa.
   über das
3. Er geht ____________ Kino.
   in das
4. Wir fahren ____________ Markt.
   zu dem
5. Der Hund ist ____________ Haus.
   in dem
6. Das Kind kommt ____________ Mutter.
   zu der

Exercise 6
Wieviel Uhr ist es?

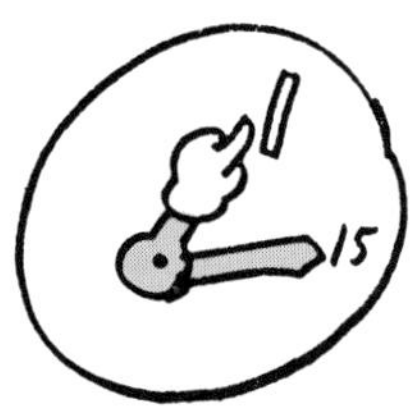

1. Es ist ____________ or ____________.

4. Es ist ____________ or ____________.

2. Es ist ____________ or ____________.

5. Es ist ____________ or ____________.

3. Es ist ____________ or ____________.

6. Es ist ____________.

ANSWERS

Exercise 4.
7. ist **8.** bist **9.** sind **10.** sind **11.** hast **12.** hat

Exercise 5.
2. übers **3.** ins **4.** zum **5.** im **6.** zur

Exercise 6.
1. Viertel zwei, fünfzehn nach eins **2.** zwei Uhr dreißig, halb drei **3.** dreiviertel drei, Viertel vor drei
4. elf Uhr dreißig, halb zwölf **5.** zwanzig nach sieben, sieben Uhr zwanzig **6.** neun Uhr neununddreißig

Remember that in Germany a 24-hour clock is used. Thus, 3 P.M. is 15 hours, or *15 Uhr*.

Exercise 7
Fill in the correct pronouns:

1. Er ist ______________ Sohn.
   my
2. Sie ist ______________ Tochter.
   our
3. Das ist ______________ Freund.
   her
4. Er ist ______________ Vater.
   his
5. Das ist ______________ Haus.
   your (polite)
6. Ist das ______________ Uhr?
   your (familiar)

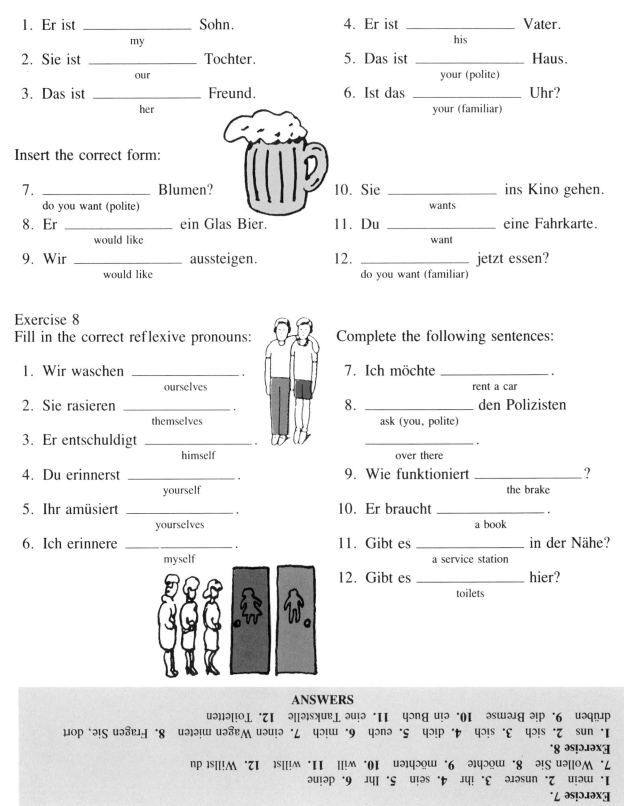

Insert the correct form:

7. ______________ Blumen?
   do you want (polite)
8. Er ______________ ein Glas Bier.
   would like
9. Wir ______________ aussteigen.
   would like
10. Sie ______________ ins Kino gehen.
    wants
11. Du ______________ eine Fahrkarte.
    want
12. ______________ jetzt essen?
    do you want (familiar)

Exercise 8
Fill in the correct reflexive pronouns:

1. Wir waschen ______________.
   ourselves
2. Sie rasieren ______________.
   themselves
3. Er entschuldigt ______________.
   himself
4. Du erinnerst ______________.
   yourself
5. Ihr amüsiert ______________.
   yourselves
6. Ich erinnere ______________.
   myself

Complete the following sentences:

7. Ich möchte ______________.
   rent a car
8. ______________ den Polizisten
   ask (you, polite)
   ______________.
   over there
9. Wie funktioniert ______________?
   the brake
10. Er braucht ______________.
    a book
11. Gibt es ______________ in der Nähe?
    a service station
12. Gibt es ______________ hier?
    toilets

ANSWERS

Exercise 7.
1. mein **2.** unsere **3.** ihr **4.** sein **5.** Ihr **6.** deine
7. Wollen Sie **8.** möchte **9.** möchten **10.** will **11.** willst **12.** Willst du

Exercise 8.
1. uns **2.** sich **3.** sich **4.** dich **5.** euch **6.** mich **7.** einen Wagen mieten **8.** Fragen Sie, dort drüben **9.** die Bremse **10.** ein Buch **11.** eine Tankstelle **12.** Toiletten

Exercise 9
Personal pronouns again:

1. Karl sieht ______________. (you (polite))
2. Wir lesen ______________. (it (the book))
3. Er hört ______________. (us)
4. Sie kauft ______________. (them)
5. Mary besucht ______________. (me)
6. Ich liebe ______________. (you (my daughter))

"Will you give it to me. . . ." (the indirect object):

7. Er gibt ______________ das Geld. (to us)
8. Sie sendet ______________ Bonbons. (to me)
9. Ich gebe ______________ Blumen. (to her)
10. Ich kaufe ______________ ein Buch. (for you (polite))
11. Er dankt ______________ für die Karte. (to you (familiar))
12. Du gibst ______________ eine Krawatte. (to him)

Exercise 10
Fill in the blanks:

1. ______________ wollen Sie sprechen? (about what)
2. ______________ sammeln Sie das? (to what purpose)

Try to translate these idiomatic expressions so that they sound as natural in German as they do in English:

3. That doesn't matter. ______________.
4. What is it about? ______________?
5. Turn left (right). ______________.
6. Drive straight ahead! ______________!
7. I am lost. ______________
8. I passed the test. ______________.
9. He has the right-of-way. ______________.
10. Fill it up, please! ______________.
11. You are right. ______________.
12. Over there. ______________.

ANSWERS

Exercise 9.
1. Sie **2.** es **3.** uns **4.** sie **5.** mich **6.** dich **7.** uns **8.** mir **9.** ihr **10.** Ihnen **11.** dir **12.** ihm

Exercise 10.
1. Worüber **2.** Wozu **3.** Das macht nichts. **4.** Worum handelt es sich? **5.** Links (Rechts) abbiegen. **6.** Fahren Sie geradeaus! **7.** Ich habe mich verirrt. **8.** Ich habe die Prüfung bestanden. **9.** Er hat das Vorrecht. **10.** Volltanken, bitte. **11.** Sie haben recht. **12.** Dort drüben.

Exercise 11
True or False?

1. ________ Ein Reporter schreibt für eine Zeitung.
2. ________ Zum Wandern braucht man einen Koffer.
3. ________ Die meisten Deutschen gehen im März auf Urlaub.
4. ________ Deutsche feiern Weihnachten zwei Tage lang.
5. ________ Jogging ist ein sehr teurer Sport.
6. ________ Die Deutschen wandern sehr gern.
7. ________ Eine Trainingsbluse ist dasselbe wie ein Sweatshirt.
8. ________ In Deutschland braucht man kein Rücklicht für Fahrräder.
9. ________ Brustschwimmen lernt man im allgemeinen zuerst.
10. ________ *Eventuell* heißt auf Englisch *eventual.*
11. ________ Fisch schneidet man immer mit dem Messer.
12. ________ Das Mittagessen ist die wichtigste Mahlzeit in Deutschland.

Exercise 12
Circle the correct answer.

1. Wohin gehen Sie, wenn Sie essen wollen?
   a. in die Garage b. ins Theater c. ins Restaurant
2. Die Tasse steht gewöhnlich auf
   a. dem Auto b. der Untertasse c. der Serviette
3. Knödel ißt man oft mit
   a. Kraut b. Sachertorte c. Tomatensaft
4. In Deutschland ist der erste Gang gewöhnlich
   a. Kuchen b. Fisch c. Suppe
5. Jause hat man gewöhnlich um
   a. zehn Uhr b. sechzehn Uhr c. zwölf Uhr mittag
6. Wasser trinkt man gewöhnlich
   a. aus einer Tasse b. aus einem Glas c. aus einem Teller

ANSWERS

Exercise 11.
1. T **2.** F **3.** F **4.** T **5.** F **6.** T **7.** T **8.** F **9.** T **10.** F **11.** F **12.** T

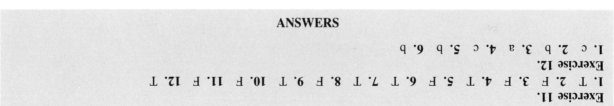

Exercise 12.
1. c **2.** b **3.** a **4.** c **5.** b **6.** b

Pick the right word and insert it where it belongs. Choose among: Bäckerei, Abzeichen, Glas, abwischen, Wanderpfade, Sport.

7. Schwimmen ist ein sehr gesunder ________________.

8. Die deutschen ________________ sind sehr gut markiert.

9. Man näht sich ein ________________ auf die Badehose.

10. Brötchen kauft man in der ________________.

11. Mit der Serviette kann man sich den Mund ________________.

12. Er bestellt ein großes ________________ Bier.

ANSWERS

7. Sport **8.** Wanderpfade **9.** Abzeichen **10.** Bäckerei **11.** abwischen **12.** Glas

AT THE STORE

(im) (ge-SHEFT)
Im Geschäft

16 *(be-KLEI-dungs-ge-shef-teh)* Bekleidungsgeschäfte

Clothing Stores

(GRŌ-sen) (MAH-seh) (GRUNT-far-ben)
Größen, Maße, Grundfarben

Sizes, Measurements, Basic Colors

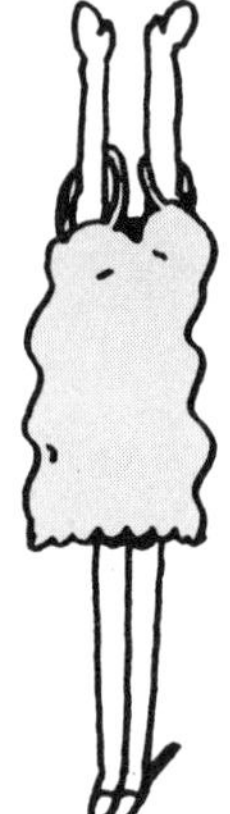

(TSEE-eh)
Ich ziehe mir einen
(UN-teR-rok)
Unterrock an.
I am putting on my slip.

Ich ziehe mir das
(hemt)
Hemd aus.
I am taking off my shirt.

(AN-klei-den) (OWS-klei-den)
SICH ANKLEIDEN—SICH AUSKLEIDEN
to get dressed / undressed

(KLEI-deR) (AN-proh-bee-ren)
Kleider anprobieren

Trying on Clothes

Ich kleide **mich** *an, du kleidest* **dich** *aus, er kleidet* **sich** *aus:* These are reflexive verbs taking the reflexive pronoun in the accusative (plural: *uns*, *euch*, *sich*).

In the case of articles of clothing:

Ich ziehe **mir** *etwas an, du ziehst* **dir** *etwas an, er probiert* **sich** *etwas an:* Here we have reflexive verbs taking the reflexive pronoun in the dative (plural: *uns*, *euch*, *sich*).

These verbs also have separable prefixes, which are separated from the verb under certain conditions. The position of the separable prefix is always at the end of the clause.

Ich *kleide* mich *an*. Ich *kleide* mich *aus*.

(MIT-gay-en) (tsoo-RÜK-kom-en) (TSOO-hō-ren)
A few other verbs with separable prefixes are *mitgehen*, *zurückkommen*, and *zuhören*. Note how they are used in sentences.

Sie *geht mit*. Er *kommt zurück*. Er *hört zu*.
along — back — listens

(HER-ren-be-klei-dung)

HERRENBEKLEIDUNG

Men's Clothes

Here are the German words for some basic items of men's clothing.

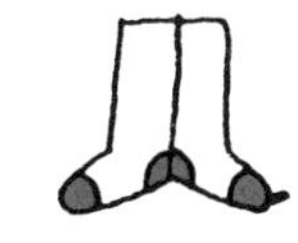

(ZOK-en)
die Socken
socks

(hemt)
das Hemd
shirt

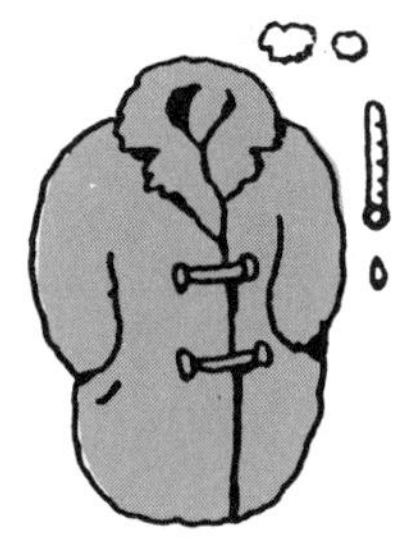

(MAN-tel)
der Mantel
overcoat

(krah-VA-teh)
die Krawatte
necktie

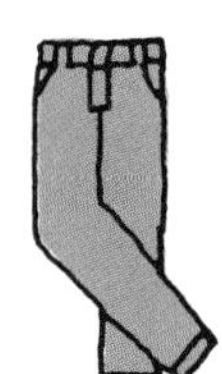

(HOH-zeh)
die Hose
pants

(TA-shen-tooch)
das Taschentuch
handkerchief

(UN-teR-hoh-zeh)
die Unterhose
underpants

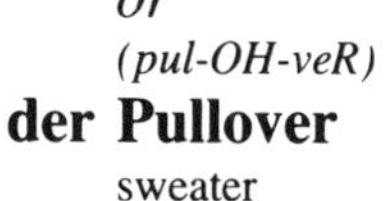

(SVET-eR)
der Sweater
or
(pul-OH-veR)
der Pullover
sweater

(SHPORT-ya-keh)
die Sportjacke
sport jacket

(UN-teR-hemt)
das Unterhemd
undershirt

(RAY-gen-shirm)
der Regenschirm
umbrella

(AN-tsook)
der Anzug
suit

(hoot)
der Hut
hat

(MÜT-seh)
die Mütze
cap

(SHTEE-fel)
die Stiefel (pl)
boots

(GÜR-tel)
der Gürtel
belt

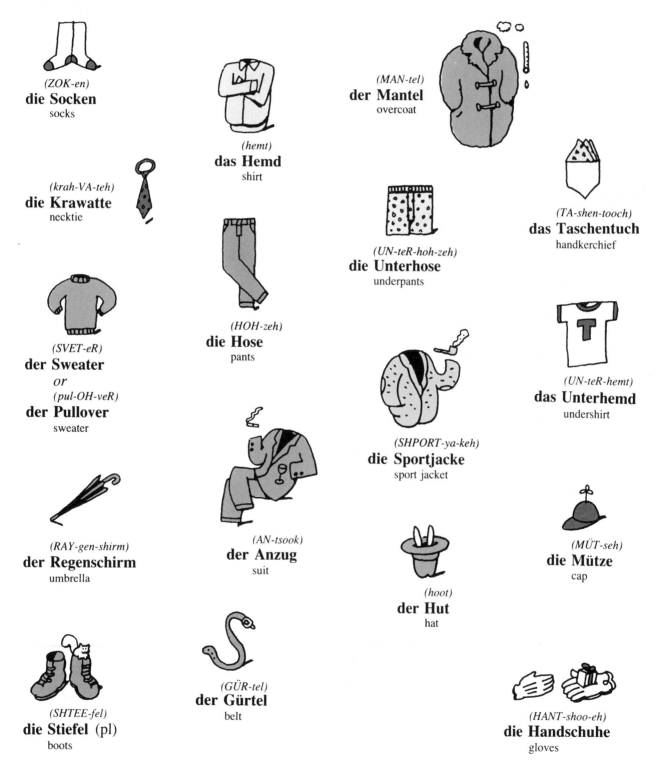

(HANT-shoo-eh)
die Handschuhe
gloves

A villager goes to a men's clothing store in the big city:

(feR-KOY-feR) *(voh-MIT)* VERKÄUFER **Womit kann ich Ihnen dienen, mein Herr?** clerk	What would you like, sir?
(KUN-deh) *(HEI-ra-teh)* *(VO-chen-en-deh)* KUNDE **Ich heirate dieses Wochenende und brauche etwas Neues zum Anziehen. Ich brauche Unterhosen und Unterhemden, auch ein weißes Hemd und eine schwarze Krawatte.** customer	I'm getting married this weekend and need new clothes. I need undershorts and undershirts, also a white shirt and a black tie.
VERKÄUFER **Brauchen Sie auch einen neuen Anzug?**	Do you need a new suit, too?
KUNDE **Ja. Zeigen Sie mir bitte einen schwarzen Anzug. Ich trage** *(TRAH-geh)* **Größe 44.**	Yes. Show me a black suit, please. I wear size 44.
VERKÄUFER **Wir haben keinen Anzug in dieser Größe. Kann ich Ihnen eine Sportjacke und eine Sporthose zeigen?**	We don't have a suit in that size. Can I show you a sport jacket and slacks?
KUNDE **Gut. Kann ich sie anprobieren?** (He tries them on, and they are too big for him.)	Good. Can I try them on?

VERKÄUFER **Sie passen Ihnen ausgezeichnet. Jetzt, glaube ich, brauchen Sie einen neuen Gürtel!**	They fit you beautifully. Now, I think, you need a new belt!

Can you tell me if these statements are correct? Write FALSCH (false) or RICHTIG (true).

1. Der Mann vom Land (villager) braucht neue Kleidung. ____________________
2. Er trägt Größe 54. ____________________
3. Er probiert die Hose an. ____________________
4. Die Hose ist ihm zu klein. ____________________
5. Er braucht keine Unterhosen. ____________________

When a man gets dressed in the morning, in what order does he put his clothes on? Write numbers over the items to show the sequence:

der Gürtel, die Socken, der Hut, die Unterhose, die Krawatte, das Hemd, die Hose

Fill in the blanks with the right form of the verb in parentheses.

1. ____________ (I need) ein Sportjacke.
2. Die Hosen ____________ (fit) mir nicht.
3. ____________ (I put) mir morgens die Kleider ____________ (on).
4. ____________ (I take) mir abends die Kleider ____________ (off).
5. Darf ich den Anzug ____________ (try on)?

Can you answer these questions?

1. Warum braucht der Mann neue Kleider?

____

2. Was für einen Anzug will er?

____

3. Was zeigt man ihm?

____

4. Was probiert er an?

____

ANSWERS

Falsch/Richtig.
1. Richtig **2.** Falsch **3.** Richtig **4.** Falsch **5.** Falsch

Getting dressed.
Unterhose, Hemd, Socken, Hose, Gürtel, Krawatte, Hut

Verbs.
1. Ich brauche **2.** passen **3.** Ich ziehe . . . an **4.** ich ziehe . . . aus **5.** anprobieren

Answers to questions.
1. er heiratet **2.** einen schwarzen Anzug **3.** eine Sportjacke und eine Sporthose **4.** eine Sportjacke und eine Sporthose

Herrengrößen

Men's Clothing Sizes

Hemden (Shirts)

AMERICAN SIZE	14	14½	15	15½	16	16½	17	17½
EUROPEAN SIZE	36	37	38	39	40	41	42	43

(AN-de-reh)
Andere Kleidung (Other clothing)

AMERICAN SIZE	34	36	38	40	42	44	46	48
EUROPEAN SIZE	44	46	48	50	52	54	56	58

If you are a man, what size shirt do you wear? Ich trage Größe ____________.

What size pants, suit, and jacket do you wear? Ich trage Größe ____________ .

If you are a woman, look for the sizes of a male friend or relative:

Er trägt Größe ____________________ für seine Hemden und Größe ____________________ für seine Hosen, Jacken und Anzüge.

Try saying these set phrases which will help you in purchasing clothes. Place the article of clothing of your choice in the blanks:

Wollen Sie mir bitte ____ zeigen?

Kann ich ____ anprobieren?

Können Sie den ____ umändern? *(UM-en-dern)* alter

Dieser ____ paßt mir nicht gut.

Fill in the blanks with the words depicted:

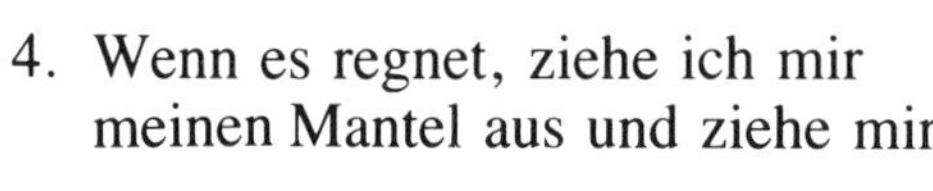

1. Wenn es kalt ist, trage ich einen ________________.
2. Wenn es kühl ist, ziehe ich mir meinen Mantel aus und ziehe mir einen ________________ an.
3. Wenn es schneit, ziehe ich mir meine ________________ an.
4. Wenn es regnet, ziehe ich mir meinen Mantel aus und ziehe mir meinen ________________ an.
5. Wenn es regnet, nehme ich auch meinen ________________ mit.

6. Wenn es heiß ist, trage ich ________________

ANSWERS

1. Mantel **2.** Sweater **3.** Stiefel **4.** Regenmantel **5.** Regenschirm **6.** kurze Hosen

(DAH-men-be-klei-dung)

DAMENBEKLEIDUNG

Women's Clothes

Grundfarben

Basic Colors

(GEL-beh) (BÜS-ten-hal-teR)
der gelbe Büstenhalter

or

(bay-HAH)
der gelbe BH
yellow bra

(ROH-teh) (HANT-ta-sheh)
die rote Handtasche
red handbag

(BLOW-eh) (kleit)
das blaue Kleid
blue dress

(GRÜ-neh) (TA-shen-tooch)
das grüne Taschentuch
green handkerchief

(GEL-beh) (HȪS-çen)
das gelbe Höschen
yellow panties

(VEI-seh) (UN-teR-rok)
der weiße Unterrock
white slip

(GRÜ-neh) (BLOO-zeh)
die grüne Bluse
green blouse

(ROH-teh) (rok)
der rote Rock
red skirt

Can you answer these questions? Example: What color is the skirt? The skirt is red. (Was für eine Farbe hat der Rock? Der Rock ist rot.)

1. Was für eine Farbe hat das Taschentuch?

____

2. Was für eine Farbe hat die Bluse?

____

Can you continue by asking and answering similar questions about remaining items of clothing above?

ANSWERS

1. Das Taschentuch ist grün. **2.** Die Bluse ist grün.

Damengrößen

Women's Clothing Sizes

Blusen (Blouses)

AMERICAN SIZE	32	34	36	38	40	42	44
EUROPEAN SIZE	40	42	44	46	48	50	52

Andere Kleidung (Other clothing)

AMERICAN SIZE	8	10	12	14	16	18
EUROPEAN SIZE	36	38	40	42	44	46

DAMEN- UND HERRENSCHUHE

Shoes for Men and Women

(eng)
Sie sind mir zu eng.
They are too narrow for me.

(DRÜ-ken)
Sie drücken mich.
They pinch me.

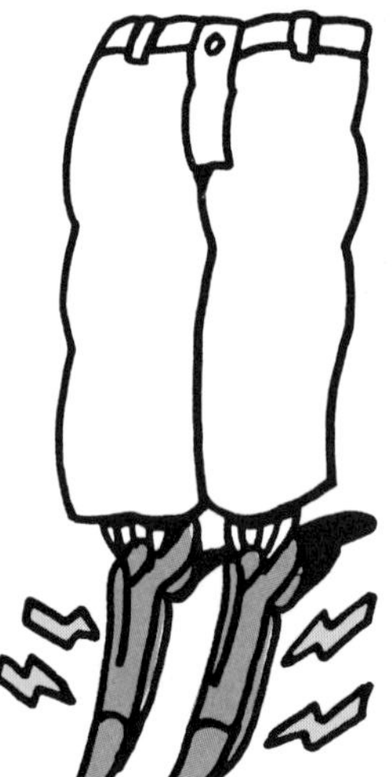

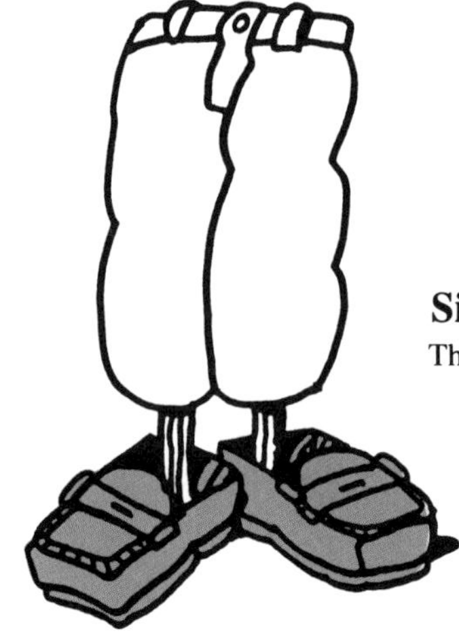

Sie sind mir zu groß.
They are too big for me.

Schuhgrößen

Shoe Sizes

Footwear for Men (shoes, boots, sandals)

AMERICAN SIZE	7	7½	8	8½	9	9½	10	10½	11	11½
GERMAN SIZE	40	41	41	42	43	43	44	44	45	46

Footwear for Women

AMERICAN SIZE	5	5½	6	6½	7	7½	8	8½	9
GERMAN SIZE	36	36½	37	37½	38	38½	39	39½	40

Welche Größe tragen Sie?
What size do you wear?

KLEIDUNG *(KLEI-dung)* FÜR DIE PARTY *(PAR-tee)*

Clothes for the Party

Mimi zieht sich für die Party bei Therese schön an. Im Schuhgeschäft probiert sie viele Schuhe an. Einige *(EIN-ig-eh)* **sind zu eng und drücken sie. Andere sind ihr zu groß. Endlich kauft sie ein Paar, das ihr gut paßt.**

Mimi is getting all dressed up for the party at Therese's. In the shoe store she tries on many shoes. Some are too narrow and pinch her. Others are too big for her. Finally she buys a pair that fits her well.

Der Verkäufer *(feR-KOY-feR)* **im Warenhaus** *(VAH-ren-hows)* **bedient sie. Sie kauft** *(kowft)* **einen blauen Rock und eine rosa Polyester-Bluse** *(po-lee-ES-teR)*. **Sie trägt** *(traykt)* **immer rosa Blusen.**

The salesman in the department store waits on her. She buys a blue skirt and a pink polyester blouse. She always wears pink blouses.

Als sie zur Party geht, findet sie, daß Therese fast dieselben Kleider anhat wie sie. Soll sie nach Hause gehen und sich andere Kleider anziehen? Oder soll sie Therese zu ihrem guten Geschmack *(ge-SHMAK)* **gratulieren** *(grah-too-LEER-en)*?

When she goes to the party, she finds that Therese has on almost the same clothes as she does. Should she go home and put on other clothes? Or should she congratulate Therese on her good taste?

We don't suppose you're overly fussy. But if you have something particular in mind, here are some words and expressions that may be helpful:

I want something in:

(BOWM-vol-eh) cotton: **Baumwolle**	*(BOWM-vol-dril)* denim: **Baumwolldrill**	*(VILT-lay-deR)* suede: **Wildleder**
(ZEI-deh) silk: **Seide**	*(NEI-lon)* nylon: **Nylon**	*(LAY-deR)* leather: **Leder**

Please take my measurement.	**Bitte nehmen Sie Maß.**
I would like something of better quality.	**Bessere Qualität, bitte.**
Do you have something handmade?	*(HANT-ge-mach-tes)* **Haben Sie etwas Handgemachtes?**
It is long (big, short, small) on me.	**Es ist zu lang (groß, kurz, klein) für mich.**
I don't like the color. I prefer green.	**Ich habe die Farbe nicht gern. Ich habe lieber grün.**

Try practicing some imaginary situations in which you might use these expressions with various articles of clothing:

You have been named the best-dressed man or woman of the year. Can you describe what you usually wear to have gained such an honor? Use expressions like *tragen*, *Schuhe anziehen*, *es paßt mir gut*, *die Farben*, *jeden Tag*, *ich ziehe an*, *ich habe lieber*, *ich habe gern*.

What does the worst-dressed man or woman wear? Be outrageous!

What articles of feminine clothing correspond, more or less, to the masculine items listed:

1. Hemd ______________________.
2. Hose ______________________.
3. Unterhose ______________________.
4. Unterhemd ______________________.

ANSWERS

1. Bluse **2.** Rock **3.** Höschen **4.** Unterrock

17 Lebensmittelgeschäfte

(LAY-bens-mit-el-ge-shef-teh)

Food Stores

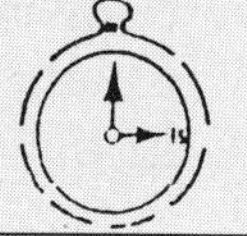

Food stores in Germany carry a wide variety of items. Shopping for food can be a lot of fun, especially if you look for local specialties.

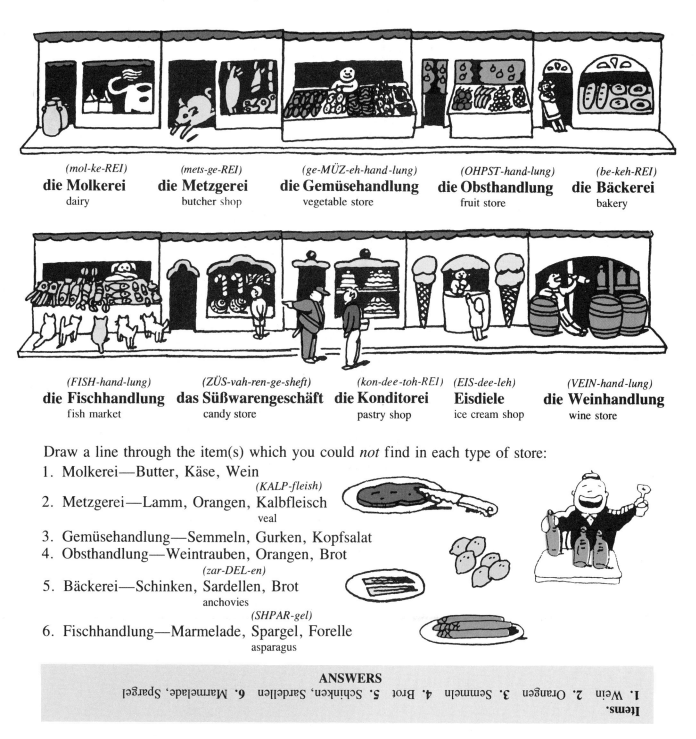

(mol-ke-REI)	*(mets-ge-REI)*	*(ge-MÜZ-eh-hand-lung)*	*(OHPST-hand-lung)*	*(be-keh-REI)*
die Molkerei	**die Metzgerei**	**die Gemüsehandlung**	**die Obsthandlung**	**die Bäckerei**
dairy	butcher shop	vegetable store	fruit store	bakery

(FISH-hand-lung)	*(ZÜS-vah-ren-ge-sheft)*	*(kon-dee-toh-REI)*	*(EIS-dee-leh)*	*(VEIN-hand-lung)*
die Fischhandlung	**das Süßwarengeschäft**	**die Konditorei**	**Eisdiele**	**die Weinhandlung**
fish market	candy store	pastry shop	ice cream shop	wine store

Draw a line through the item(s) which you could *not* find in each type of store:

1. Molkerei—Butter, Käse, Wein
2. Metzgerei—Lamm, Orangen, Kalbfleisch *(KALP-fleish)* veal
3. Gemüsehandlung—Semmeln, Gurken, Kopfsalat
4. Obsthandlung—Weintrauben, Orangen, Brot
5. Bäckerei—Schinken, Sardellen *(zar-DEL-en)* anchovies, Brot
6. Fischhandlung—Marmelade, Spargel *(SHPAR-gel)* asparagus, Forelle

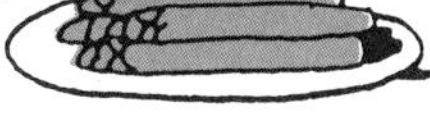

ANSWERS

Items. **1.** Wein **2.** Orangen **3.** Semmeln **4.** Brot **5.** Schinken, Sardellen **6.** Marmelade, Spargel

7. Süßwarengeschäft—Süßigkeiten, Tomaten, Mineralwasser
8. Konditorei—Reis, Milch, Torten
9. Eisdiele—Sardellen, Salate, Eis
10. Weinhandlung—Backhuhn, Flaschen, *(shpi-NAHT)* Spinat
spinach

In Germany there are supermarkets, but not as many as in the United States. Many Germans still do their shopping at a number of specialized stores rather than at one supermarket.

Here are some adjectives that describe food:

(frish)	*(feR-DOR-ben)*	*(ALT-bak-en)*
frisch	**verdorben**	**altbacken**
fresh	spoiled	stale

How could you complain about the following situations?

1. You have bought a rotten tomato. Diese Tomate ist ____________________.
2. The bread you bought is not fresh. Dieses Brot ist nicht ____________________.
3. The cake you bought is stale. Dieser Kuchen ist ____________________.

(ge-VIÇ-teh) *(MAH-seh)*

GEWICHTE UND MASSE

Weights and Measures

(VEE-gen)
wiegen
to weigh

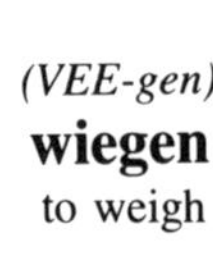

(ge-VIÇT)
das Gewicht
weight

Although it has not yet caught on fully in the U.S., the metric system is the standard means for measuring in many foreign countries, including Germany. Here are two of the most common weights and measures:

a kilogram = 2.2 U.S. pounds

(KEE-loh-gram)
das Kilogramm *or* **das Kilo**

a liter = 1.1 U.S. quarts

(LEE-teR)
das Liter

ANSWERS

Items.
7. Tomaten, Mineralwasser **8.** Reis, Milch **9.** Sardellen, Salate **10.** Backhuhn, Spinat

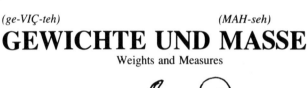

Situations.
1. verdorben **2.** frisch **3.** altbacken

(pfunt)
A kilogram is made up of 1000 grams; it is sometimes divided into two pounds *(das Pfund)* of 500 grams each. The German pound is slightly heavier than the U.S. pound.

How many kilos do you weigh? ________ How much water do you drink a day? ______

Here are some expressions to use when buying food. Try writing them out:

(DUT-sent)
ein Dutzend ____________________
dozen

(HAL-bes)
ein halbes Dutzend ________________
half dozen

ein Kilo ____________________

ein halbes Kilo ________________

ein halbes Pfund ________________
half a pound

ein Liter ____________________

(veekt)
Wieviel wiegt es? ________________
How much does it weigh?

Wieviel kostet es? ________________
How much does it cost?

Es ist zu viel. ________________
It's too much.

Ich möchte (gern) ________________
I would like

Wieviel kosten sie per Dutzend? ________________________________
How much are they per dozen?

IM LEBENSMITTELGESCHÄFT

At the Grocery Store

PLEASE NOTE: In German the **of** in the following expressions is not translated: A cake of soap is **ein Stück Seife** *(ZEI-feh)* (*not* ein Stück von Seife), a liter of milk **ein Liter Milch.**

Ask the clerk for the items in the pictures. Use the names of the containers they come in or the unit of measurement. Try asking some questions like:

Wieviel kostet das (kosten sie)?
How much does it (do they) cost?

Wieviel wiegt das (wiegen sie)?
How much does it (do they) weigh?

Wieviel kosten sie pro Dutzend, pro Kiste, etc.
How much are they per dozen, per box, etc.?

(shtük) (ZEI-feh)
ein Stück Seife
a cake of soap

(KIR-shen) (owf) (dayR) (VAH-geh)
die Kirschen auf der Waage
cherries on the scales

(DOH-zeh)
eine Dose Gemüse
a can of vegetables

(pah-KAYT) (TSUK-eR)
ein Paket Zucker
a package of sugar

(PAK-ung)
eine Packung Eier
a carton of eggs

(HAL-bes) (KEE-loh) (KIR-shen)
ein halbes Kilo Kirschen
half a kilo of cherries

(HAL-bes) (DU-tsent) (tsi-TROH-nen)
ein halbes Dutzend Zitronen
half a dozen lemons

(KA-fay)
der Kaffee
coffee

(LEE-teR) (milç)
ein Liter Milch
a liter of milk

(ein-eh) (SHACH-tel) (kayks)
eine Schachtel Keks
a box of cookies

(ROL-eh) (toy-LE-ten-pah-peeR)
eine Rolle Toilettenpapier
a roll of toilet paper

1. Ich möchte (gern) ______________ (cherries). Wieviel ____________________ (do they cost)?
2. Ich brauche _________ (a roll of toilet paper). Wieviel ____________________ (does it cost)?
3. Ich möchte (gern) _________ (a half dozen lemons).
4. Wir brauchen __________________ (a cake of soap).
5. Ich suche (look for) *(ZOO-cheh)* ____________________ (eggs).
6. Haben Sie ____________________________ (sugar)?

Try practicing these requests further on a sheet of paper until you feel you know them.

Nowadays, it is not always necessary to go to different stores to buy groceries. Germany now has North American style supermarkets where we can buy them in one place: bakery items, meat, eggs, a box of cookies, a roll of toilet paper, a liter of milk, a half-dozen oranges, a kilo of sugar, a package of candy. But it is still interesting to go to the open-air markets to see the great variety of poultry, fruit, vegetables, and other products the farmers sell each day. It is a good way to observe the foods typical of the country or the region.

Indicate the correctness of the following statements by writing RICHTIG or FALSCH.

1. Es gibt keine Supermärkte *(ZU-peR-merk-teh)* (supermarkets) in Deutschland. ______________________________

ANSWERS

Wieviel?
1. Kirschen, kosten sie **2.** eine Rolle Toilettenpapier, kostet das **3.** ein halbes Dutzend Zitronen **4.** ein Stück Seife **5.** Eier **6.** Zucker

Richtig/Falsch.
1. Falsch

2. Viele Deutsche kaufen Lebensmittel in kleinen Geschäften. ______________

3. Keks kauft man in einer Schachtel. ______________

4. Produkte der Umgebung (um-GAY-bung) region kauft man nur im Supermarkt. ______________

5. Die Deutschen wiegen Milch auf einer Waage. ______________

Suppose you're making out a grocery list. Fill in the blanks below with the things you want and the quantity. Example: Zwei Kilo Kirschen.

______________ ______________ ______________

______________ ______________ ______________

In many German cities you can find open-air markets where local farmers sell their produce. In some cities local specialties are sold by street vendors. For instance, in Hamburg you can buy smoked eel, a local specialty, from street vendors.

As we've noted, there are numerous specialty stores in Germany. What stores would you visit to buy the following items?

1. Wir finden *Semmeln* in der ______________.
2. Sie verkaufen (fer-KOW-fen) sell *Schinken* in der ______________.
3. Wenn wir frische *Erdbeeren* brauchen, gehen wir zur ______________.
4. Sie verkaufen *Sahne* in der ______________.
5. Wenn wir *Tomaten* wollen, gehen wir zur ______________.
6. Wenn wir *Kuchen* brauchen, kaufen wir ihn in der ______________.

ANSWERS

Richtig/Falsch.
2. Richtig **3.** Richtig **4.** Falsch **5.** Falsch

Stores.
1. Bäckerei **2.** Metzgerei **3.** Obsthandlung **4.** Molkerei **5.** Gemüsehandlung **6.** Konditorei

Can you make up questions which would bring about these responses?

1. Sie kosten 2 Mark per Kilo.
____

2. Sie wiegen ein halbes Pfund.
____

Can you guess what we call the person who works in the following stores?

1. in der Konditorei ______________

2. in der Metzgerei ______________

3. in der Bäckerei ______________

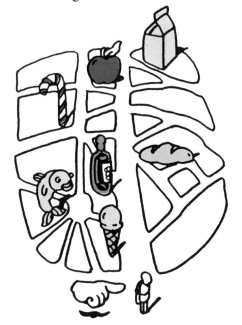

Let's have a little fun.

You are on a food-shopping trip. Fill in the blanks in the following sentences to indicate how you'd get to various stores. You are standing near the ice-cream shop as you start your trip.

Do you remember?
links = left
rechts = right
geradeaus = straight ahead

Ich möchte zuerst zur Fischhandlung. Ich gehe an der Eisdiele vorbei und dann ______________ um die Ecke. Ich kaufe zwei Forellen in der Fischhandlung. Dann möchte ich das Süßwarengeschäft besuchen. Ich gehe links und dann ______________. Dann gehe ich ______________ zur Obsthandlung, wo ich viele Äpfel kaufe. Dann muß ich ______________ und dann ______________, um Milch zu kaufen. Ich möchte auch Brot kaufen. Ich gehe erst ______________, dann ______________ bis zur Bäckerei. Die Weinhandlung ist in der Nähe; ich kaufe eine Flasche Wein und dann gehe ich ______________ nach Hause.

ANSWERS

Questions.
1. Wieviel kosten die Tomaten?
2. Wieviel wiegen sie?

Stores.
1. Konditor 2. Metzger 3. Bäcker

Shopping trip.
links, geradeaus, links, links, rechts, rechts, rechts, links, rechts

(droh-ge-REE) *(ah-poh-TAY-keh)*

18 Die Drogerie / Die Apotheke

Drugstore Pharmacy

IN DER DROGERIE

At the Drugstore

(HEI-dee) *(KAHR-in)*
Heidi and Karin go into a drugstore and head for the beauty aids. Heidi looks at herself in the mirror.

(REI-ni-gungs-kraym) HEIDI **Ich muß eine Dose Reinigungskrem** *(pah-PEER-ta-shen-tüç-eR)* **und Papiertaschentücher kaufen.**	I must buy a jar of cold cream and paper tissues.
(fer-VEN-deh) KARIN **Ich verwende nie Reinigungskrem. Sie ist zu teuer. Kaufst du immer dein Make-up hier? Das ist ein Geschäft für die Reichen; die Artikel kosten sehr viel.**	I never use cold cream. It's too expensive. Do you always buy your makeup here? This is a shop for the rich; the articles cost a lot.
(pro-DUK-teh) HEIDI **Du hast recht, aber gute Produkte sind teuer.**	You're right, but good products are costly.
KARIN **Ich sag dir was. Ich kaufe nichts in dieser Drogerie. Die Preise sind zu hoch hier.**	I'll tell you something. I'm not buying anything in this drugstore. The prices are too high here.
DER VERKÄUFER **Guten Tag, meine Damen. Womit kann ich Ihnen dienen?**	Hello, ladies. What would you like?

HEIDI	(kam) **Ich brauche einen Kamm, eine** (HAHR-bürs-teh) **Haarbürste und eine Dose** (HAHR-shpray) **Haarspray.** **Ich möchte auch gern eine** (TSAHN-bürs-teh) **Zahnbürste** (TSAHN-pas-teh) **und Zahnpaste kaufen. Wieviel macht das?**	I need a comb, a hair brush, and a can of hair spray. I'd also like to buy a toothbrush and toothpaste. How much does that come to?
VERKÄUFER	**Die Zahnbürste kostet 4 Mark und die Zahnpaste 3 Mark fünfzig.**	The toothbrush costs 4 marks and the toothpaste 3 marks fifty.
KARIN	**Siehst du? Das kostet dich eine Menge Geld.**	You see? That'll cost you a lot of money.
HEIDI	**Jetzt möchte ich gern das Make-up sehen.** (roož) **Rouge,** (LIP-en-shtift) **Lippenstift,** (ma-SKAH-ra) **Maskara, bitte. O ja, auch** (NAH-gel-lak) **Nagellack** (NAH-gel-lak-ent-fern-eR) **und Nagellackentferner.**	Now I'd like to see the makeup. Rouge, lipstick, mascara, please. Oh, yes, nail polish and nail polish remover, too.
KARIN	**Aber du gibst zu viel aus.**	But you're spending too much.
HEIDI	**Ja, ich weiß. Aber ich brauche diese** (ZA-chen) **Sachen.**	Yes, I know. But I need these things.

Show whether the statements are TRUE or FALSE:

1. Ich kann Papiertaschentücher in einer Drogerie kaufen. ____________
2. Wir finden Make-up in der (kos-MAY-tik-ap-tei-lung) Kosmetikabteilung (beauty-aid section). ____________
3. Die Preise in der Drogerie sind hoch. ____________
4. Karin will in der Drogerie nichts ausgeben. ____________
5. Heidi kauft nie etwas in einer Drogerie. ____________

ANSWERS

True/false. 1. T 2. T 3. T 4. T 5. F

Let's try to answer the following questions.

1. Was kann man für die Zähne in einer Drogerie kaufen? (2)

_______________, _______________

(be-NUTS-en)
2. Was benutzen Frauen auf ihren Fingernägeln? (2)
use

_______________, _______________

(ge-SIÇT)
3. Was sind die drei Schönheitsmittel, die Frauen auf Gesicht, Lippen und Augen benutzen? (3)
face

_______________, _______________, _______________

4. Was benutzen Frauen für ihr Haar? (3)

_______________, _______________, _______________

(MÜ-sen)
Müssen
must, have to

The following modal verb is very useful:

ich muß du mußt er } sie } muß es }	wir müssen ihr müßt sie müssen
Sie müssen	

Here are a couple examples:

Ich muß etwas kaufen.
I must buy something.

(TSAHN-artst)
Sie müssen zum Zahnarzt.
You (polite) have to go to the dentist.

ANSWERS

Questions.
1. Zahnbürste, Zahnpaste **2.** Nagellack, Nagellackentferner **3.** Rouge, Lippenstift, Maskara
4. Haarspray, Haarbürste, Kamm

Can you answer the questions?

1. Wo müssen Sie Brot kaufen? ______________________________

2. Wo muß man Fleisch kaufen? ______________________________

3. Was muß man benutzen, um Nagellack zu entfernen? *(ent-FERN-en)* remove

____

4. Wohin muß man gehen, um Make-up zu kaufen?

____

Study the following dialogue, set in a German drugstore. Write the name of the toilet articles on the line indicated.

HEINRICH **Haben Sie Süßigkeiten?**

VERKÄUFER **Nein, wir haben keine Süßigkeiten. Um Süßigkeiten zu kaufen, müssen Sie ins Süßwarengeschäft gehen.**

HEINRICH **Und wie steht es mit Zigaretten und Streichhölzern?** *(SHTREIÇ-hölts-eRn)* matches

VERKÄUFER **Um Zigaretten zu kaufen, müssen Sie in die Tabakhandlung gehen.**

HEINRICH **Dann möchte ich gern ein Deodorantspray kaufen, einen Rasierapparat, Rasierkrem, und einige Rasierklingen.**

(rah-ZEER-ap-pa-raht)
der Rasierapparat
razor

____

(rah-ZEER-kling-en)
die Rasierklingen
razor blades

____

(day-o-do-RANT-spray)
das Deodorantspray

____

ANSWERS

1. In einer Bäckerei. **2.** In einer Metzgerei. **3.** Man muß Nagellackentferner benutzen. **4.** Man muß zur Drogerie gehen.

VERKÄUFER **Wie wäre es mit einem elektrischen Rasierapparat?**

HEINRICH **Nein, dafür bin ich zu altmodisch.** *(ALT-moh-dish)* old-fashioned

(eh-LEK-tri-sheh) **der elektrische** *(rah-ZEER-ap-pa-raht)* **Rasierapparat**
electric razor

____

Let's try a few more questions.

1. Was finden Sie in der Tabakhandlung? (2)

______________________, ______________________

2. Was benutzt ein Mann zum Rasieren? (3)

______________________, ______________________, ______________________

3. Wo kauft man Süßigkeiten?

____

IN DER APOTHEKE

At the Pharmacy

At the pharmacy your prescription (**das Rezept**) *(re-TSEPT)* will be filled. Write the name of each of the drugstore items on the line indicated.

(as-pi-REEN)
Aspirin
aspirin

____

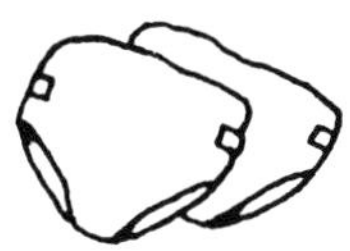

(VIN-deln)
die Windeln
diapers

____

(KÖRP-eR-poo-deR)
das Körperpuder
talcum powder

____

(HEFT-pflas-teR)
das Heftpflaster
adhesive bandage

____

(tayR-moh-MAY-teR)
das Thermometer
thermometer

____

(SI-çeR-heits-nah-deln)
die Sicherheitsnadeln
safety pins

____

ANSWERS

1. Zigaretten, Streichhölzer **2.** einen Rasierapparat, Rasierklingen, Rasierkrem **3.** In der Süßwarenhandlung.

Here are some useful phrases for making purchases at the pharmacy.

Ich brauche etwas *gegen* . . .

(er-KEL-tung) **eine Erkältung** cold	*(fer-SHTOP-fung)* **die Verstopfung** constipation	*(HALS-shmer-tsen)* **die Halsschmerzen** sore throat

Here's a short paragraph about Marie's trip to a pharmacy.

Marie geht in die Apotheke, um einiges zu kaufen. Sie verlangt *(feR-LANKT)* **Heftpflaster, Alkohol und ein Thermometer. Sie sagt dem Verkäufer, sie hat Kopfschmerzen,** *(KOPF-shmerts-en)* **und sie verlangt auch Aspirin.**

Marie goes into the pharmacy to buy a few things. She asks for adhesive bandages, rubbing alcohol, and a thermometer. She tells the clerk she has a headache, and also asks for aspirin.

Marie sagt dazu, *(da-TSU)* **daß sie sich morgens öfters** *(ÖF-teRs)* **nicht wohl** *(vohl)* **fühlt und daß sie Gewicht** *(ge-VIÇT)* **zunimmt.** *(TSU-nimt)*

Marie adds that she often doesn't feel well in the morning and that she is putting on weight.

Und der Verkäufer denkt, sie ist schwanger, *(SHVANG-eR)* **und sagt zu Marie „Vielleicht sollen Sie lieber Körperpuder, Sicherheitsnadeln und Windeln für das Baby kaufen."**

And the clerk thinks she is pregnant, and says to Marie, "Perhaps you should rather buy talcum powder, safety pins, and diapers for the baby."

Here are some expressions to use in a drugstore or pharmacy.

Ich habe . . .

(DURÇ-fal) **Durchfall** diarrhea	*(TSU-keR-krank-heit)* **Zuckerkrankheit** diabetes	*(HOOS-ten)* **Husten** cough	*(FEE-beR)* **Fieber** fever
(KREMP-feh) **Krämpfe** cramps	*(KOPF-shmerts-en)* **Kopfschmerzen** headache	*(SHNIT-vun-deh)* **eine Schnittwunde** cut	*(ZON-en-brant)* **einen Sonnenbrand** sunburn
(GRI-peh) **die Grippe** flu	*(TSAHN-shmer-tsen)* **Zahnschmerzen** toothache		

Ich möchte . . . kaufen.

(MAH-gen-zoy-reh) **etwas gegen Magensäure** antacid	*(an-tee-ZEP-ti-kum)* **ein Antiseptikum** antiseptic	*(YOHT-tink-tooR)* **Jodtinktur** iodine
(HEFT-pflas-teR) **Heftpflaster** adhesive bandages	*(VAT-eh)* **Watte** cotton	*(SHAY-reh)* **eine Schere** scissors

Ich muß . . . kaufen.

(AP-für-mi-tel) **ein Abführmittel** laxative	*(MOH-nats-bin-den)* **Monatsbinden** sanitary napkins	*(TAM-pongs)* **Tampons** tampons
(in-zu-LEEN) **Insulin** insulin	*(HOO-sten-zee-rup)* **Hustensirup** cough syrup	

Match the ailment (column 1) with the item or items (column 2) you would most likely ask for at the pharmacy.

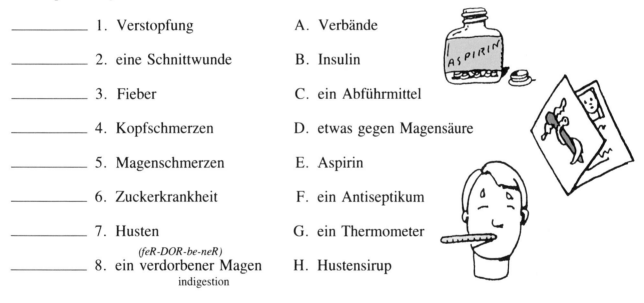

________	1. Verstopfung	A. Verbände
________	2. eine Schnittwunde	B. Insulin
________	3. Fieber	C. ein Abführmittel
________	4. Kopfschmerzen	D. etwas gegen Magensäure
________	5. Magenschmerzen	E. Aspirin
________	6. Zuckerkrankheit	F. ein Antiseptikum
________	7. Husten	G. ein Thermometer
________	8. ein verdorbener Magen *(feR-DOR-be-neR)* indigestion	H. Hustensirup

Can you recall these items you might want to buy at the pharmacy?

1. _ _ _ _ _ _ _ (aspirin) 2. _ _ _ _ _ _ _ (insulin) 3. _ _ _ _ _ _ _ _ _ _ (iodine) 4. _ _ _ _ _ _ _ _ _ _ _ (cough syrup)

ANSWERS

Matching. 1. C **2.** A, F **3.** E **4.** E **5.** D, E **6.** B **7.** H **8.** D

Medical items. 1. Aspirin **2.** Insulin **3.** Jodtinktur **4.** Hustensirup

Now try the same with these ailments:

1. __________ 2. _______ 3. ________ 4. ______
diarrhea flu headache cough

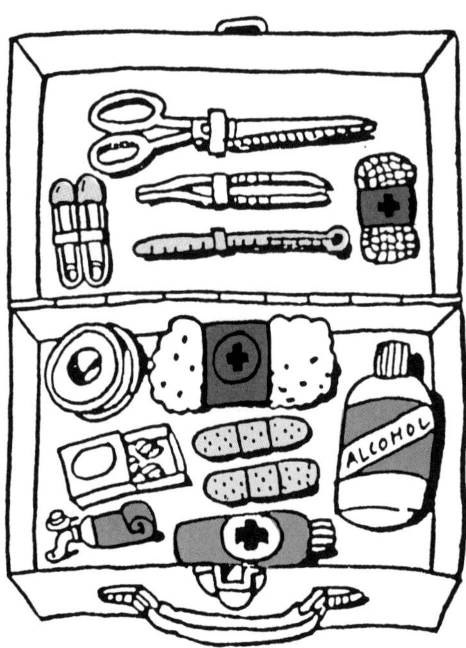

Answer the following questions in German:

1. What are two items for feminine hygiene?

_______________, _______________

2. What things might you need for a minor cut or abrasion?

_______________, _______________

3. Can you name three ailments that could cause a fever?

_______________, _______________, _______________

ANSWERS

Ailments. 1. Durchfall **2.** Grippe **3.** Kopfschmerzen **4.** Husten
Questions.
1. Monatsbinden, Tampons **2.** Jodtinktur, Heftpflaster **3.** Erkältung, Halsschmerzen, Grippe

19

(ve-sheh-REI-en)
Wäschereien und
Laundries and

(ÇAY-mish-eh) *(REI-ni-gung)*
Chemische Reinigung
Dry Cleaning

(VASH-mah-shee-neh)
die Waschmaschine
washing machine

(VASH-en)
waschen
to wash

(TROK-nen)
trocknen
to dry

(TRO-ken-ma-shee-neh)
die Trockenmaschine
drier

Hotel laundering and cleaning services in Germany, Austria, and Switzerland are more than adequate all through the year. It usually takes three days for clothing to be returned.

The better hotels offer a one-day service if the customer is willing to pay about 50% more for it. Outside the hotel, laundry and cleaning establishments are plentiful.

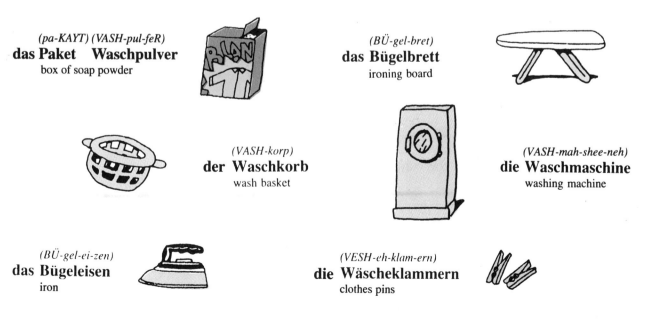

(pa-KAYT) (VASH-pul-feR)
das Paket Waschpulver
box of soap powder

(BÜ-gel-bret)
das Bügelbrett
ironing board

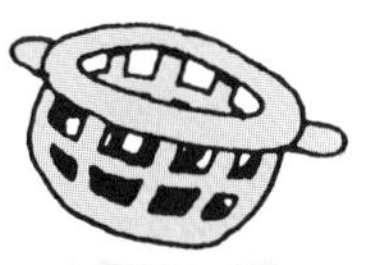

(VASH-korp)
der Waschkorb
wash basket

(VASH-mah-shee-neh)
die Waschmaschine
washing machine

(BÜ-gel-ei-zen)
das Bügeleisen
iron

(VESH-eh-klam-ern)
die Wäscheklammern
clothes pins

(ve-sheh-REI)

WÄSCHEREI UND CHEMISCHE REINIGUNG IM HOTEL

Since you may not want to spend time in laundromats, you will probably prefer to use the laundry services of the hotels where you stay. In that case, these expressions may be useful:

Haben Sie hier eine Wäscherei?	Do you have a laundry here?
Ich habe etwas zum Waschen.	I have some laundry to wash.
Können Sie einen Knopf an meinem Hemd annähen? *(AN-nay-en)* annähen = sew on	Can you sew a button on my shirt?
Können Sie den Ärmel dieser Bluse flicken? *(ER-mel)* Ärmel = sleeve; *(FLIK-en)* flicken = mend	Can you mend the sleeve of this blouse?
Ich will keine Stärke in meinen Hemden. *(SHTERK-eh)* Stärke = starch; *(HEM-den)*	I don't want any starch in my shirts.
Bitte bügeln Sie dieses Hemd noch einmal. *(hemt)* Hemd = shirt	Please iron this shirt again.
Bitte bringen Sie diesen Anzug zur Reinigung. *(REI-ni-gung)*	Please take this suit to the cleaners.
Können Sie diesen Fleck herausnehmen? *(flek)* Fleck = spot; *(he-ROWS-nay-men)* herausnehmen = take out	Can you take this spot out?

Try filling in the blanks with the key words from the sentences above. Then read the sentences aloud:

1. Können Sie diesen ________ (spot) herausnehmen?
2. Können Sie meine Hemden ________ (wash)?
3. Können Sie einen Knopf an meinem Hemd ________ (sew)?
4. Können Sie diesen Anzug zur ________ (cleaners) bringen?
5. Wollen Sie dieses Hemd noch einmal ________ (iron)?
6. Können Sie den ________ (spot) aus dieser Bluse ________ (take out)?
7. Ich habe etwas Unterwäsche zum ________ (wash).
8. Ich will keine ________ (starch) in meinen Hemden.

ANSWERS

Fill-ins.
1. Fleck **2.** waschen **3.** annähen **4.** Reinigung **5.** bügeln **6.** Fleck, herausnehmen **7.** waschen
8. Stärke

(be-SHVAYR-den)

BESCHWERDEN

Complaints

Hans schickt seine Kleidung immer zur Hotelwäscherei. Dieses Mal gibt es Probleme. Da gibt es eine
(feR-VEKS-lung)
Verwechslung und viele Kleidungsstücke, die man ihm
(ge-HÖ-ren)
zurückschickt, gehören einer
(payR-ZOHN) (be-SHVAYRT)
anderen Person. Er beschwert sich beim Manager. Erstens
(traykt)
trägt er niemals Büstenhalter oder Höschen. Außerdem haben seine Hemden zu viel Stärke und
(roo-ee-NEERT) (feR-ZENGT)
eines ist ruiniert; es ist versengt.
(FAY-len)
Auch fehlen ihm zwei Socken, eine rote und eine grüne. Der Anzug, den er von der Reinigung bekommt, hat noch immer einen Fleck am
(grunt)
Ärmel. Er hat Grund, sich zu beschweren, glauben Sie nicht?

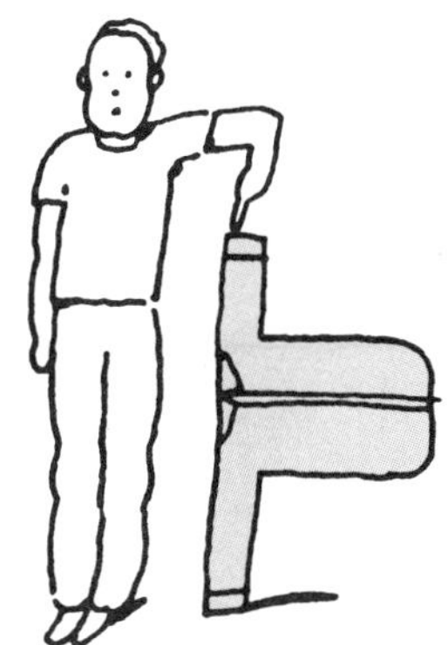

Hans always sends his clothes to the hotel laundry service. This time there are problems. There is a mix-up, and many of the clothes they return to him belong to another person. He complains to the the manager. In the first place, he never wears bras or panties. Besides, his shirts have too much starch in them and one is ruined; it's scorched. Also, he is missing two socks, one red and one green. The suit he receives from the cleaner's still has a spot on the sleeve. He has reason to complain, don't you think?

Here are some phrases to use if you have a complaint.

I have a complaint.
Ich habe eine Beschwerde.

These clothes are someone else's.
Diese Kleidung gehört jemand anders.

My clothes are ruined.
Meine Kleidung ist ruiniert.

There's a button missing.
Da fehlt ein Knopf.

There is a mix-up.
Da gibt es eine Verwechslung.

This shirt has too much starch.
Dieses Hemd hat zuviel Stärke.

This shirt is scorched.
Dieses Hemd ist versengt.

I'm missing a pair of socks.
Mir fehlt ein Paar Socken.

Circle the most appropriate complaint dealing with the laundry and dry cleaner.

1. Diesem Hemd fehlt ein Wäscheleine / Fleck / Knopf
2. Das Hemd ist rot / versengt / zugemacht
3. Da ist eine ein Knopf / Waschmaschine / ein Fleck auf meinem Anzug.
4. Ich habe gern / Mir fehlen meine Unterhosen. / Ich trage
5. Das Hemd hat zuviel Baumwolle / Stärke / Rouge
6. Diese Anzüge gehören jemand anders / uns / meinen Freunden

ANSWERS

Complaints.
1. Knopf **2.** versengt **3.** Fleck **4.** mir fehlen **5.** Stärke **6.** jemand anders

Can you put the following words in the right order to form sensible sentences?

1. Verwechslung, es, eine, da, gibt

____

2. fehlen, drei Hemden, mir

____

3. dieses Hemdes, flicken, können Sie, den Ärmel

____

4. Knopf, annähen, diesen, man muß

____

5. bügeln, Kleidung, meine, waschen, ich muß, und

____

   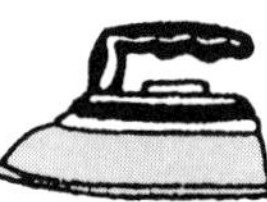 

This should be a snap! Can you draw lines from the words in Column 1 to those in Column 2 which are related to them? Some words in Column 1 may be related to more than one entry in Column 2.

1. Waschmaschine	A. Hemd
2. Fleck	B. hängen
3. Waschkorb	C. die Wäsche trocknen
4. Beschwerde	D. Reinigungsanstalt
5. Bügeleisen	E. die Kleidung waschen
6. nähen	F. die Kleidung zur Wäscheleine tragen
7. Stärke	G. Kleider fehlen mir
8. Trockenmaschine	H. die Kleider bügeln
9. Wäscheleine	I. Knopf
10. Ärmel	J. Waschpulver

ANSWERS

Sentence order.
1. Da gibt es eine Verwechslung. **2.** Mir fehlen drei Hemden. **3.** Können Sie den Ärmel dieses Hemdes flicken? **4.** Man muß diesen Knopf annähen. **5.** Ich muß meine Kleidung waschen und bügeln.

Matching.
1. A, E, J **2.** A, D, E, J **3.** E, F **4.** G **5.** A, D, H **6.** A, I **7.** A **8.** A, C, E **9.** A, B, C, F **10.** A, H, I

20

Der Damensalon Der Friseur

(DAH-men-zah-long) (fri-ZÖR)

The Beauty Shop — Hairdresser

Der Herrensalon Der Friseur

(HER-en-zah-long)

Hair Stylist — Barber

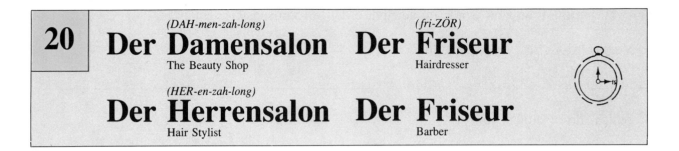

Der Damensalon

(hahR)	(lang)	(brown)	(kurts)	(blont)
das Haar	**lang**	**braun**	**kurz**	**blond**
hair	long	brown	short	blond

Josephine goes to the hairdresser.

FRISEUR **Was wünschen Sie, gnädige Frau?**
(VÜN-shen) wish; (GNAY-di-geh) madam

JOSEPHINE **Waschen und Legen, bitte, und Auffrischen. Können Sie mir auch eine Maniküre geben?**
(LAY-gen) set; (OWF-fri-shen) touch up

FRISEUR **Sie sind jetzt eine Brünette; was für eine Farbe wünschen Sie für die Haarspülung? Dieselbe Farbe oder ein wenig dunkler?**
(brü-NE-teh); (HAHR-shpü-lung) rinse; (DUNK-leR) darker

(ge-ZIÇTS-ma-sa-žeh)
die Gesichtsmassage
facial massage

(ma-ni-KÜ-reh)
die Maniküre
manicure

(LOK-en-vik-el)
die Lockenwickel
curlers

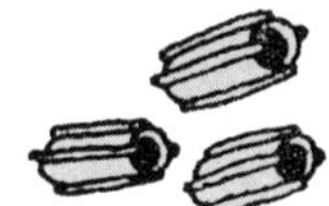

(HEL-eR)
JOSEPHINE **Ein wenig heller, bitte. Und ich**
lighter

(LOK-en)
möchte Locken auf der Seite und
curls

(VEL-en) (OH-ben)
Wellen oben. Können Sie hinten ein
waves on top

(AP-shnei-den)
wenig abschneiden? Ich habe langes
cut off

Haar nicht gern. Ich habe es lieber kurz.

(zelbst) *(AN-show-en)*
sich selbst im Spiegel anschauen
to look at oneself in the mirror

Eine Stunde später bürstet der

Friseur Josephines Haar aus, und

Josephine schaut sich im Spiegel an.

(HAHR-trok-neR)
der Haartrockner
hair dryer

(GO-tes) (VI-len)
JOSEPHINE **Um Gottes willen! Ich bin blond!**
good grief

(DOW-eR-vel-eh)
die Dauerwelle
permanent

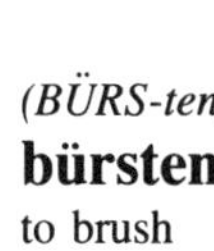

NOTE: If the hairdresser is a woman, she is
(fri-ZÖ-zeh)
called *die Friseuse*.

(sham-POO)
das Shampoo
shampoo

(HAHR-bürs-teh)
die Haarbürste
brush

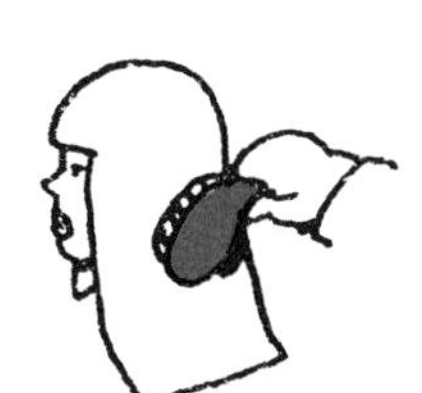

(BÜRS-ten)
bürsten
to brush

Here are some useful expressions a woman might want to know before she goes to the beauty shop. Try writing them out:

I'd like to make an appointment for tomorrow.

(ter-MEEN)
Ich möchte einen Termin für morgen machen.
appointment

Can you wash and cut my hair?

Können Sie mir die Haare waschen und schneiden?

Don't apply any hairspray.

(HAHR-shpray)

Verwenden Sie kein Haarspray.

hairspray

I would like my hair in bangs. I would like a bun.

(POH-nee) *(KNOH-ten)*

Ich möchte einen Pony. Ich möchte einen Knoten.

bangs bun

Here are some German words about hair styling:

legen	to set
der Spiegel	mirror
der Pony	bangs
die Maniküre	manicure
das Haarspray	hairspray

kastanienbraun	auburn
der Haarschnitt	haircut
die Lockenwickel	curlers
die Locken	curls
bürsten	to brush

Let's try a quick exercise. Fill in the blanks by using the words you have learned in this unit.

1. Morgen gehe ich zum ______________ (beauty shop).
2. Ich muß einen ______________ (appointment) machen.
3. Ich brauche einen ______________ (haircut).
4. Ich habe ______________ (long) Haar nicht gern.
5. Ich möchte auch, daß man mir das Haar wäscht und ______________ (sets) und ______________ (auburn) tönt *(tönt)* (tints).
6. Ich habe es lieber ______________ (short) auf den Seiten und ______________ (long) hinten.
7. Vorne trage ich einen ______________ (bangs).
8. Die Friseuse ______________ (brushes) mein Haar und verwendet etwas ______________ (hairspray).
9. Dann schaue ich mich im ______________ (mirror) an.

ANSWERS

1. Damensalon **2.** Termin **3.** Haarschnitt **4.** langes **5.** legt, kastanienbraun **6.** kurz, lang **7.** Pony **8.** bürstet, Haarspray **9.** Spiegel

(HAHR-pflay-geh)
DIE HAARPFLEGE
hair care

There are plenty of beauty salons throughout Germany to suit every conceivable taste, need, and pocketbook. Since German hairdressers have to pass strict exams before being admitted to the profession, they can generally be depended on for competence and cleanliness.

What are known as Unisex Hairdressers in the United States are more modestly referred to as *Damen- und Herrensalons.* You won't find many of them.

Here are some more terms that might come in handy:

to trim lightly	**nachschneiden**	tint, to tint	*(TÖ-nung)* **die Tönung, tönen**
to blow dry	*(FÖ-nen)* **fönen**	body wave	*(SHTÜTS-vel-eh)* **die Stützwelle**

DER HERRENSALON
Hair Stylist

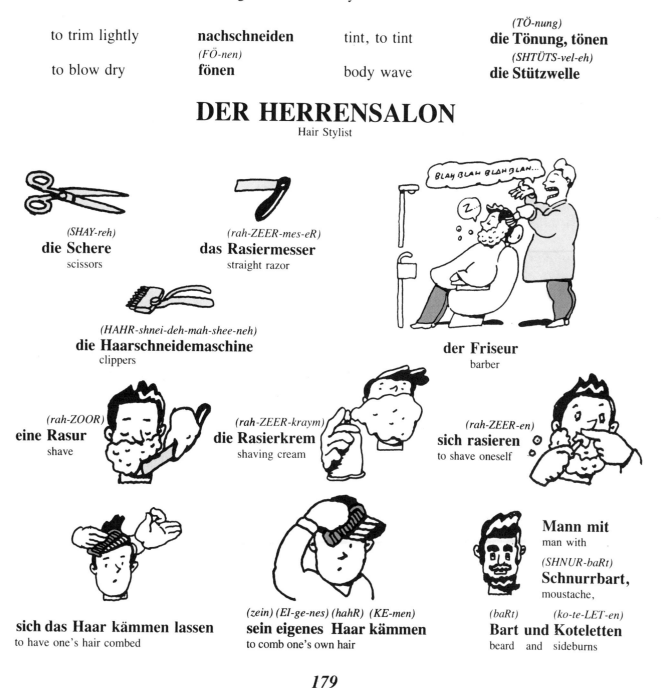

(SHAY-reh)
die Schere
scissors

(rah-ZEER-mes-eR)
das Rasiermesser
straight razor

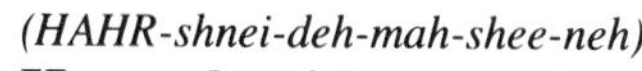

(HAHR-shnei-deh-mah-shee-neh)
die Haarschneidemaschine
clippers

der Friseur
barber

(rah-ZOOR)
eine Rasur
shave

(rah-ZEER-kraym)
die Rasierkrem
shaving cream

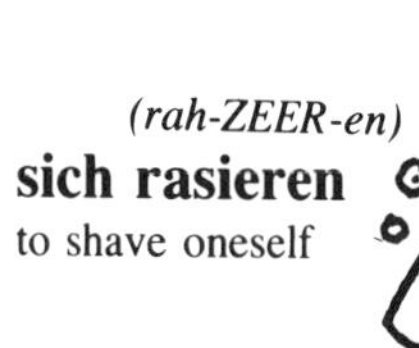

(rah-ZEER-en)
sich rasieren
to shave oneself

sich das Haar kämmen lassen
to have one's hair combed

(zein) (EI-ge-nes) (hahR) (KE-men)
sein eigenes Haar kämmen
to comb one's own hair

Mann mit
man with
(SHNUR-baRt)
Schnurrbart,
moustache,
(baRt) (ko-te-LET-en)
Bart und Koteletten
beard and sideburns

(SHTUTS-en)
stutzen
to trim

(HAHR-shnit)
ein Haarschnitt
hair cut

(GLAT-seh)
die Glatze
bald head

Here's a tale about Anton's trip to the hair stylist. Auf Deutsch, natürlich!

Anton geht zum Friseur, weil er einen Haarschnitt braucht. Zuerst rasiert ihn der Friseur mit einem Rasiermesser und stutzt seinen Bart, seinen Schnurrbart und seine Koteletten mit der Haarschneidemaschine. Dann wäscht er ihm die Haare und gibt ihm einen Haarschnitt. Weil Anton sein Haar sehr gern kurz trägt, schneidet der Friseur viel von oben und hinten ab. Anton ist sehr *(MÜD-eh)* **müde und schläft im** *(shtool)* **Stuhl ein.**

Anton goes to the barber because he needs a haircut. First the barber shaves him with a straight razor and trims his beard, his moustache, and his sideburns with the clippers. Then he gives him a shampoo and a haircut. Because Anton likes to wear his hair short the barber cuts off a lot on top and in back. Anton is very tired and falls asleep in the chair.

Der Friseur schneidet mehr und mehr. *(ENT-liç)* **Endlich sagt er: „Also, mein Herr." Anton schaut sich im Spiegel an und sieht, daß er ganz kahl ist.**

The barber cuts more and more. Finally he says, "There you are, sir." Anton looks at himself in the mirror and sees that he is entirely bald.

(SHUL-diç) **„Wieviel bin ich Ihnen schuldig," fragt er.**	"What do I owe you?" he asks.
Der Friseur sagt: „Sieben Mark. Wissen Sie, ich glaube nicht, daß Sie sehr bald zurück sind."	The barber says, "Seven marks. You know something, I don't think you'll be back very soon."

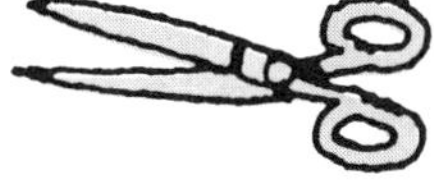

(feR-ZOO-chen) *(FOL-gen-den)* *(FRAH-gen)*
Versuchen Sie, die folgenden Fragen zu beantworten.
try following questions

1. Warum geht Anton zum Friseur? ______________________
2. *(VOH-mit)* Womit (with what) stutzt der Friseur seinen Bart? ______________________
3. Warum schneidet der Friseur viel ab? ______________________
4. Wo schaut sich Anton an? ______________________
5. Was sieht er dann? ______________________
6. Wieviel muß Anton bezahlen? ______________________

Here are some expressions that might come in handy:

Wo gibt es einen guten Friseur?	Where is a good barber?
Wer kommt jetzt dran?	Whose turn is it now?
Ich brauche einen Haarschnitt.	I need a haircut.
Ich brauche eine Rasur.	I need a shave.
Hinten lang und vorne kurz.	Long in back, short in front.
Schneiden Sie ein wenig mehr hier.	Cut a little bit more here.
Bitte verwenden Sie nicht die Haarschneidemaschine.	Please don't use the clippers.
So ist es gerade richtig.	It's fine that way.
Wieviel bin ich Ihnen schuldig?	How much do I owe you?

ANSWERS

Beim Friseur.
1. Er braucht einen Haarschnitt. **2.** Mit der Haarschneidemaschine. **3.** Weil Anton sein Haar gern kurz trägt. **4.** Im Spiegel **5.** Daß er ganz kahl ist **6.** Sieben Mark.

(mayR)
Mehr Fragen.
more

1. Was soll der Friseur nicht verwenden? ______________________

2. Womit rasiert ihn der Friseur? ______________________

3. Was stutzt er mit der Haarschneidemaschine?

______________________, ______________________, ______________________

Can you answer these questions in German?

1. What color is your hair? ______________________

2. How do you wear your hair? Long, short, or medium length? ______________________

3. Do you like long or short sideburns? ______________________

4. What does the barber use to cut hair? ______________________

5. What does the beautician put on the hair when she sets it? ______________________

6. What do you need if your hair is dirty? ______________________

Try putting the following fragments in the proper order so that they make sense:

1. Maniküre, mir, können Sie, geben, eine?

____

2. Spiegel, mich, möchte, anschauen, gern, ich, im

____

ANSWERS

Fill-ins.
1. die Haarschneidemaschine **2.** mit dem Rasiermesser **3.** Bart, Schnurrbart und Koteletten
Questions.
1. blond, rot, braun, schwarz **2.** lang, kurz, mittel **3.** lange, kurze, Koteletten **4.** die Schere, die Haarschneidemaschine **5.** Haarspray **6.** ein Shampoo
Fragments.
1. Können Sie mir eine Maniküre geben? **2.** Ich möchte mich gern im Spiegel anschauen.

3. muß, Termin, einen, morgen, machen, für, ich

---

4. Haar, um, schneiden, Schere, verwendet, Friseur, der, das, zu, die

---

Und nun (*noon*, now) ein kleines Rätsel (*RAY-tsel*, puzzle). Übersetzen (*ü-beR-ZE-tsen*, translate) Sie die folgenden Wörter. Der erste Buchstabe (*BOOCH-shtah-beh*, letter) ist schon da.

1. bald
2. curls
3. to trim
4. mirror
5. to set
6. permanent
7. bald head
8. hair dryer
9. to brush
10. blond

1. K
2. L
3. S
4. S
5. L
6. D
7. G
8. H
9. B
10. B

ANSWERS

Fragments.
3. Ich muß für morgen einen Termin machen.
4. Der Friseur verwendet die Schere, um das Haar zu schneiden.

Puzzle.
1. kahl **2.** Locken **3.** stutzen **4.** Spiegel **5.** legen **6.** Dauerwelle **7.** Glatze **8.** Haartrockner
9. bürsten **10.** blond

21 Der Kiosk

(kee-OSK)

The Newsstand

Die Papierwarenhandlung

(pah-PEER-vah-ren-hand-lung)

The Stationery Store

AM KIOSK IN WIEN

At the Newsstand in Vienna

(TSEI-tung)
die Zeitung
newspaper

(POST-kar-teh)
die Postkarte
postcard

(AN-ziçts-kar-teh)
die Ansichtskarte
picture postcard

JUNGER MANN **Entschuldigen Sie. Haben Sie Zeitungen** *(TSEI-tung-en)* **in Englisch?** — Excuse me. Do you have newspapers in English?

BESITZER *(be-ZITS-eR)* DES KIOSKS (owner) **Ja, wir haben eine gute Auswahl** *(OWS-vahl)* **von Zeitungen aus England und den U.S.A.** *(oo-es-AH)* — Yes, we have a nice selection of newspapers from England and the U.S.

JUNGER MANN **Ich möchte auch einige Ansichtskarten von Wien kaufen.** — I would also like to buy a few picture postcards of Vienna.

BESITZER **Hier ist eine gute Auswahl von Bildern der** *(HOWPT-shtat)* **Hauptstadt Österreichs.**

Here is a good selection of picture postcards of the capital of Austria.

(BREEF-mar-ken)
Briefmarken
postage stamps

JUNGER MANN **Verkaufen Sie Briefmarken?**

Do you sell postage stamps?

BESITZER **Ja, aber heute habe ich keine Luftpostmarken.** (pointing) **Die können Sie in der** *(tra-FIK)* ***Trafik** kaufen.**

Yes, but I don't have any air mail stamps today. You can buy them in the *Trafik*.

JUNGER MANN *(TAH-bak)* **Und Tabak? Ich möchte gern eine Packung amerikanischer Zigaretten kaufen.**

And tobacco? I would like to buy a pack of American cigarettes.

(tsi-ga-RET-en-pah-kung)
die Zigarettenpackung
package of cigarettes

BESITZER **Die können Sie auch in der *Trafik* kaufen.**

You can buy them in the *Trafik*, too.

JUNGER MANN *(FÜ-ren)* **Führen Sie auch** *(ma-ga-TSEE-neh)* **Magazine mit Fotos? *Playboy*,** *(BEI-shpeel)* **zum Beispiel? Es ist nicht für mich, es ist für meinen Großvater.**

Do you carry illustrated magazines, too? *Playboy*, for example? It isn't for me; it's for my grandfather.

(ma-ga-TSEEN)
das Magazin
magazine

BESITZER (with eyebrows raised) **Ja, natürlich.**

Yes, of course.

***NOTE:** In Austria, tobacco products are a government monopoly and can be sold in a *Trafik* or *Tabak-Trafik* only; in Germany, they can be sold in a *Tabakladen* (tobacco shop) or at a kiosk where postage stamps are also available.

JUNGER MANN **Ich nehme die Zeitung, die Ansichtskarten und das Magazin. Wieviel bin ich Ihnen schuldig?**	I'll take the newspaper, the picture postcards, and the magazine. What do I owe you?

Try reading aloud several times the conversation between the youth and the owner of the kiosk. When you feel confident of its meaning, see if you can fill in the missing words below:

1. *Junger Mann:* Entschuldigen Sie. Haben Sie ________________ in Englisch?
2. *Besitzer:* Ja, wir haben eine Auswahl von Zeitungen aus ________________.
3. *Junger Mann:* Ich möchte auch gern ________________ von Wien kaufen.
4. Haben Sie ______________________?
5. *Besitzer:* Sie können sie in der ________________ kaufen. Die haben auch ______________________, wenn Sie eine Packung ________________ brauchen.
6. *Junger Mann:* ________________ (I'll take) die Ansichtskarten, eine Zeitung und dieses ________________ mit Fotos. Wieviel bin ich Ihnen ________________?

Try answering the following questions in German.

1. What types of reading material can you buy at a kiosk?

______________________________, ______________________________

2. Besides at the post office, where else can you buy postage stamps?

______________________________, ______________________________

3. What handy phrase can you use to beg someone's pardon or excuse yourself?

____

4. If you want your friends back home to know you're abroad, what might you send them?

____

ANSWERS

Missing words.
1. Zeitungen **2.** England und den U.S.A. **3.** Ansichtskarten **4.** Briefmarken **5.** Tabak-Trafik, Tabak, Zigaretten **6.** Ich nehme, Magazin, schuldig

Questions.
1. Zeitungen, Magazine **2.** in der Tabak-Trafik, im Kiosk **3.** Entschuldigen Sie, bitte. **4.** Ansichtskarten

5. What must you put on your postcards if you want them to arrive back home? ______________

6. If you want postcards to arrive quickly in the U.S., what should you put on them? __________

7. When you are ready to pay for an item, what do you say?

____

IN DER PAPIERWARENHANDLUNG

At the Stationery Store

Here are some items you can purchase at a stationery store. Be sure that you write the new words in the blanks under the pictures and say them aloud several times:

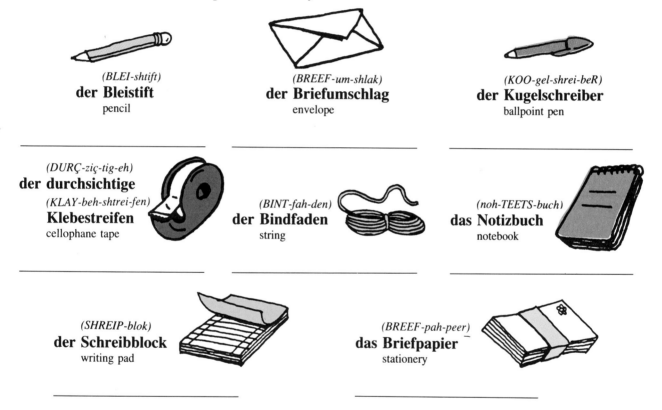

(BLEI-shtift)
der Bleistift
pencil

____

(BREEF-um-shlak)
der Briefumschlag
envelope

____

(KOO-gel-shrei-beR)
der Kugelschreiber
ballpoint pen

____

(DURÇ-ziç-tig-eh)
der durchsichtige
(KLAY-beh-shtrei-fen)
Klebestreifen
cellophane tape

____

(BINT-fah-den)
der Bindfaden
string

____

(noh-TEETS-buch)
das Notizbuch
notebook

____

(SHREIP-blok)
der Schreibblock
writing pad

____

(BREEF-pah-peer)
das Briefpapier
stationery

____

Words you have just learned are contained in the following paragraph.

Wenn ich einen Kugelschreiber oder einen Bleistift brauche, gehe ich in die Papierwarenhandlung. Wenn ich

If I need a ball-point pen or a pencil, I go to the stationery store. When I

ANSWERS

5. Briefmarken **6.** Luftpostmarken **7.** Wieviel bin ich Ihnen schuldig?

einen Brief schreiben will, benutze ich Briefpapier und ich stecke *(SHTE-keh)* **den Brief in einen Briefumschlag. In der Papierwarenhandlung verkauft man auch Notizbücher** *(noh-TEETS-bü-çeR)***. Ich kann Notizen in einem Notizbuch oder auf einem Schreibblock machen. Wenn ich ein Paket machen will, brauche ich Klebestreifen. Um etwas zu verlangen, sage ich: „Ich möchte ____________________ kaufen.“**

want to write a letter, I use letter paper, and I stick the letter in an envelope. Notebooks are sold in the stationery store, too. I can make notes in a notebook or on a pad. If I want to prepare a package, I need tape. To ask for something, I say: "I would like to buy ______________________________."

Please answer in German:

1. What two instruments can you use for writing?

   ____________________, ____________________

2. If you write a letter, what do you write on? ____________________
3. What three things can you use to prepare a package? ____________________, ____________________, ____________________
4. What do you put a letter in before you mail it? ____________________
5. What two things can you write notes on? ____________________ ____________________
6. Where can you buy a ball-point pen? ____________________

ANSWERS

1. Bleistift, Kugelschreiber **2.** Briefpapier **3.** Papier, Klebestreifen, Bindfaden **4.** Briefumschlag **5.** Notizbuch, Schreibblock **6.** in der Papierwarenhandlung

You've learned a lot about items sold at a newsstand and a stationery store. Can you list ten items they carry that are made of paper?

1. ______________________ 6. ______________________

2. ______________________ 7. ______________________

3. ______________________ 8. ______________________

4. ______________________ 9. ______________________

5. ______________________ 10. ______________________

EVA	**Wo, um Gottes willen, bekomme ich Zigaretten?**	Where, for heaven's sake, do I get cigarettes?
OTTO	(overhearing her) **In der Tabak-Trafik. Geradeaus, bis zum Damenbekleidungsgeschäft, dann nach rechts an der Papierhandlung vorbei, wo Sie nach links abbiegen.**	In the Tabak-Trafik. Straight ahead to the women's clothing store, then to the right, past the stationery store where you make a left turn.

ANSWERS

Zeitung, Magazin, Postkarte, Ansichtskarte, Briefumschlag, Notizbuch, Schreibblock, Klebestreifen, Briefmarke, Luftpostmarke

EVA **Danke schön. Sie haben mir das Leben gerettet.**
Thanks a lot. You saved my life.

OTTO **Brauchen Sie noch etwas?**
Do you need anything else?

EVA **Ja. Ein Brot.**
Yes. A loaf of bread.

OTTO **Aha. Also auf dem Weg zurück biegen Sie links ab, gehen Sie ein bißchen** *(BIS-çen)* **geradeaus, und dann nach rechts. Sie sehen sofort** *(zoh-FORT)* **die Bäckerei.**
Aha. Well, on the way back you make a left, go a little straight ahead, and then right. You'll see the bakery right away.

EVA **Herzlichen Dank.**
Thanks a lot.

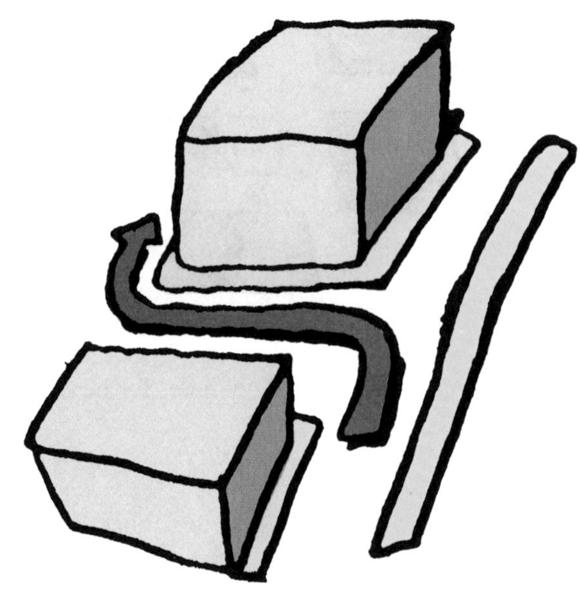

22 Der Juwelier (yoo-vay-LEER) Der Uhrmacher (OOR-ma-cher)

The Jeweler — The Watchmaker

DER JUWELIER

Let's look at a dialogue in a jewelry store. There are a number of new words, but some are very similar to English. Remember to read the dialogue out loud.

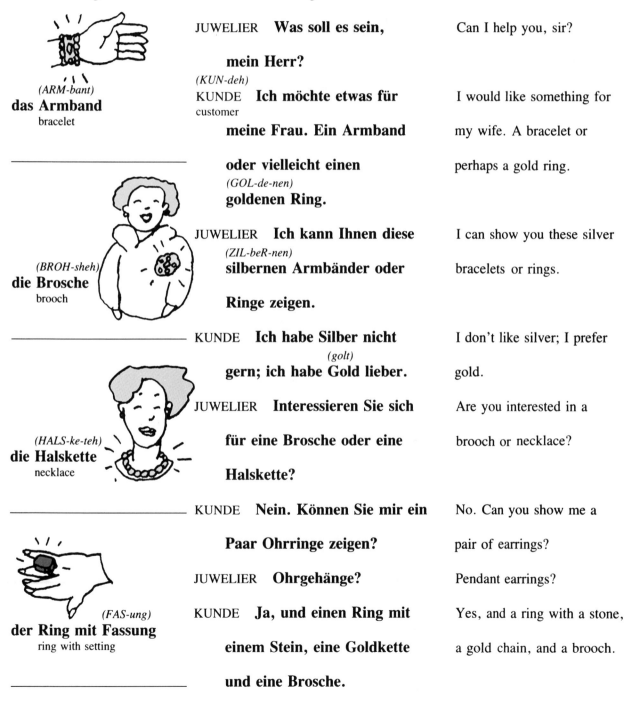

(ARM-bant)
das Armband
bracelet

(BROH-sheh)
die Brosche
brooch

(HALS-ke-teh)
die Halskette
necklace

(FAS-ung)
der Ring mit Fassung
ring with setting

JUWELIER	**Was soll es sein, mein Herr?**	Can I help you, sir?
KUNDE *(KUN-deh)* customer	**Ich möchte etwas für meine Frau. Ein Armband oder vielleicht einen goldenen** *(GOL-de-nen)* **Ring.**	I would like something for my wife. A bracelet or perhaps a gold ring.
JUWELIER	**Ich kann Ihnen diese silbernen** *(ZIL-beR-nen)* **Armbänder oder Ringe zeigen.**	I can show you these silver bracelets or rings.
KUNDE	**Ich habe Silber nicht gern; ich habe Gold** *(golt)* **lieber.**	I don't like silver; I prefer gold.
JUWELIER	**Interessieren Sie sich für eine Brosche oder eine Halskette?**	Are you interested in a brooch or necklace?
KUNDE	**Nein. Können Sie mir ein Paar Ohrringe zeigen?**	No. Can you show me a pair of earrings?
JUWELIER	**Ohrgehänge?**	Pendant earrings?
KUNDE	**Ja, und einen Ring mit einem Stein, eine Goldkette und eine Brosche.**	Yes, and a ring with a stone, a gold chain, and a brooch.

JUWELIER **Diese Ohrgehänge, dieser Ring und diese Goldkette passen sehr gut** *(tsu-ein-AN-deR)* **zueinander.**

These pendant earrings, this ring, and this gold chain go very well together.

KUNDE **Gut. Wieviel kosten sie?**

Good. What do they cost?

JUWELIER **4000 Mark.**

4000 marks.

KUNDE **Die kosten sehr viel. Na ja, ich möchte meiner Frau** *(FROY-deh)* **eine Freude machen. Ich nehme den** *(shmook)* **Schmuck. (Er nimmt etwas aus der** *(TA-sheh)* **Tasche.) Aber ich bezahle nicht! Hände hoch! Ich habe** *(re-VOL-veR)* **einen Revolver.**

They cost a lot. Oh well, I want to please my wife. I'll take the jewelry. (He takes something out of his pocket.) But I'm not paying! Hands up! I have a revolver!

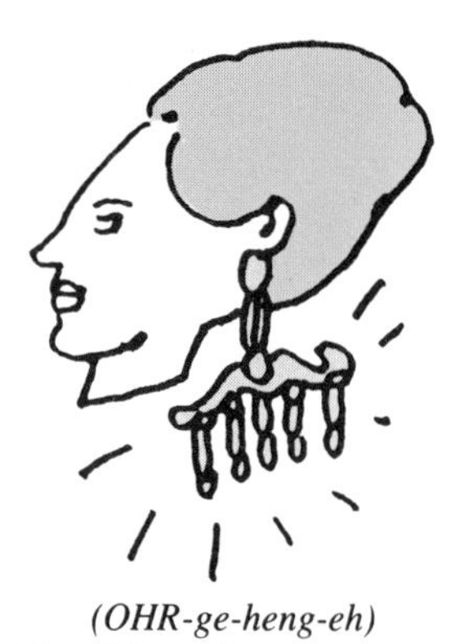

(OHR-ge-heng-eh)
die Ohrgehänge
pendant earrings

____

(KE-teh)
die Kette
chain

____

(ring) (OH-neh) (shtein)
ein Ring ohne Stein
ring without a stone

____

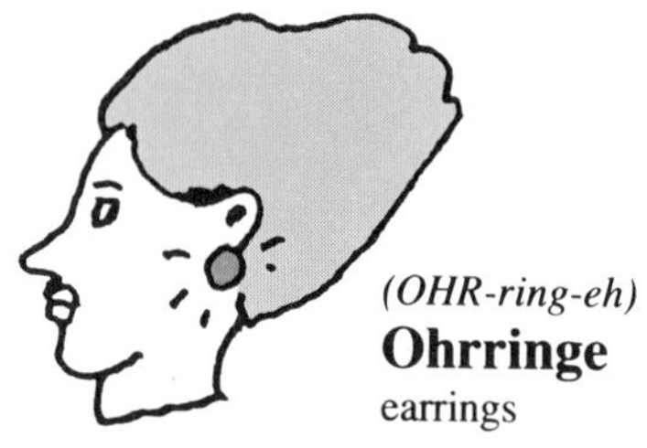

(OHR-ring-eh)
Ohrringe
earrings

____

Practice writing the new words on the lines provided under the pictures:

(dee-a-MANT)
der Diamant
diamond

____

(PER-leh)
die Perle
pearl

____

(ZA-feer)
der Saphir
sapphire

____

(smah-RAKT)
der Smaragd
emerald

____

(roo-BEEN)
der Rubin
ruby

____

(TOH-pahs)
der Topas
topaz

____

(golt)
das Gold
gold

____

(plah-TEEN)
das Platin
platinum

____

(ZIL-beR)
das Silber
silver

____

Here are a couple questions about jewelry. They should be easy.

1. Name two items of jewelry you might wear on your fingers:

   ______________________, ______________________

2. What two sorts of jewelry do women wear on their ears?

   ______________________, ______________________

3. What items of jewelry are worn around the neck?

   ______________________, ______________________

4. What might a woman pin on her dress? ______________________

You've been introduced to the names of precious stones. Do you remember them? Try writing the German word next to the English.

1. diamond ______________
2. pearl ______________
3. sapphire ______________
4. emerald ______________
5. ruby ______________
6. topaz ______________

ANSWERS

Questions.
1. Ring mit Stein (mit Fassung), Ring ohne Stein **2.** Ohrringe, Ohrgehänge **3.** Goldkette, Perlenkette
4. eine Brosche

Precious stones.
1. der Diamant **2.** die Perle **3.** der Saphir **4.** der Smaragd **5.** der Rubin **6.** der Topas

Can you give the German word for the following precious metals?

1. gold ________ 2. silver ________ 3. platinum ________

Can you match the stone with its color? Draw a line from the stone to its corresponding color:

1. Smaragd	A. weiß
2. Rubin	B. blau
3. Topas	C. grün
4. Saphir	D. rot
5. Perle	E. gelb

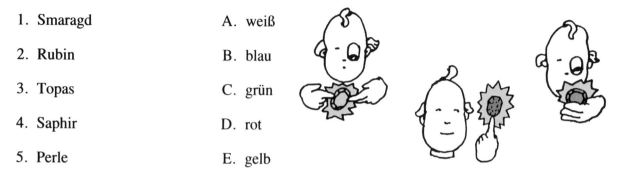

Here you have some useful phrases you might want to use at the jeweler's. Try saying them aloud, and write them in the space provided.

Haben Sie einen Ring mit einem Diamanten (einem Smaragd, etc.)?

____

Können Sie mir ein goldenes (silbernes) Armband zeigen?

____

Ich suche eine silberne (goldene) Halskette.

____

Ich interessiere mich für ein Paar Ohrringe.

____

(kah-RAHT)
Wieviel Karat (carats) hat es?

____

Imagine now that you are looking for something quite specific at the jeweler's. How would you begin your conversation? Once you've found what you want, what else do you need to ask?

ANSWERS

Precious metals.
1. das Gold **2.** das Silber **3.** das Platin
Matching.
1. C **2.** D **3.** E **4.** B **5.** A

DER UHRMACHER

The Watchmaker

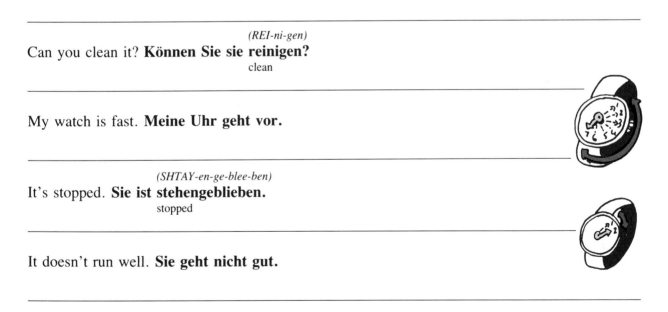

(VEK-eR)
der Wecker
alarm clock

(ARM-bant-ooR)
die Armbanduhr
wrist watch

der Uhrmacher
watchmaker

(OOR-mach-eR-lah-den)
der Uhrmacherladen
watchmaker's shop

Practice writing the new words by filling in the blanks near the pictures. Once you have done this, read aloud the sentences below. They may help you when you visit the watchmaker's. After you have practiced them aloud, try writing them out in the spaces provided:

Can you fix this watch for me? **Können Sie mir diese Uhr reparieren?**

(REI-ni-gen)
Can you clean it? **Können Sie sie reinigen?**
clean

My watch is fast. **Meine Uhr geht vor.**

(SHTAY-en-ge-blee-ben)
It's stopped. **Sie ist stehengeblieben.**
stopped

It doesn't run well. **Sie geht nicht gut.**

Notice that in German watches and clocks don't run. They take their time and walk. The verb *gehen*, in its literal sense, means "to walk."

(OWF-tsee-en)
I can't wind it. **Ich kann sie nicht aufziehen.**
wind

My alarm clock is slow. **Mein Wecker geht nach.**

(OOR-glas)
I need a crystal. **Ich brauche ein Uhrglas.**
crystal

When will it be ready? **Wann wird sie fertig sein?**

(KVI-tung)
Can you give me a receipt? **Können Sie mir eine Quittung geben?**
receipt

Try reading the following paragraph to see if you understand it. You may want to refer to the previous sentences.

(MANÇ-mal)
Meine Armbanduhr geht nicht gut. Manchmal geht sie vor; manchmal geht sie nach.
sometimes
Heute bleibt sie auch stehen, und ich kann sie nicht aufziehen. Ich bringe sie zum
(dort)
Uhrmacher und der Uhrmacher repariert sie. Er reinigt sie auch. Wenn ich die Uhr dort
(LA-seh) (lohs) there
lasse, gibt er mir auch eine Quittung. Was ist mit deiner Uhr los, wenn du immer spät
leave what is the matter with your watch
ankommst?

The following German sentences about watches need to be completed. Give them a try.

1. Meine Uhr ______________________ gut; sie ______________________.
   (is not running well) (is slow)

2. When you always seem to be early for appointments, what might be the matter?

   Meine Uhr ______________________.
   (is fast)

3. When the hands of your watch don't move, how do you describe the problem?

   Meine Uhr bleibt ______________________.
   (is stopped)

   Ich muß sie ______________________.
   (wind)

4. Where do you take your watch for repairs?

   Ich nehme meine Uhr zum ______________________.
   (watchmaker)

5. What is the man called who works on your watch?

   Er heißt ______________________.
   (watchmaker)

6. When you leave your watch, what does the watchmaker give you?

   Er gibt mir eine ______________________.
   (receipt)

ANSWERS

Fill-in.

1. geht nicht gut, geht nach **2.** geht vor **3.** stehen, aufziehen **4.** Uhrmacher **5.** der Uhrmacher **6.** Quittung

23 Der Geschenkartikelladen

(ge-SHENK-ar-tee-kel-lah-den)
Der Geschenkartikelladen
Gift Shop

(moo-ZEEK-ge-sheft)
Das Musikgeschäft
Music Store

(FOH-toh-ge-sheft)
Das Photogeschäft
Photo Shop

IM GESCHENKARTIKELLADEN

At the Gift Shop

Here are some words that will come in handy at a gift shop.

(ge-SHENK)
das Geschenk
gift

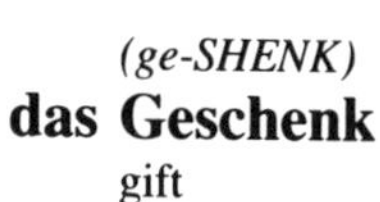

(ring)
der Ring
ring

(shahl)
der Schal
scarf

(GELT-tash-eh)
die Geldtasche
or
(port-mon-NAY)
das Portemonnaie
wallet (purse)

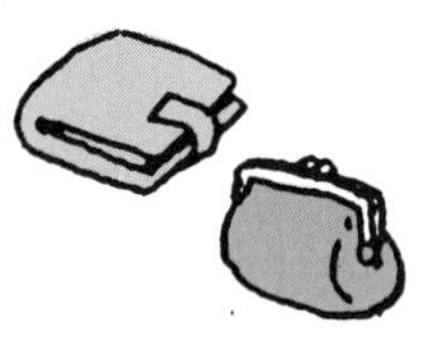

(par-FÜM)
das Parfüm
perfume

(par-FÜM-tser-shtoy-beR)
der Parfümzerstäuber
atomizer

(HANT-tash-eh)
die Handtasche
handbag

(SHLÜS-el-ring)
der Schlüsselring
key ring

(AN-heng-eR)
der Anhänger
pendant

(bilt)
das Bild
picture

(NIP-sa-chen)
die Nippsachen
knick-knacks

(TOY-eR) **teuer**	expensive	**die Figurine**	figurine
(PREIS-vayRt) **preiswert**	a good value	**der Schmuck**	jewelry
(TÜ-pish) **typisch**	typical		

VERKÄUFER	*(be-HILF-liç)* **Kann ich Ihnen behilflich sein?**	Can I help you?
TOURISTIN	**Ich möchte etwas typisch** *(ÖS-teR-rei-çish-es)* **österreichisches.**	I would like something typically Austrian.
VERKÄUFER	**Für einen Herrn oder für eine Dame?**	For a gentleman or for a lady?
TOURISTIN	**Eine Dame.**	A lady.
VERKÄUFER	**Vielleicht eine Petit-Point-** *(HANT-ta-sheh)* **Handtasche? Oder ein** *(me-dal-YONG)* **Medaillon? Das kommt von den österreichischen** *(VERK-shte-ten)* **Werkstätten. Oder einen** *(shahl)* **Schal?**	**Maybe an embroidered evening handbag?** Or a locket? This one comes from the Austrian jewelry factories. Or a scarf?
TOURISTIN	**Wieviel kostet der Schal?**	How much is the scarf?
VERKÄUFER	**500 Schilling.**	500 schillings.
TOURISTIN	**Zeigen Sie mir diesen.**	Show me that one.
VERKÄUFER	**Gern. Der ist sehr** *(hüpsh)* **hübsch und kostet etwas weniger. 450 Schilling.**	Gladly. This one is very pretty, and costs somewhat less. 450 schillings.
TOURISTIN	**Sie haben recht. Der Schal ist sehr hübsch und preiswert. Ich kaufe ihn.**	You are right. The scarf is very pretty and a good value. I'll buy it.
VERKÄUFER	**Wollen sie auch Parfüm kaufen? Wir haben eine gute** *(OWS-vahl)* **Auswahl.**	Would you also like to buy perfume? We have a good selection.

TOURISTIN	**Nein, danke. Ich kaufe nie** *(nee)*	No thanks. I never buy perfume.
	Parfüm. Mein Mann kauft es für mich.	My husband buys it for me.

Did you notice? The tourist in this dialogue is a woman, so we added *-in* to *Tourist* to form *Touristin* (female tourist).

IM MUSIKGESCHÄFT

At the Music Store

Some of the more important words to remember when shopping at a music store:

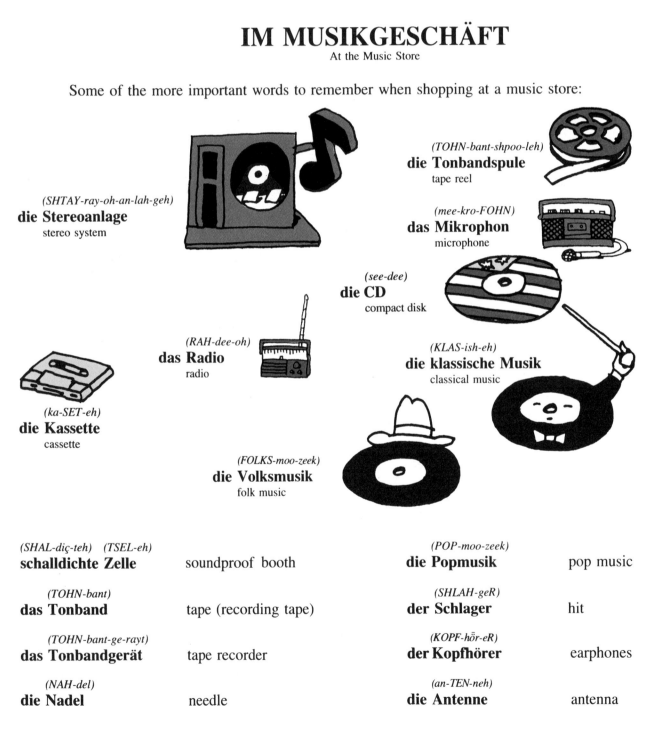

(SHAL-diç-teh) (TSEL-eh) **schalldichte Zelle**	soundproof booth	*(POP-moo-zeek)* **die Popmusik**	pop music
(TOHN-bant) **das Tonband**	tape (recording tape)	*(SHLAH-geR)* **der Schlager**	hit
(TOHN-bant-ge-rayt) **das Tonbandgerät**	tape recorder	*(KOPF-hőr-eR)* **der Kopfhörer**	earphones
(NAH-del) **die Nadel**	needle	*(an-TEN-neh)* **die Antenne**	antenna

Let's read a paragraph about listening to records.

Herr Müller hat klassische Musik sehr gern, und er hat nicht viel Geld. Er hat keine Stereoanlage. Jeden Samstag nachmittag nimmt er den Bus oder die U-Bahn und besucht ein Schallplatten- oder Musikgeschäft in einem anderen Stadtteil. Er nimmt drei oder vier Platten, setzt sich in eine schalldichte Zelle und hört seinen *(LEEP-lings-kom-poh-nis-ten)* **Lieblingskomponisten zwei oder drei Stunden lang zu. Dann geht er glücklich nach Hause und freut sich auf das** *(kon-TSAYRT)* **Konzert nächste Woche.**

Mr. Müller likes classical music very much, and he does not have much money. He doesn't have a stereo system. Every Saturday afternoon he takes the bus or the subway and visits a record- or music store in a different part of town. He takes three or four records, sits down in a booth, and listens to his favorite composers for two or three hours. Then he goes home happily and looks forward to next week's concert.

Now, see if you can answer the following questions. *Auf Deutsch, bitte.*

1. Was tut Herr Müller jeden Samstag? ______________________________

____

2. Ist Herr Müller reich? ______________________________

____

3. Wem hört er zwei oder drei Stunden lang zu? ______________________________

____

4. Warum ist er glücklich, wenn er nach Hause geht? ______________________________

____

ANSWERS

1. Er besucht ein Schallplatten– oder Musikgeschäft. **2.** Nein, er ist nicht reich. **3.** Er hört seinen Lieblingskomponisten zwei oder drei Stunden lang zu. **4.** Weil er sich auf das Konzert nächste Woche freut.

(ROK-moo-zeek)
ROCKMUSIK
Rock Music

VERKÄUFER	**Womit kann ich Ihnen dienen?**	What can I do for you?
TOURISTIN	**Geben Sie mir den größten deutschen Schlager. Für einen jungen Amerikaner.**	Give me the biggest German hit. For a young American.
VERKÄUFER	**Ich habe gerade was Sie brauchen. Hier. Der größte Schlager von Rocky Rock.**	I have just what you need. Here. The biggest hit of Rocky Rock.
TOURISTIN	**Wer ist das?**	Who is that?
VERKÄUFER	**Ein großer Rockstar. Die Platte kommt mit Garantie.** *(gah-ran-TEE)*	A great rockstar. The record comes with a warranty.
TOURISTIN	**Was für eine Garantie?**	What kind of warranty?
VERKÄUFER	**Ihr Trommelfell kaputt nach zweimal Hören oder Ihr Geld zurück.** *(TRO-mel-fel) (ka-PUT)*	Your eardrums will be split after listening twice, or your money back.

IM PHOTOGESCHÄFT
At the Photo Shop

Let's learn some words about photography.

(foh-toh-grah-FEE) **die Photographie (Fotografie)**	photography
(foh-toh-GRAHF) **der Photograph (Fotograf)**	photographer
(GLANTS-pah-peeR) **das Glanzpapier**	glossy paper
(ma-TEERT) **mattiert**	matte
(shvarts) (veis) **in schwarz und weiß**	black and white
(FARP-film) **der Farbfilm**	color film
(OWS-lö-zeR) **der Auslöser**	shutter release
(be-LIÇ-tung) **die Belichtung**	exposure
(ZOO-cheR) **der Sucher**	viewfinder
(ent-FER-nungs-me-seR) **der Entfernungsmesser**	range finder
(BLITS-liçt) **das Blitzlicht**	flash

Here's a short dialogue that might take place at a photo shop. Don't forget to read it aloud. Your German probably sounds pretty good by now.

KUNDE **Möchten Sie diesen Film** *(ent-VIK-eln)* **entwickeln?** — Would you develop this film?

VERKÄUFER **Diapositive oder Abzüge?** — Slides or prints?

KUNDE **Abzüge.** — Prints

VERKÄUFER **7 mal 11 cm?** — 7 by 11 centimeters?

KUNDE *(ge-NOW)* **Genau. Wann sind sie fertig?** — Exactly. When will they be ready?

VERKÄUFER **In drei Tagen. Hier ist Ihr** *(shein)* **Schein.** — In three days. Here is your receipt.

KUNDE **Geben Sie mir auch einen** *(FÜNF-unt-drei-siç)* **fünfunddreißig** *(mil-lee-MAY-teR)* **millimeter (35 mm) Film, 20** *(OWF-nah-men)* **Aufnahmen, in schwarz und weiß.** — Give me also a roll of 35 mm film, 20 exposures, in black and white.

VERKÄUFER **Sehr gut. Noch etwas?** — Very well. Anything else?

KUNDE **Nein, danke. Das wäre es.** — No, thank you. That will be all.

(AP-tsook) *(ko-PEE)*
der Abzug (die Kopie)
print

(KAH-me-ra)
die Kamera
camera

(veR-GRÖ-se-rung)
die Vergrößerung
enlargement

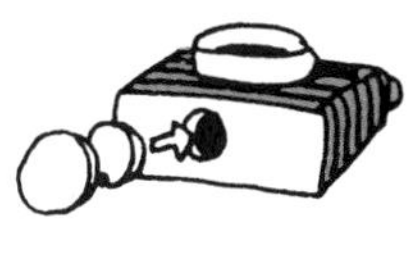

(ba-te-REE)
die Batterie
battery

(dee-ah-poh-zi-TEEF)
das Diapositiv
slide

(film)
der Film
film

Here's a good way to review this unit. Choose gifts for the following people:

1. your mother: ____________________________
2. your grandfather: ____________________________
3. your nephew (teenage boy): ____________________________
4. your niece (teenage girl): ____________________________
5. your uncle who brought you a pink elephant last time (he knows you like German *Schnaps*): ____________________________

(shnaps)

Word Hunt. There are seven German words in this puzzle. Can you find them?

C	L	P	F	A	N	D	A
O	T	O	N	B	A	N	D
P	A	P	O	Z	D	E	O
F	L	M	N	U	E	G	R
L	A	U	T	G	L	O	T
R	L	S	T	A	D	T	N
S	I	I	R	G	O	N	E
I	T	K	L	M	K	L	A

ANSWERS

Word hunt.
Tonband, Popmusik, Abzug, Nadel, dort, laut, Stadt

24 Reparaturen: Optiker Schuhmacher

(re-pah-rah-TOO-ren) **Reparaturen:** Repair Services

(OP-ti-keR) **Optiker** Optometrist

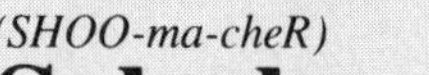

(SHOO-ma-cheR) **Schuhmacher** Shoemaker

As you travel, you'll want to learn about each new city you visit. Here are some useful tips on getting to know a city.

(OWS-ge-tseich-ne-teh) (me-TOH-deh) **Eine ausgezeichnete Methode, eine fremde**	An excellent method of getting acquainted
Stadt kennenzulernen, ist es, dort zu Fuß	with a foreign city is by walking. You
(feR-SHVIN-det) **zu gehen. Man verschwindet in der Menge;**	disappear in the crowd; you observe the
(be-OH-bach-tet) (ge-ZIÇ-teR) **man beobachtet die Gesichter der Leute,**	faces of the people, walk into stores, examine
geht in Geschäfte hinein, sieht die	the produce in open-air markets,
Produkte auf den offenen Märkten an,	stop as long as you wish to read
bleibt solange stehen, wie man will, um die	inscriptions on statues. To the American,
(IN-shrif-ten) (DENK-may-lern) **Inschriften an den Denkmälern zu lesen.**	who is accustomed to taking his car for
Für den Amerikaner, der daran gewöhnt	everything, this can be an
ist, bei Schritt und Tritt sein Auto zu nehmen,	entirely novel experience.
(eR-LAYP-nis) **kann das ein ganz neues Erlebnis sein.**	

Did you get some good ideas about familiarizing yourself with a new city? Look at the following statements and write in the blank whether each is *richtig* *(RIÇ-tiç)* (true) or *falsch* *(falsh)* (false).

1. Man kann eine fremde Stadt kennenlernen, wenn man dort zu Fuß geht. ________________
2. Es ist eine gute Idee *(ee-DAY)* idea, die Gesichter der Leute zu beobachten. ________________
3. Man soll nicht in Geschäfte hineingehen. ________________
4. Denkmäler haben Inschriften. ________________
5. Amerikaner fahren lieber als zu Fuß zu gehen. ________________

BEIM OPTIKER

At the Optometrist

(OP-ti-keR)
der Optiker
optometrist (optician)

(ZON-en-bril-eh)
die Sonnenbrille
sun glasses

(RAH-men)
der Rahmen
frame

(kon-TAKT-lin-zeh)
die Kontaktlinse
contact lens

If you wear glasses or contact lenses, you probably won't have any trouble with them on your trip. But look at the following dialogue closely just in case you need to visit an optometrist.

TOURISTIN	**Der Rahmen** *(RAH-men)* **und ein Glas von meiner Brille** *(BRIL-eh)* **sind kaputt. Sehen Sie?**	The frame and a lens of my glasses are broken. You see?
OPTIKER	**Wie ist das passiert?**	How did it happen?

ANSWERS

1. richtig **2.** richtig **3.** falsch **4.** richtig **5.** richtig

(VAY-rent)
TOURISTIN **In der U-Bahn während der**
(HOWPT-feR-kehrs-tseit) *(drenkt)*
Hauptverkehrszeit. Jemand drängt
(ZOY-leh)
mich und ich stoße gegen eine Säule
an. Ich weiß nicht, was ich tun soll.
(übeR-HOWPT)
Ich sehe überhaupt nichts ohne Brille.

In the subway during the rush hour. Somebody pushes me and I hit a pillar. I don't know what to do. I can't see anything without glasses.

(eR-ZATS-bril-eh)
OPTIKER **Haben Sie eine Ersatzbrille?**

Do you have a spare pair?

(LEI-deR)
TOURISTIN **Leider nicht.**

Unfortunately not.

OPTIKER **Also gut. Setzen Sie sich dort**
(zoh-FORT)
hin. Ich versuche, das sofort zu
reparieren. Aber Ihre Brille ist
(leiçt) *(tseR-BREÇ-liç)*
leicht zerbrechlich. Sie müssen
(FOHR-ziç-tiç)
vorsichtig sein.

Okay. Sit down over there. I'll try to repair this immediately. But your glasses are very fragile. You must be careful.

TOURISTIN **Vielen Dank. Ich bin Ihnen**
(VIRK-liç)
wirklich sehr dankbar.

Thank you. I am really grateful to you.

OPTIKER **Kann ich Ihnen einen Rat**
geben?

May I give you some advice?

TOURISTIN **Ja?**

Yes?

OPTIKER **Nehmen Sie nächstes Mal**
während des Hauptverkehrs ein Taxi.

Take a taxi next time during rush hour.

Which entry in Column 2 goes best with each entry in Column 1?

1. Wie lange haben Sie offen?	A. Morgen, wenn möglich.
2. Wann brauchen Sie die Brille?	B. Vielen Dank.
3. Haben Sie eine Ersatzbrille.	C. Der Rahmen und eine Linse.
4. Was ist kaputt?	D. Bis sechs Uhr abends.
5. Hier haben Sie die Brille.	E. Leider nicht.

ANSWERS

Matching. 1. D 2. A 3. E 4. C 5. B

Fill in the correct words:

1. Der Rahmen und ein ________________ sind gesprungen.
2. Der Optiker versucht, die Brille zu ________________.
3. Die Dame sieht fast nichts ohne ________________.
4. Leider hat sie keine ________________.
5. Die U-Bahn in dieser Stadt ist immer sehr ________________.

BEIM SCHUHMACHER

At the Shoemaker

(SHOO-mach-eR)
der Schuhmacher
shoemaker

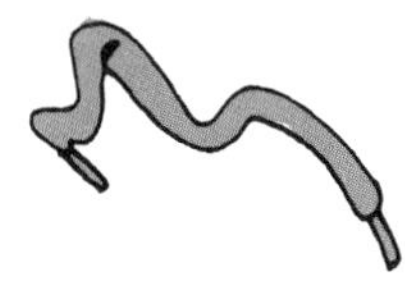

(SHNÜR-zen-kel)
der Schnürsenkel
shoelace

(zan-DAH-leh)
die Sandale
sandal

(pahR) (SHOO-eh)
ein Paar Schuhe
a pair of shoes

You are more likely to have trouble with your shoes while traveling than with your eyeglasses. So read the following dialogue for hints on how to speak with a shoemaker.

TOURISTIN **Guten Tag. Der Absatz** *(AP-zats)* **von meinem Schuh ist kaputt. Können Sie ihn reparieren?**	Hello. My shoe's heel is broken. Can you repair it?
SCHUHMACHER **Lassen Sie mal sehen. Ich glaube nicht. Das ist Plastik** *(PLAS-tik)*. **Wann brauchen Sie Ihre Schuhe?**	Let's see. I don't think so. It's plastic. When do you need your shoes?
TOURISTIN **Morgen, wenn möglich. Ich bleibe nur ein paar Tage hier. Ich bin Touristin** *(too-RIS-tin)*.	Tomorrow if possible. I am staying only for a few days. I am a tourist.

ANSWERS

Fill-in. 1. Glas **2.** reparieren **3.** Brille **4.** Ersatzbrille **5.** voll

SCHUHMACHER **Ich kann versuchen, ihn** *(proh-vee-ZOH-rish) (AN-tsoo-lei-men)* **provisorisch anzuleimen.**	I can try to glue it temporarily.
TOURISTIN **Das ist alles, was ich brauche. Wie lange haben Sie offen?**	That's all I need. How long are you open?
SCHUHMACHER **Bis 19 Uhr.**	Till 7 P.M.
TOURISTIN **Wunderbar! Dann komme ich später zurück.**	Perfect. I'll come back later.
SCHUHMACHER **Gut.**	Good.
TOURISTIN **Können Sie auch Schuhe schnell** *(be-ZOH-len)* **neu besohlen?**	Can you also quickly put new soles on shoes?
SCHUHMACHER **Aber natürlich.**	Of course.
TOURISTIN **Dann bringe ich Ihnen die Schuhe meines Mannes.**	Then I'll bring you my husband's shoes.

Which expression or word does not belong?

1. Absatz, Schuhe, Brille, Sandalen
2. sofort, gleich, diesen Moment, ich bin Ihnen dankbar
3. ersetzen, reparieren, anleimen, stoßen
4. Optiker, Schuhmacher, Tourist, offen

ANSWERS

1. Brille **2.** ich bin Ihnen dankbar **3.** stoßen **4.** offen

ESSENTIAL SERVICES

(DEENST-leis-tun-gen)
Wichtige Dienstleistungen

25 das Bankwesen

(BANK-vay-zen)
Banking

BANKNOTEN UND MÜNZEN

(BANK-noh-ten) (unt) (MÜN-tsen)
Bills and Coins

(courtesy of Ernst Klett Verlag, Stuttgart)

The basic unit of currency in Germany is the mark, known as the Deutsche Mark or DM. It is divided into 100 pfennigs.

(pa-PEER-gelt)
DAS PAPIERGELD
bills

(BANK-noh-ten) *(FOL-gen-den)* *(NEN-veR-teh)*
Deutsche Banknoten haben die folgenden Nennwerte.
bank notes / following / denominations

5 Mark	100 Mark
10 Mark	500 Mark
20 Mark	1 000 Mark
50 Mark	

(KLEIN-gelt)
DAS KLEINGELD
change

(MÜN-tsen) *(UM-lowf)*
Die folgenden Münzen sind im Umlauf.
coins / circulation

Pfennig:	**Mark:**
(PFE-niç)	*(mark)*
1 Pfennig	1 Mark
2 Pfennig	2 Mark
5 Pfennig	5 Mark
10 Pfennig	
50 Pfennig	

(BAN-ken) *(GELT-vek-sel)*
BANKEN, GELDWECHSEL
Banks, Exchanging Money
(REI-zeh-sheks)
UND REISESCHECKS
and Traveler's Checks

(DOY-tsheh) (BUN-des-bank)
The central bank of Germany is the **Deutsche Bundesbank,** headquartered in Frankfurt.
German Federal Bank
The country has many banks that deal with the public, and most offer a wide range of services. The largest banks are the *Deutsche Bank, Dresdner Bank,* and *Commerzbank.* In addition, many foreign banks, including U.S. banks, have offices in Germany. You can exchange currency at banks and also at smaller exchange offices. Credit cards are accepted by major establishments and by many other businesses. But Germans use credit cards much less than Americans, so be prepared to pay in cash during your daily excursions. Banking and money conditions are similar in Austria and Switzerland.

Menschen und Dinge
People and Things

das Geld
money

(BANK-be-am-teh) *(BANK-be-am-tin)*
der Bankbeamte, die Bankbeamtin

bank employee

die Bank
bank

die Reiseschecks
traveler's checks

(dee-REK-tohR)
der Direktor
manager

(AN-lei-eh) *(DAR-layn)*
die Anleihe, das Darlehn
loan

(EIN-tsah-lungs-be-layk)
der Einzahlungsbeleg
deposit slip

(KA-sen-shal-teR)
der Kassenschalter
teller's window

(Ka-SEE-reR) *(ka-SEE-reR-in)*
der Kassierer, die Kassiererin
teller (cashier)

(AP-hay-bungs-be-layk)
der Abhebungsbeleg
withdrawal slip

(BANK-noh-teh) *(GELT-shein)*
die Banknote, der Geldschein
bill

(BAHR-gelt)
das Bargeld
cash

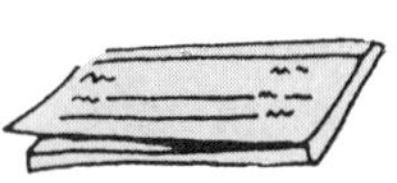

(SHEK-booch)
das Scheckbuch
checkbook

Wie man . . .

How to . . .

(VEK-seln) *(TOW-shen)*
wechseln, tauschen
to exchange

(VEK-sel-koors)
der Wechselkurs
rate of exchange

(TSAH-len)
zahlen
to pay

(eR-ÖF-nen)
ein Konto eröffnen
to open an account

(EIN-tsah-lung)
die Einzahlung
deposit

(day-poh-NEE-ren)
einzahlen, deponieren
to deposit

(AP-hay-ben)
abheben
to withdraw

(un-teR-SHREI-ben)
unterschreiben
to sign

(EIN-lö-zen)
einen Scheck einlösen
to cash a check

You've been introduced to a number of useful words. See if you remember them by circling the term that correctly describes each of the following pictures.

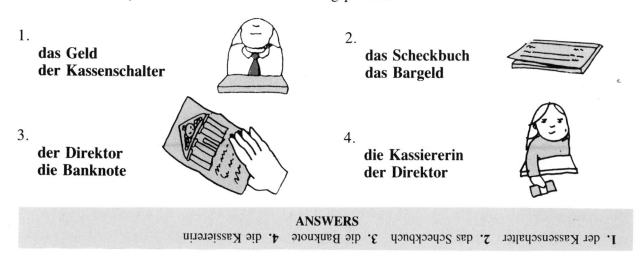

1.
das Geld
der Kassenschalter

2.
das Scheckbuch
das Bargeld

3.
der Direktor
die Banknote

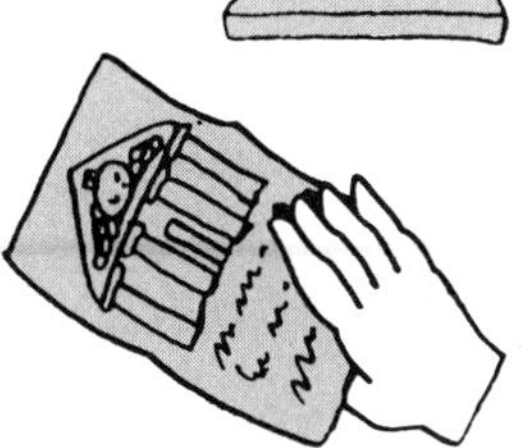

4.
die Kassiererin
der Direktor

ANSWERS

1. der Kassenschalter **2.** das Scheckbuch **3.** die Banknote **4.** die Kassiererin

5.

der Einzahlungsbeleg
der Abhebungsbeleg

6.

die Reiseschecks
das Bargeld

Now, try to complete the following:

1. Ich möchte zehn U.S. Dollars ________________. (exchange)
2. Ich möchte 100 Mark ________________. (withdraw)
3. Ich möchte einen Reisescheck ________________. (cash)
4. Ich möchte 300 Mark ________________. (deposit)

GELD WECHSELN

Changing Money

JULIE (to teller at a bank in Munich)

Können Sie mir diesen Reisescheck für 100 Dollar in Mark umwechseln?	Can you change this traveler's check for $100 into marks?
KASSIERER **Ich brauche Ihren Paß.**	I need your passport.
JULIE **Warum?**	Why?
KASSIERER **Persönlicher Ausweis.** *(OWS-veis)*	Personal identification.
JULIE **Was meinen Sie?**	What do you mean?

ANSWERS

5. der Einzahlungsbeleg **6.** die Reiseschecks

Completion.
1. wechseln **2.** abheben **3.** einlösen **4.** einzahlen

KASSIERER *(ee-den-tee-TAYT)* **Ihre Identität.**	Your identity.
JULIE **Ah.—Ich habe ihn vergessen. Im Hotel.**	Ah.—I forgot it. At the hotel.
KASSIERER **Es tut mir leid. Haben Sie etwas anderes zur** *(ee-den-ti-fi-TSEE-rung)* **Identifizierung?**	I am sorry. Do you have something else to identify yourself with?
JULIE **Ich hab' ein** *(MUT-eR-mahl)* **Muttermal an der rechten** *(SHUL-teR)* **Schulter.**	I have a mole on the right shoulder.

der Paß
passport

Try to fill in the missing dialogue parts without looking them up:

1. „Können Sie mir diesen ________________ für 100 Dollar in Mark ________________?"
2. „Ich brauche Ihren ________________."
3. „Ich habe ihn ________________."
4. „Ich hab' ein Muttermal an der rechten ________________."

(vits)
EIN KLEINER WITZ
joke

(day-fi-nit-see-OHN) **Definition einer Bank**	Definition of a bank
Eine Bank ist eine *(in-sti-toot-see-OHN)* **Institution, wo man Geld borgen kann, wenn man** *(be-VEI-zen)* **beweisen kann, daß man es nicht braucht.**	A bank is an institution where one can borrow money if one can prove that one does not need it.

ANSWERS

Dialogue. **1.** Reisescheck, umwechseln **2.** Paß **3.** vergessen **4.** Schulter

Are the following statements about the dialogue true or false?

1. Julie möchte einen Reisescheck in Mark umwechseln. __________
2. Der Kassierer sagt, er braucht ihren Paß. __________
3. Julie versteht den Mann sofort. __________
4. Sie hat ihren Paß bei sich. __________
5. Sie holt den Paß vom Hotel. __________
6. Der Beamte gibt ihr das Geld ohne Paß. __________
7. Julie hat ein Muttermal an der linken Schulter. __________
8. Der Beamte sagt, „Es tut mir leid." __________

Pick the right word:

9. In den meisten Ländern braucht man als persönlichen Ausweis
   a. eine Flugkarte b. eine Postkarte c. einen Paß
10. Wie heißt der Mann in der Bank, der Ihnen das Geld wechselt?
    a. der Kassierer b. der Direktor c. der Kellner
11. Was bekommt man zurück, wenn man Geld bei der Bank deponiert hat?
    a. einen Abhebungsbeleg b. einen Einzahlungsbeleg c. Bargeld
12. Was bekommt man, wenn man einen Scheck einlöst?
    a. einen neuen Scheck b. Bargeld c. nichts

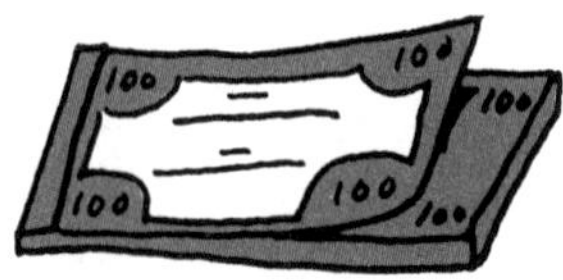

ANSWERS

True/false.
1. T **2.** T **3.** F **4.** F **5.** F **6.** F **7.** F **8.** T
Right word.
9. c **10.** a **11.** b **12.** b.

Here's a short story about banking.

Mein Freund in München erzählt *(eR-TSAYLT)* **mir die folgende Geschichte:** *(ge-SHIÇ-teh)*
Vorige *(FOH-ri-geh)* **Woche eröffnet mein junger Sohn zum ersten Mal in seinem Leben ein Konto bei der Bank. Heute fragt er mich, ganz aufgeregt:** *(OWF-ge-raykt)*
„Vati, warum sagst du mir, ich soll mein Geld bei so einer Bank einzahlen?"
„Was meinst du?" frage ich ihn.
„Die Bank ist doch bankrott," *(bank-ROT)* **sagt er.**
„Wieso? Das ist doch die stärkste *(SHTERK-steh)* **Bank in Deutschland."**
„Hier. Schau dir diesen Scheck an," antwortet er.
„Mein Scheck für 30 Mark. Die Bank schickt ihn mir zurück und schau, Vati: mit Aufdruck *(OWF-druk)* ***keine Deckung*****."**

My friend in Munich tells me the following story:
Last week my young son opens an account at the bank for the first time in his life. Today he asks me, all excited:
''Dad, why did you tell me to deposit my money with such a bank?''
''What do you mean?'' I ask him.
''The bank is bankrupt,'' he says.
''How come? That is the strongest bank in Germany.''
''Here. Look at this check,'' he replies.
''My check for 30 marks. The bank sends it back to me, and look, dad: Printed on it is *no funds*.''

Please fill in the missing words:

1. Vorige Woche ________________ mein Sohn ein Konto.
2. Warum soll ich das Geld bei so einer Bank ________________?
3. Das ist doch die stärkste ________________ in Deutschland.
4. Die Bank schickt mir den Scheck ________________.
5. Der Scheck hat einen Aufdruck: ________________.

ANSWERS

Missing words. 1. eröffnet **2.** einzahlen **3.** Bank **4.** zurück **5.** keine Deckung

Bitte beantworten Sie die folgenden Fragen. *(FRAH-gen)* questions

1. Wer erzählt die Geschichte? ______________________
2. Wo eröffnet der Junge das Konto? ______________________
3. Wann eröffnet er das Konto? ______________________
4. Warum ist der Junge ganz aufgeregt? ______________________
5. Was tut die Bank mit dem Scheck? ______________________
6. Was steht auf dem Scheck? ______________________

Match each word in Column 1 with the proper English translation in Column 2.

1. **der Wechselkurs**	A. teller's window
2. **der Reisescheck**	B. to withdraw
3. **der Kassenschalter**	C. exchange rate
4. **abheben**	D. traveler's check
5. **unterschreiben**	E. deposit
6. **die Einzahlung**	F. no funds
7. **keine Deckung**	G. to sign
8. **das Darlehn**	H. cashier
9. **der Kassierer**	I. manager
10. **der Direktor**	J. loan

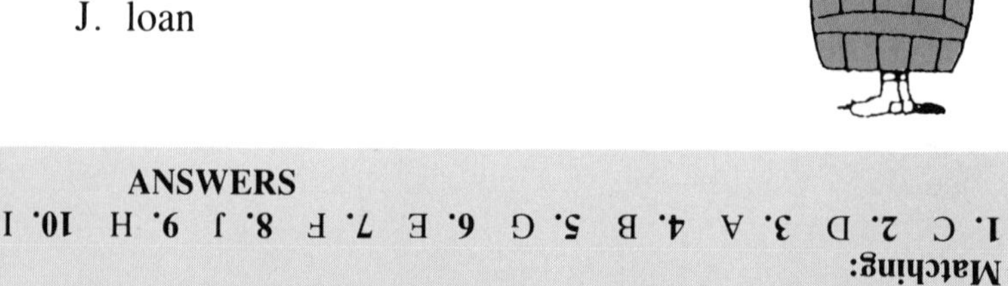

ANSWERS

Fragen.
1. mein Freund **2.** bei der Bank **3.** vorige Woche **4.** Er glaubt, die Bank ist bankrott. **5.** Sie schickt ihn zurück. **6.** keine Deckung

Matching:
1. C **2.** D **3.** A **4.** B **5.** G **6.** E **7.** F **8.** J **9.** H **10.** I

And here is a puzzle you'll enjoy. Just enter the German translation of each English term. We've supplied the first letter of each German word.

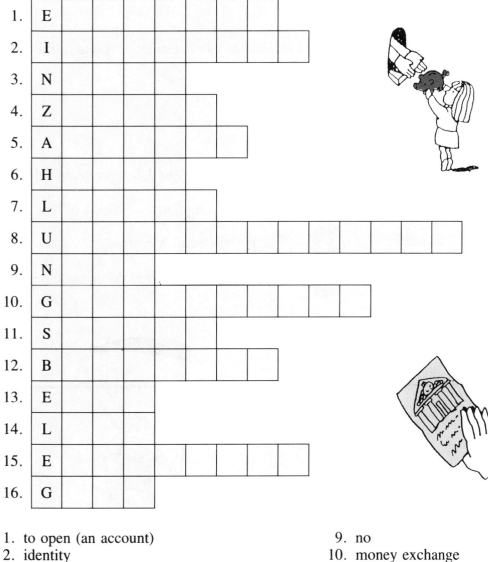

1.	E
2.	I
3.	N
4.	Z
5.	A
6.	H
7.	L
8.	U
9.	N
10.	G
11.	S
12.	B
13.	E
14.	L
15.	E
16.	G

1. to open (an account)
2. identity
3. not
4. to pay
5. loan
6. hotel
7. unfortunately
8. to sign
9. no
10. money exchange
11. check
12. bill (bank note)
13. corner
14. long
15. to deposit
16. money

ANSWERS

Puzzle.
1. eröffnen **2.** Identität **3.** nicht **4.** zahlen **5.** Anleihe **6.** Hotel **7.** leider **8.** unterschreiben
9. nein **10.** Geldwechsel **11.** Scheck **12.** Banknote **13.** Ecke **14.** lang **15.** einzahlen **16.** Geld

26 Die Post

(post)

Postal Service

The German postal service (Deutsche Post AG) is known for its efficiency. It is one of the largest service enterprises in Europe.

The following story is about an amateur letter carrier.

(root) (shpriçt) (U-lee)

Ruth spricht mit ihrem Sohn Uli, fünf Jahre alt.

Ruth talks to her son Uli, five years old.

(frü)

„Was machst du so früh, Uli?"

"What are you doing so early, Uli?"

(BREEF-tray-geR)(MA-mee)

„Ich spiele Briefträger, Mami."

"Playing mailman, Mommy."

„Briefträger? Wie kannst du das ohne Briefe machen?"

"Mailman? How can you do that without letters?"

„Aber ich habe ja Briefe."

"But I do have letters."

„Was für Briefe?"

"What kind of letters?"

(KAS-ten)

„Die in dem Kasten in deinem Zimmer, ein ganzes Paket, mit einem schönen rosa Band um sie herum . . ."

"The ones in the big box in your room, whole package, with a beautiful pink ribbon around them . . ."

„Und mit denen spielst du Briefträger?"

"And with those you play mailman?"

(MU-tee)

„Ja, Mutti. Ich steck' einen Brief nach dem anderen auf der Straße unter jede Haustür."

"Yes, Mommy. I put one letter after another under each front door on the street."

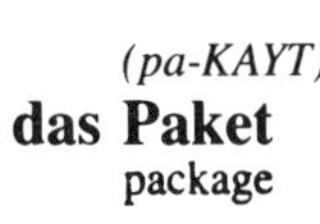

(pa-KAYT)
das Paket
package

(BREEF-tray-geR)
der Briefträger
letter carrier

(BREEF-kas-ten)
der Briefkasten
mailbox

John wants to mail a package to the U.S.A., and Alois takes him to the post office.

(AH-loh-is) ALOIS **Wissen Sie, daß die Post** *(be-FÖR-deRt)* **täglich Millionen Briefe befördert?**	Do you know that the postal service forwards millions of letters a day?
JOHN *(fan-TAS-tish)* **Fantastisch!**	Fantastic!
ALOIS **Die Deutsche Post AG ist einer der** *(DEENST-leis-tungs-be-tree-beh)* *(oy-ROH-pa)* **größten Dienstleistungsbetriebe in Europa.**	The German postal service is one of the biggest service enterprises in Europe.
JOHN **Großartig!**	Great.

(They arrive at the post office.)

ALOIS *(pah-KAYT-an-nah-meh)* **Also hier haben Sie die Paketannahme.**	Here you have the parcel post window.
(POST-be-am-teR) POSTBEAMTER (postal employee) **Wollen Sie bitte diese** *(OWS-fül-en)* **Paketkarte ausfüllen?**	Would you please complete this parcel form?
JOHN **Sehr gut. Haben Sie auch Briefmarken?**	Very good. Do you also have stamps?
POSTBEAMTER **Die bekommen Sie beim Briefmarkenschalter dort drüben.**	Those you get at the stamp window over there.

JOHN	**Auch Postkarten?**	Postal cards also?
POSTBEAMTER	**Ja, natürlich.**	Yes, of course.
JOHN	*(shok-oh-LAH-deh)* **Großartig! Und auch Schokolade?**	Great! And also chocolate?
POSTBEAMTER	**Leider nicht.**	Unfortunately not.

Bitte nicht vergessen

Please Don't Forget

das Postfach
post office box

der Beamte
employee

die Briefe
letters

(POST-vert-tsei-çen)
die Briefmarke *or* **das Postwertzeichen**
postage stamp

(mil-YOHN) **eine Million**	one million
Millionen	millions
(BREEF-kas-ten-lay-rung) **die Briefkastenleerung**	mail collection
(POR-toh) **das Porto**	postage
Die Post kommt zweimal täglich.	Mail is delivered twice daily.
Der Postbeamte leert den Briefkasten.	The postal worker empties the mailbox.

(NÜTS-li-çeh) (OWS-drü-keh)
Nützliche Ausdrücke
Useful Expressions

Bitte gehen Sie doch.
The *doch* in this sentence is hard to translate. It often expresses interest or impatience: Please *do* go. There are other little words like this, sometimes called flavoring or intensifying particles, e.g., *denn* in *Gehst du denn nicht?* Aren't you going? Replying to this, one might say (expressing annoyance): *Ich gehe ja.* I *am* going!

Haben Sie etwas dagegen?	Do you mind?
Ich habe nichts dagegen.	I don't mind; I have no objection to it.

Here's a quick quiz about the German postal service.

Fill in the correct German words:

1. Die Deutsche Post befördert Millionen ________________ täglich.
2. Sie ist einer der größten Dienstleistungsbetriebe in ________________.

3. John will auch ________________ kaufen.
4. Die Deutsche Post ist ein ________________.
   service enterprise
5. Mit dem Paket geht man zur ________________.
   parcel post window
6. Leute, die fürs Postamt arbeiten, heißen ________________.
   postal employees

Draw lines between the matching English and German:

1. Deutsche Post	A. to forward
2. Dienstleistungsbetrieb	B. post office box
3. Paketannahme	C. postal card
4. Postbeamter	D. service enterprise
5. Briefmarke	E. German postal service
6. befördern	F. postal employee
7. Postfach	G. postage
8. Porto	H. parcel post window
9. Postkarte	I. postage stamp

ANSWERS

Fill-in. 1. Briefe **2.** Europa **3.** Briefmarken **4.** Dienstleistungsbetrieb **5.** Paketannahme **6.** Postbeamte

Matching. 1. E **2.** D **3.** H **4.** F **5.** I **6.** A **7.** B **8.** G **9.** C

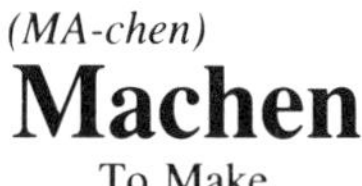

(MA-chen)

Machen

To Make

Machen is one of the most useful words in the German language. It can have a number of meanings.

Geschäfte machen mit	to do business with
Mach' dir nichts daraus! *(da-ROWS)*	Don't worry about it.
Das macht nichts!	It doesn't matter.
Mach's gut!	Take care of yourself.
Da kann man nichts machen.	It can't be helped.
Laß mich nur machen!	Leave it to me!
Wie geht's? Es macht sich.	How are things? Pretty good. So-so.
Gemacht!	Agreed! Okay!

27 Der Telefondienst
(te-le-FOHN-deenst)
Telephone Service

(HA-loh) *(HA-loh)*
HALLO...HALLO?
Hello . . . Hello?

anrufen **telefonieren**	to make a telephone call
Bleiben Sie am Apparat.	Hold the line; don't hang up.
(fer-MIT-lung) **Hallo, Vermittlung.** **Hallo, Fräulein.**	Hello, operator?
(ORTS-ge-shprayç) (FERN-ge-shprayç) **das Ortsgespräch, Ferngespräch**	local call; long distance call
(ER-ge-shprayç) **das R-Gespräch**	collect call, reverse charges
Hören Sie mich jetzt besser?	Can you hear me better now?
(FOHR-an-mel-dung) **mit Voranmeldung**	person-to-person
(a-pa-RAHT) (be-ZETST) **Der Apparat ist besetzt.**	The line is busy.
(VAY-len) **eine Nummer wählen**	to dial a number

On the telephone, it is customary to say *zwo* *(tsvoh)* instead of *zwei* if you use the number 2. The reason is that *zwei* and *drei* sound alike on the phone. *Zwo* prevents confusion.

John and Mary would like to pay a visit to their relatives in Munich, but John has to call them first.

JOHN (to a passerby in the street) **Können Sie mir bitte sagen,**	Could you please tell me
wo ich einen öffentlichen	where I find a public
(FERN-shpre-çeR) **Fernsprecher finde?**	telephone?
VORBEIGEHENDER **Dort drüben**	Over there at the street
an der Straßenecke ist eine	corner there is a telephone
(tay-lay-FOHN-tse-leh) **Telefonzelle.**	booth.
JOHN **Dort?**	There?
VORBEIGEHENDER **Ja, die gelb**	Yes, the one that is painted
(AN-ge-shtri-çe-neh) **angestrichene. Kann ich**	yellow.
(be-HILF-liç) **Ihnen behilflich sein?**	May I help you?
JOHN **Danke, nein. Sehr liebenswürdig.** *(LEE-bens-vür-diç)*	No, thank you. You're very kind. I'll find it.
Ich find' sie schon. Komm, Mary.	Come, Mary.

(at the booth)

MARY **Hast du Münzen?**	Do you have coins?
JOHN **Ja—also willst du**	Yes—do you want to wait
draußen warten? Für zwei	outside? For two it is a bit small.
ist es ein bißchen eng.	

(he takes off the receiver, inserts the money, and dials)

Franz? Kann ich bitte mit	Franz? Can I speak with
Franz sprechen?	Franz, please?
Franz—Grüß dich! Ja, wir	Franz—Hi!
sind in München. Um 17 Uhr? . . .	Yes, we are in Munich. At 17 hours (5 P.M.)? . . .
Wunderbar. Bis später.	Great. Until later.

Fill in the correct German word:

1. Die Telefonzelle ist  ____________________ angestrichen.

2. Mary fragt John: ,,Hast du genug 

____________________?"

3. Man findet die Nummer im  ____________________.

4. Wann werden sie die Verwandten besuchen? Um ____________________.

5. Beim Telefonieren sagt man ____________________ anstatt zwei.

6. Wie sagt man 1½ auf Deutsch? ____________________.

7. Wie sagt man ½? ____________________

8. Und wie sagt man ⅓? ____________________

ORTSGESPRÄCH ODER FERNGESPRÄCH?

Local or Long Distance?

John and Mary are back at the hotel at 21 hours. There is still time to place a call to his cousin Lotte in Stuttgart.

JOHN	**Hallo, Fräulein.**	Hello, operator.
FRÄULEIN	**Ortsgespräch oder Ferngespräch?**	Local call or long distance?
JOHN	**Ferngespräch.**	Long distance.

ANSWERS

Fill-in.
1. gelb **2.** Münzen **3.** Telefonbuch **4.** 17 Uhr **5.** zwo **6.** anderthalb **7.** ein halb **8.** ein Drittel

FRÄULEIN	**Mit Voranmeldung?**	Person-to-person?
JOHN	**Ja, bitte.**	Yes, please.
FRÄULEIN	**Ein R-Gespräch?**	Collect?
JOHN	**Nein, das geht auf meine Hotelrechnung.**	No; that goes on my hotel bill.
FRÄULEIN	**Namen und Nummer, bitte.**	Name and number, please.
JOHN	**Lotte Müller, 84-56-13. Meine Nummer ist 63-47-82. Wie lange muß ich warten?**	Lotte Müller, 84-56-13. My number is 63-47-82. How long do I have to wait?
FRÄULEIN	**Einen Moment, bitte. Bleiben Sie am Apparat. Ich verbinde Sie. . . . Keine Antwort.**	One moment, please. Stay on the line. I'll connect you . . . . No answer.
JOHN	**Danke. Ich versuche später nochmals.**	Thank you. I'll try again later.

Circle the correct answer for the following questions.

1. Mit welcher Farbe ist der öffentliche Fernsprecher angestrichen?
   a. blau b. gelb c. rot
2. Von wo telefoniert er Franz?
   a. vom Hotel b. vom Kino c. von einer Telefonzelle
3. Wann sollen sie bei den Verwandten sein?
   a. um 13 Uhr b. um 7 Uhr c. um 17 Uhr
4. Mit wem telefoniert er um 9 Uhr abends?
   a. mit seiner Kusine Lotte b. mit seinem Bruder Paul c. mit seiner Tante Lilly
5. Wie schreiben Sie die Zahl 33 aus?
   a. dreißig-drei b. dreiunddreißig c. dreißigunddrei
6. *(fer-GLEI-çen)*
   Vergleichen Sie (compare) ein Ortsgespräch mit einem Ferngespräch:
   a. Ein Ortsgespräch ist billiger. b. Ein Ferngespräch ist billiger. c. Sie kosten dasselbe.

ANSWERS

1. b **2.** c **3.** c **4.** a **5.** b **6.** a

Bitte nicht vergessen . . .

Please don't forget . . .

die Adresse address

der Apparat phone

der Moment moment

die Auskunft information

die Nummer number

das Telefon telephone

das Telefonbuch telephone book

Wie spät ist es?
or
Wieviel Uhr ist es?

die gelb angestrichene Telefonzelle the yellow telephone booth

Draw lines between the matching words or expressions.

1. der Fernsprecher	A. local call
2. eine Nummer wählen	B. street corner
3. die Auskunft	C. telephone
4. das Ortsgespräch	D. to dial
5. die Münzen	E. public
6. die Straßenecke	F. information
7. öffentlich	G. kind
8. liebenswürdig	H. coins

ANSWERS

Matching. 1. C 2. D 3. F 4. A 5. H 6. B 7. E 8. G

Frau Hauser tries to call a grocery store.

Hallo? Frau Hauser hier, Schillerstraße 115. Schicken Sie mir bitte ein kleines Huhn zum Grillen *(GRIL-en)*. **Haben Sie nicht. Das ist schade** *(SHAH-deh)*. **Also vielleicht ein Pfund gekochten** *(ge-KOCH-ten)* **Schinken, dünn** *(dün)* **geschnitten** *(ge-SHNIT-en)*— **Haben Sie auch nicht. Wieso? Das ist doch unmöglich. Also dann eventuell ein Pfund mageres** *(MAH-ger-es)* **Hackfleisch** *(HAK-fleish)*—**auch kein Hackfleisch?? Es ist nicht zu glauben! Ist denn das nicht Herr Blunz, der Metzger? Sie sind Blunz, der Blumenhändler** *(BLOOM-en-hend-leR)*? **Ach, bitte verzeihen** *(feR-TSEI-en)* **Sie mir. Aber warum sagen Sie nicht sofort, daß Sie nicht Fleisch verkaufen? . . . Weil ich so viel rede! Sie sind ja frech** *(freç)*!

Hello? This is Frau Hauser, 115 Schillerstraße. Send me, please, a small chicken for grilling. You don't have it. That's too bad. Well, maybe a pound of boiled ham, sliced thin—you don't have that either. How come? That's impossible. Maybe a pound of lean hamburger—no hamburger?? That's incredible! Isn't this Herr Blunz, the butcher? You are Blunz, the florist? Oh, please excuse me. But why didn't you say right away that you don't sell meat? . . . Because I talk so much! You are really impertinent!

Ein Rätsel

Here's an interesting change of pace—a word-search puzzle. Find the nouns with or without their articles. Circle them. The nouns are not capitalized in this puzzle.

1. the street corner
2. number
3. the information
4. moment
5. the address
6. the man
7. one quarter

a	e	z	m	b	o	r	n	l	p	r	b	o	n
d	i	e	a	u	s	k	u	n	f	t	z	i	u
s	n	l	n	m	i	k	l	s	c	o	n	r	m
a	v	b	n	o	n	a	z	r	s	t	m	u	m
d	i	e	s	t	r	a	ß	e	n	e	c	k	e
a	e	c	k	l	m	o	p	r	s	t	v	u	r
n	r	g	i	a	m	o	i	s	t	n	m	l	z
s	t	a	g	h	u	n	m	s	p	r	a	l	t
d	e	r	m	a	n	n	p	o	r	s	g	g	n
e	l	n	m	o	m	e	n	t	p	l	a	e	i
d	i	e	a	d	r	e	s	s	e	g	s	o	p

ANSWERS

Puzzle

1. die Straßenecke **2.** Nummer **3.** die Auskunft **4.** Moment **5.** die Adresse **6.** der Mann **7.** ein Viertel

28 Der Zahnarzt Der Arzt Das Krankenhaus

(TSAHN-artst) **Der Zahnarzt** — Dentist

(artst) **Der Arzt** — Doctor

(KRAN-ken-hows) **Das Krankenhaus** — Hospital

EINE KURZE ANATOMIEÜBUNG

(ah-nah-toh-MEE-ü-bung)

A Short Lesson in Anatomy

Kurt und Trude are testing each other on the parts of the human body.

KURT **Also wer fängt an, du oder ich?** — Well, who'll start, you or I?

TRUDE **Du fragst mich zuerst.** — You ask me first.

KURT **Gut. Also was hast du da?** — Good. What do you have here?

TRUDE **Die Haare.** (HAH-reh) — The hair.

KURT **Zwischen den Haaren und den Augen?** (OW-gen) — Between the hair and the eyes?

TRUDE **Die Stirn.** (shtirn) — The forehead.

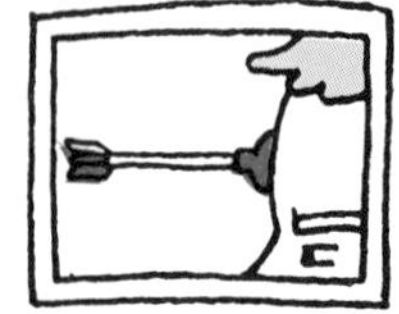

KURT **Über den Augen. . .?** — Over the eyes . . .?

(OW-gen-brow-en)
TRUDE **Die Augenbrauen.** — The eyebrows.

KURT **Und was macht man zu,** — And what does one

wenn man schläft? — close when sleeping?

(OW-gen-lee-deR)
TRUDE **Die Augenlider.** — The eyelids.

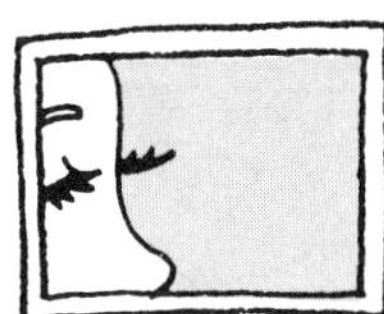

KURT **Und auf den Augenlidern** — And on the eyelids

haben wir . . . — we have . . .

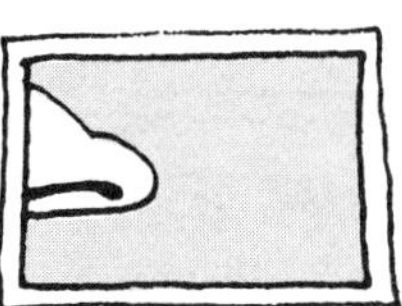

(VIM-pern)
TRUDE **Wimpern.** — lashes.

KURT **Und zwischen** — And between

den Augen ist . . . — the eyes is . . .

(NAH-zeh)
TRUDE **die Nase.** — the nose.

KURT **Und zwischen der Nase** — And between the nose

(munt)
und dem Mund — and the mouth

tragen viele Männer . . . — many men wear . . .

(SHNUR-bart)
TRUDE **einen Schnurrbart.** — a moustache.

KURT **Du hast zwei** — You have two

(OH-ren)
TRUDE **Ohren** — ears

KURT **und zwei** — and two

(VAN-gen) *(BA-ken)*
TRUDE **Wangen (oder Backen).** — cheeks.

KURT **Aber du hast nur ein** — But you have only one

(ge-ZIÇT)
TRUDE **Gesicht** — face

KURT **und nur einen** — and only one

(kopf)
TRUDE **Kopf.** — head.

KURT **Wenn du lachst,** — When you laugh, one sees the

sieht man die

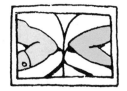

	(TSAY-neh)		
TRUDE	**Zähne.**	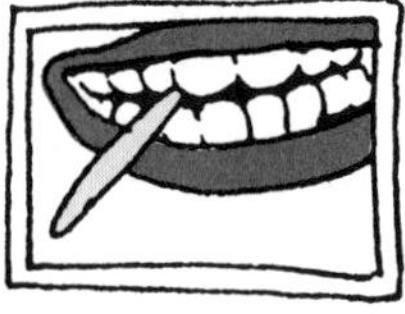	teeth.
KURT	**Wenn du zum**		When you go to
	Doktor gehst, zeigst du ihm die		the doctor, you
	(TSUNG-eh)		
TRUDE	**Zunge, aaah. . . .**		show him your tongue, aaah. . . .
KURT	**Das ist das**	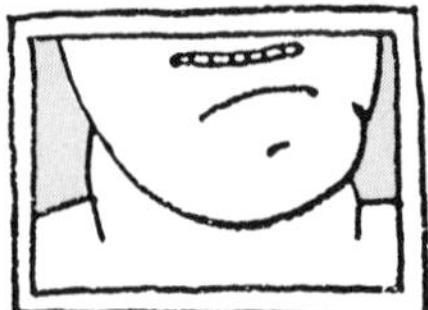	This is the
	(kin)		
TRUDE	**Kinn,**		chin,
KURT	**und das ist der**		and that is the
	(hals)		
TRUDE	**Hals.**		neck.
KURT	**Hier sind zwei**	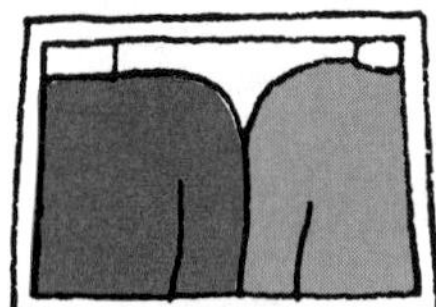	Here are two
	(SHUL-teRn)		
TRUDE	**Schultern,**		shoulders,
KURT	**vier**		four
	(AR-meh)		
TRUDE	**Arme**		arms,
KURT	**und zwei**		and two
	(EL-boh-gen)		
TRUDE	**Ellbogen.**		elbows.
KURT	**Hier sind zwei**		Here are two
	(HEN-deh)		
TRUDE	**Hände**		hands
KURT	**und zehn**		and ten
	(FING-eR)		
TRUDE	**Finger.**		fingers.
KURT	**Jetzt komm' *ich* dran.**		Now it's *my* turn.
TRUDE	**Also das ist der**		This is the

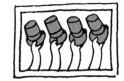

KURT **Rücken,** *(RÜK-en)*

TRUDE **und da vorne ist die** *(FOR-neh)*

KURT **Brust.** *(brust)*

TRUDE **Etwas tut dir weh, wenn du zuviel Kuchen ißt:**

KURT **Der Magen.** *(MAH-gen)*

TRUDE **Und etwas tiefer ist der**

KURT **Bauch.** *(bowch)*

TRUDE **Und da hinten hast du den**

KURT **Popo.** *(poh-POH)*

TRUDE **Und von hier bis hier hast du zwei**

KURT **Schenkel.** *(SHEN-kel)*

TRUDE **Dann hast du zwei**

KURT **Knie.** *(KNEE-eh)*

TRUDE **Und weiter unten sind**

KURT **die zwei Waden.** *(VAH-den)*

TRUDE **Dann kommen die zwei**

KURT **Knöchel.** *(KNÖ-çel)*

TRUDE **Und darunter sind die großen**

KURT **Füße** *(FÜS-eh)*

TRUDE **mit den zehn**

KURT **Zehen.** *(TSAY-en)*

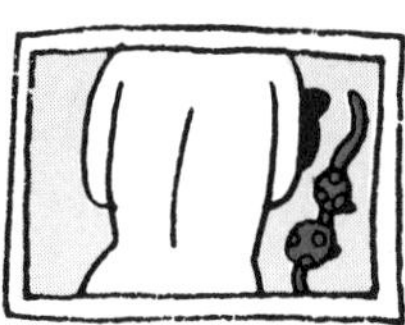

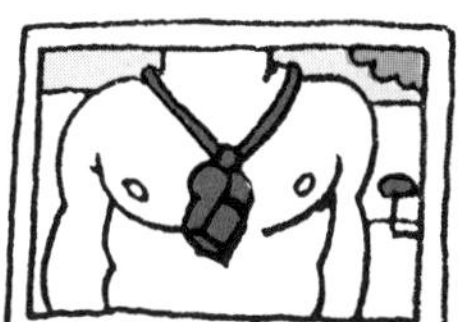

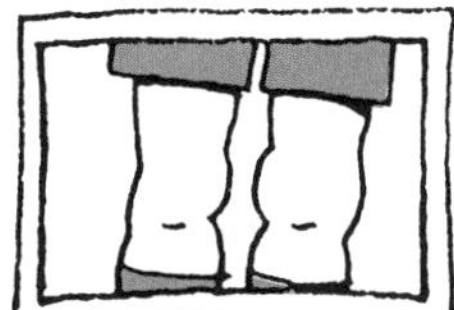

back,

and here in front is the

chest.

Something hurts you, when you eat too much cake:

the stomach.

and a little lower is the

belly.

And there in the back you have the

fanny.

And from here to here you have two

thighs.

Then you have two

knees.

And farther down are the

two calves.

Then come the two

ankles.

And under them are the big

feet

with the ten

toes.

Draw lines between the matching words:

1.	**die Stirn**	A.	tongue
2.	**die Zehen**	B.	face
3.	**der Mund**	C.	eyelids
4.	**die Knöchel**	D.	forehead
5.	**die Zunge**	E.	ankles
6.	**die Augenlider**	F.	toes
7.	**der Magen**	G.	stomach
8.	**das Gesicht**	H.	mouth
9.	**der Schnurrbart**	I.	teeth
10.	**die Zähne**	J.	moustache

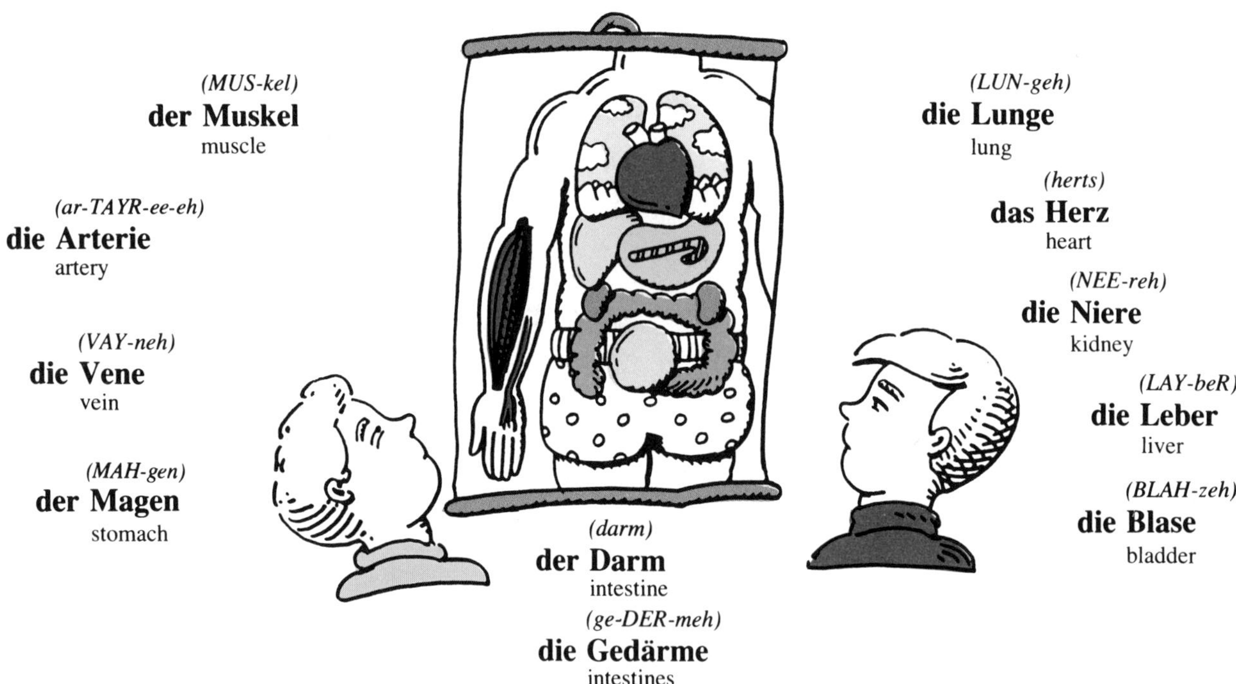

A very comprehensive system of compulsory health insurance pays all or part of the cost of medical and dental care, medications, laboratory tests, and hospitalization for the insured and his or her family, which means for nearly every citizen of the Federal Republic.

ANSWERS

Matching. **1.** D **2.** F **3.** H **4.** E **5.** A **6.** C **7.** G **8.** B **9.** J **10.** I

The procedures for getting medical care are relatively simple. Most Germans go to their (KRAN-ken-kas-en-artst) *Krankenkassenarzt* (health insurance fund doctor) for their medical or dental needs. A (KRAN-ken-shein) *Krankenschein* (medical certificate) is prepared by the physician for prescriptions, and, if necessary, a stay in the hospital. The patient is free to choose his or her own doctor from a sizable number of general practitioners or specialists.

While traveling in Germany, Austria, or Switzerland, you should have no difficulty receiving adequate medical care. Noncitizens are not covered by the German health-insurance system. Medical fees vary greatly and are set by the physician or dentist you consult. Your best bet would be to ask a German friend for a recommendation.

DER ZAHNARZT: MUND (munt) AUFMACHEN! (OWF-ma-chen)

Open Wide!

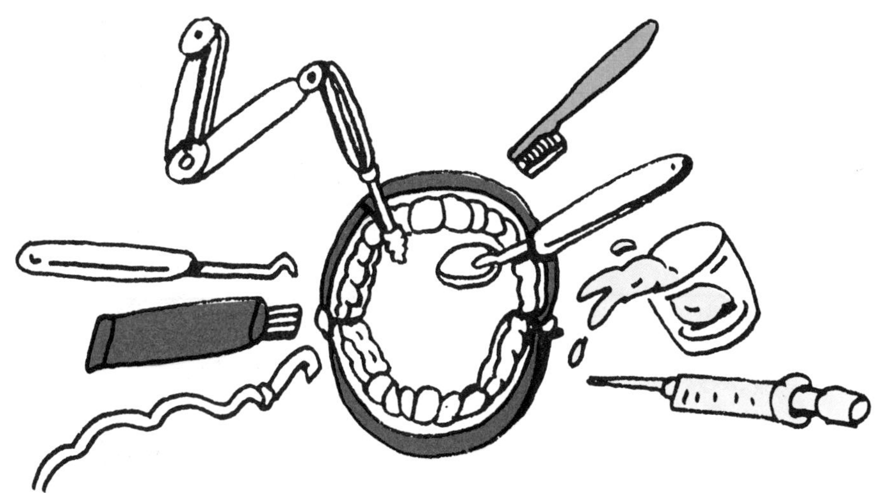

John has a toothache. His cousin recommends a dentist with whom she is most satisfied. John's appointment is today at 14 hours.

JOHN (to receptionist)

(AN-ge-mel-det)
Ich bin angemeldet. — I have an appointment.

(SHPREÇ-shtun-den-hil-feh) (emp-FANGS-dah-meh)
SPRECHSTUNDENHILFE or EMPFANGSDAME
receptionist

Mit Dr. Scherer? — With Dr. Scherer?

JOHN **Ja, für 14 Uhr.** — Yes, for 14 hours (2 P.M.).

SPRECHSTUNDENHILFE **Ihr Name, bitte?** — Your name, please?

JOHN **John Wagner.** — John Wagner.

SPRECHSTUNDENHILFE **Lassen Sie mich im**
(tayr-MEEN-kah-len-deR)
Terminkalender nachsehen. 14 Uhr, stimmt. Wir haben heute eine Menge
(pah-tsee-EN-ten)
Patienten. Bitte nehmen Sie Platz. Sind Sie zum erstenmal hier?

Let me look in the appointment book. 14 hours, right. We have a lot of patients today. Please take a seat. Is this your first visit?

JOHN **Ja.**

Yes.

SPRECHSTUNDENHILFE **Wollen Sie bitte diese Karte ausfüllen?**

Please fill out this card.

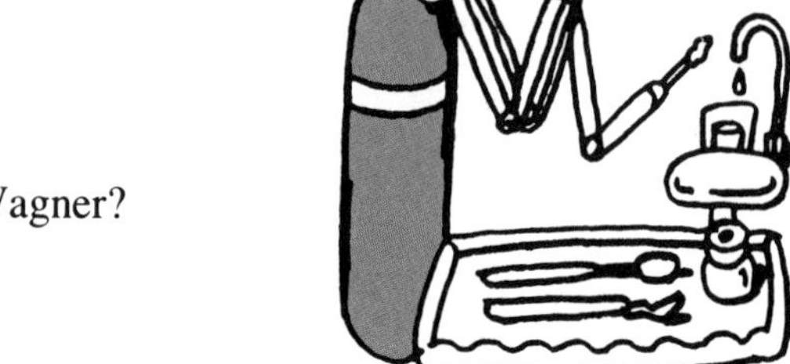

(after one hour)

(TSAHN-artst-helf-eR-in)
ZAHNARZTHELFERIN **Herr Wagner?**
Dental Assistant

Mr. Wagner?

JOHN **Ja?**

Yes?

ZAHNARZTHELFERIN **In diesen Stuhl, bitte. Der Arzt ist gleich hier.**

In this chair, please. The doctor will be here soon.

(after fifteen minutes)

(TSAHN-artst)
ZAHNARZT **Herr Wagner?**
Dentist

Mr. Wagner?

Also wo tut es weh? Hier? Lassen Sie
(shmertst)
mich sehen. Schmerzt das? Und das?
(VA-kelt)
Ja—also, das wackelt auch ein
(FÜL-ung)
bißchen. Sie haben die Füllung
(feR-LOH-ren)
verloren. Ich gebe Ihnen eine
(SHPRI-tseh) (ÖRT-li-çeh) (be-TOY-bung)
Spritze für örtliche Betäubung. Jetzt warten wir ein bißchen, und
(BRÜ-keh)
dann füllen wir den Zahn. Die Brücke
(KROH-neh)
sitzt nicht recht und die Krone hier
(DURÇ-ge-bis-en)
ist halb durchgebissen.

Well, where does it hurt? Here? Let me look. Does this hurt? And that? Yes—well, This wobbles a bit. You have lost the filling. I'll give give you an injection for local anaesthesia. Now we'll wait a little, and then we'll fill the tooth. The bridge doesn't sit right, and the crown here is half bitten through.

In zwei bis drei Jahren brauchen Sie wahrscheinlich eine Zahnprothese. *(TSAHN-proh-tay-zeh)*

In two to three years you'll probably need dentures.

JOHN **Da freu' ich mich schon.**

I'm looking forward to it.

ZAHNARZT **Auf Wiedersehen, Herr Wagner. Und schöne Ferien!**

So long, Mr. Wagner. And have a nice vacation.

BITTE „AAAH" SAGEN!

Say "Aaaah," Please.

Mary has developed a sore throat. While waiting at the doctor's office, she speaks with another patient.

PATIENT **Ja, Dr. List ist eine sehr gute Ärztin.**

Yes, Dr. List is a very good physician.

MARY **Ist sie Spezialistin?**

Is she a specialist?

PATIENT **Nein, sie ist praktische Ärztin.**

No, she is in general practice.

EMPFANGSDAME **Frau Wagner? Frau Doktor wird gleich da sein.**

Mrs. Wagner? The doctor will be here soon.

DR. LIST **Frau Wagner? Ich bin Dr. List. Schön, Sie kennenzulernen.** *(KEN-en-tsu-ler-nen)* **Wie kann ich Ihnen helfen?**

Mrs. Wagner? I am Dr. List. Nice to meet you. How can I help you?

MARY **Ich kann kaum reden.**

I can hardly talk.

DR. LIST **Öffnen Sie bitte den Mund. Sagen Sie „Aaaah." Gut. Ja, das ist ein wenig gerötet.** *(ge-RÖ-tet)* **Wie fühlen Sie sich sonst?**

Open your mouth, please. Say "Aaaah." Good. Yes, this is a little red. How do you feel otherwise?

MARY **Scheußlich.** *(SHOYS-liç)* **Eine verstopfte** *(fer-SHTOPF-teh)* **Nase und Kopfweh.** *(KOPF-vay)*

Rotten. A stuffed-up nose and a headache.

DR. LIST **Fieber?**

Fever?

MARY **Nein. Die Temperatur ist ganz normal.**

No. The temperature is quite normal.

DR. LIST **Na ja. Hier ist ein Rezept. Nehmen Sie die Medizin** *(me-di-TSEEN)* **dreimal täglich.** *(TAYG-liç)*

Okay. Here is a prescription. Take the medicine three times a day.

MARY **Danke schön!**

Thank you.

Let's try a few questions about the dialogues in this unit.

True or False?

1. John ist um 16 Uhr angemeldet. ________
2. Er hat eine Füllung verloren. ________
3. Er bekommt eine Spritze. ________
4. Dr. List ist eine Spezialistin. ________
5. Mary hat Zahnschmerzen. ________

ANSWERS

1. F 2. T 3. T 4. F 5. F

Bitte nicht vergessen . . .

Please don't forget . . .

(artst)
der Arzt — doctor (man)

(ERTS-tin)
die Ärztin — doctor (woman)

(pah-tsi-ENT)
der Patient — patient

(PRAK-sis)
die Praxis — practice

(roo-TEE-neh)
die Routine — routine

(shpets-ee-a-LIST) *(FAÇ-artst)*
der Spezialist *or* **der Fachartzt** — specialist

(tem-peR-ah-TOOR)
die Temperatur — temperature

(çi-RURK)
der Chirurg — surgeon

(HARN-proh-beh)
die Harnprobe — urine specimen

(ge-VIÇT)
das Gewicht — weight

(ray-TSEPT)
das Rezept — prescription

(un-teR-ZOO-chung)
die Untersuchung — (medical) examination

(me-di-TSEEN)
die Medizin — medicine

(RÖNT-gen-owf-nah-meh)
der Röntgenaufnahme — Xray

(KAR-teh)
die Karte
card

(FEE-beR)
das Fieber
fever

(BLOOT-druk)
der Blutdruck
blood pressure

(KRAN-ken-hows-heeR-ahR-çee)
DIE KRANKENHAUSHIERARCHIE

Hospital Hierarchy

(SHEF-artst)
der Chefarzt
medical director

(OH-beR-artst)
der Oberarzt
assistant medical director

(artst)
der Arzt
physician on the hospital staff

(ze-kun-DAHR-artst)
der Sekundararzt
hospital physician (in Austria) without his own ward

(a-sis-TENTS-artst) *(HILFS-artst)*
der Assistenzarzt, der Hilfsarzt
assistant physician on the hospital staff

(PFLIÇT-a-sis-ten-ten)
die Pflichtassistenten
interns

(OH-beR-shves-ter)
die Oberschwester
head nurse

(KRAN-ken-shves-teR) *(SHVES-teR)*
die Krankenschwester, die Schwester
nurse

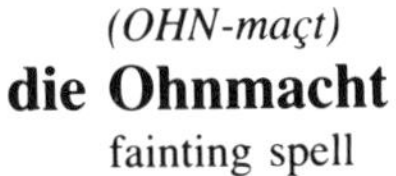

(OHN-maçt)
die Ohnmacht
fainting spell

(HERTS-an-fal)
der Herzanfall
heart attack

Andreas, Aunt Sophie's husband, has a fainting spell. The ambulance takes him to the hospital; Sophie and Mary are in the waiting room.

SOPHIE **Nein, er ist nicht herzkrank.** *(HERTS-krank)* **Ich rufe** *(ROOF-eh)* **sofort** *(zoh-FORT)* **den Doktor an, bestelle einen Krankenwagen, und zehn Minuten später ist Andreas** *(an-DRAY-as)* **im Krankenhaus.**	No, he doesn't have heart trouble. I call the doctor right away, send for an ambulance, and ten minutes later Andreas is in the hospital.
MARY **Wo ist er jetzt?**	Where is he now?
SOPHIE **In der Intensivstation.** *(in-ten-ZEEF-shtah-tsee-ohn)*	In the intensive care unit.
MARY **Sprichst du mit dem Arzt?**	Do you speak with the doctor?
SOPHIE **Nur ganz kurz. Ich glaube, man untersucht** *(un-ter-ZUCHT)* **ihn jetzt.**	Only quite briefly. I think they are examining him now.
MARY **Hier kommt die Krankenschwester.**	The nurse is coming.
KRANKENSCHWESTER **Sie können jetzt in sein Zimmer gehen.**	You may go into his room now.
SOPHIE **Danke, Schwester. Wie geht's meinem Mann?**	Thank you, nurse. How is my husband?
KRANKENSCHWESTER **Gut, Frau Kleist. Der Doktor ist sehr zufrieden.** *(tsoo-FREED-en)*	Fine, Mrs. Kleist. The doctor is very satisfied.
(in the room)	
SOPHIE (to Andreas) **Wie fühlst du dich, Liebster?**	How do you feel, darling?

ANDREAS **Nicht schlecht.** — Not bad.

DR. SCHMITT **Machen Sie sich keine großen** *(ZOHRG-en)* **Sorgen, Frau Kleist. Ihr Mann ist** *(eR-SHÖPFT)* **erschöpft. Er braucht vor allem** *(BET-roo-eh)* **Bettruhe. Und mit dem Rauchen muß Schluß sein. Also—Frau Kleist, gehen Sie nach Hause und ruhen Sie sich aus.** — There is no need to worry too much, Mrs. Kleist. Your husband is exhausted. He needs bed rest above all. And there must be an end to his smoking. OK—Frau Kleist, you go home and get some rest.

Here are some questions about the dialogues in this unit.

1. Was hat John verloren?
   a. ein Buch b. Geld c. eine Füllung
2. Was ist mit Johns Brücke los?
   a. Sie sitzt nicht recht. b. Sie ist in Ordnung. c. Er braucht keine.
3. Was braucht er in zwei bis drei Jahren?
   a. eine Goldkrone b. eine Zahnprothese c. nichts
4. Wer ist in Dr. Scherers Wartezimmer?
   a. nur John b. nur drei Patienten c. eine Menge Patienten
5. Warum geht Mary zum Arzt? Sie hat
   a. Bauchschmerzen b. Halsschmerzen c. Ohrenschmerzen
6. Wer hat einen Herzanfall?
   a. Andreas b. John c. Sophie
7. Später braucht Andreas vielleicht
   a. Schokolade jeden Tag b. einen Herzschrittmacher c. eine gute Zigarre

ANSWERS

1. c 2. a 3. b 4. c 5. b 6. a 7. b

(KOH-mi-sheh) (ge-SHIÇ-teh)

Eine komische Geschichte

A Strange Story

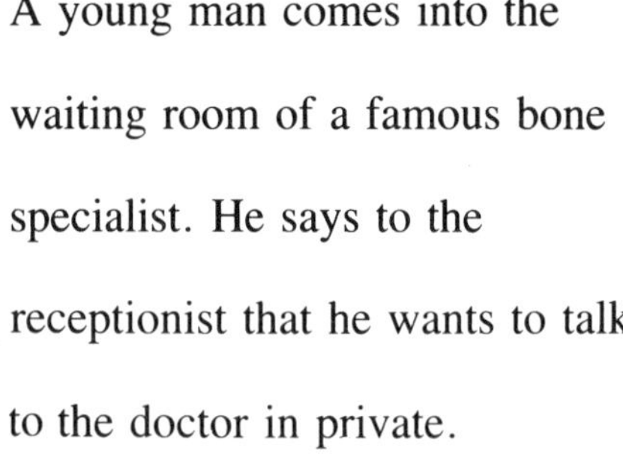

Ein junger Mann kommt in das Wartezimmer eines berühmten *(be-RÜMT-en)* **Knochenspezialisten.** *(KNOCH-en-shpe-tsee-a-LIST-en)* **Er sagt der Sprechstundenhilfe, er möchte den Arzt privat** *(pree-VAHT)* **sprechen.**

A young man comes into the waiting room of a famous bone specialist. He says to the receptionist that he wants to talk to the doctor in private.

„Gehen Sie in dieses Zimmer hier, ziehen Sie sich aus und warten Sie."

Go into this room here, get undressed, and wait."

„Aber—"

"But—"

„Was ist los mit Ihnen?" fragt ihn der Doktor.

"What's the matter with you?" the doctor asks him.

„Ich bin hier," antwortet der junge Mann, „weil ich Ihr Abonnement *(a-bo-ne-MANG)* **für den *Stern* erneuern** *(eR-NOY-ern)* **möchte."**

"I am here," replies the young man, "because I would like to renew your subscription to *Stern* magazine."

Können sie diese Fragen beanworten?

1. Wer kommt ins Wartezimmer? ______________________
2. Was sagt er der Sprechstundenhilfe? ______________________
3. Wen möchte er gern privat sprechen? ______________________
4. Wo zieht der junge Mann sich aus? ______________________
5. Was antwortet er dem Arzt? ______________________

ANSWERS

1. ein junger Mann **2.** Er möchte den Arzt privat sprechen. **3.** den Arzt **4.** in einem Zimmer
5. Ich bin hier, weil ich Ihr Abonnement für den *Stern* erneuern möchte.

BEFORE YOU LEAVE

(fohR) (AP-reiz-eh)

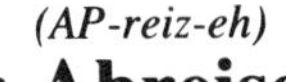

Vor der Abreise

You've learned a lot of German by now—probably much more than you realize. This section is a very important final step in the learning process—a step in which you review and solidify your understanding of your new language.

We've organized the section around basic situations tourists encounter. For each situation there are a number of questions about appropriate German expressions. If you have difficulty remembering what to say in a particular situation, review the relevant unit in this book.

Good luck!

Und gute Reise!

(zi-tu-at-si-OHN)

SITUATION 1: Leute kennenlernen

Getting to Know People

1. It is afternoon, and you meet someone. What do you say in order to start a conversation?
   A. Guten Tag. ☐
   B. Auf Wiedersehen. ☐
   C. Bitte. ☐

2. You meet someone you'd like to get to know better. You might say:
   A. Ich bin müde. ☐
   B. Möchten Sie mit mir essen? ☐
   C. Die Katze ist groß. ☐

3. Someone asks you how you are. Which of the following is *not* possible as an answer?
   A. Danke, nicht schlecht. ☐
   B. Danke, sehr gut. ☐
   C. Danke, guten Tag. ☐

4. And how do you say good-bye?
   A. Danke ☐
   B. Auf Wiedersehen ☐

ANSWERS

Situation 1. 1. A 2. B 3. C 4. B

SITUATION 2: Ankunft

Arrival

1. You do not have a reservation at the hotel. What do you say?
   A. Wie geht's, mein Herr? ☐
   B. Entschuldigen Sie, bitte. Ich habe keine Reservierung. ☐
   C. Guten Tag, mein Herr. Wie heißen Sie? ☐

2. You want to say that you really need a room. You say:
   A. Ich brauche dringend ein Zimmer, bitte. ☐
   B. Bitte, ich brauche kein Badezimmer. ☐

3. You want to inquire about price. So you say:
   A. Ihr Name, bitte? ☐
   B. Wo ist das Badezimmer? ☐
   C. Können Sie mir sagen, wieviel das Zimmer kostet? ☐

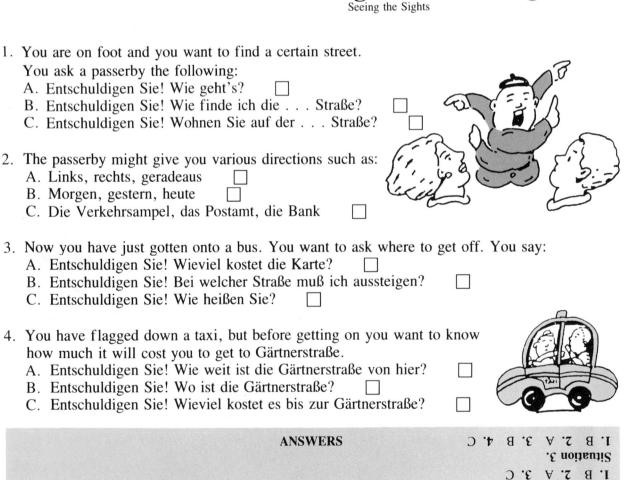

SITUATION 3: Sehenswürdigkeiten besichtigen

Seeing the Sights

1. You are on foot and you want to find a certain street.
   You ask a passerby the following:
   A. Entschuldigen Sie! Wie geht's? ☐
   B. Entschuldigen Sie! Wie finde ich die . . . Straße? ☐
   C. Entschuldigen Sie! Wohnen Sie auf der . . . Straße? ☐

2. The passerby might give you various directions such as:
   A. Links, rechts, geradeaus ☐
   B. Morgen, gestern, heute ☐
   C. Die Verkehrsampel, das Postamt, die Bank ☐

3. Now you have just gotten onto a bus. You want to ask where to get off. You say:
   A. Entschuldigen Sie! Wieviel kostet die Karte? ☐
   B. Entschuldigen Sie! Bei welcher Straße muß ich aussteigen? ☐
   C. Entschuldigen Sie! Wie heißen Sie? ☐

4. You have flagged down a taxi, but before getting on you want to know how much it will cost you to get to Gärtnerstraße.
   A. Entschuldigen Sie! Wie weit ist die Gärtnerstraße von hier? ☐
   B. Entschuldigen Sie! Wo ist die Gärtnerstraße? ☐
   C. Entschuldigen Sie! Wieviel kostet es bis zur Gärtnerstraße? ☐

ANSWERS

Situation 2.
1. B **2.** A **3.** C

Situation 3.
1. B **2.** A **3.** B **4.** C

5. You have forgotten your watch. You stop a passerby to ask what time it is. You say:
   A. Entschuldigen Sie! Können Sie mir sagen, wieviel Uhr es ist? ☐
   B. Entschuldigen Sie! Haben Sie eine Uhr? ☐
   C. Entschuldigen Sie! Haben Sie Zeit? ☐

6. The passerby would *not* answer:
   A. Es ist zwei Uhr fünfundzwanzig. ☐
   B Es ist Mittwoch. ☐
   C. Es ist halb zwei. ☐

7. You are at the train station and want to buy a ticket. You might say:
   A. Entschuldigen Sie! Wieviel kostet eine Fahrkarte nach Wien? ☐
   B. Entschuldigen Sie! Wo ist Wien? ☐
   C. Entschuldigen Sie! Wo bin ich hier? ☐

8. The clerk answers that there is no seat left on the train. He might say something like:
   A. Es tut mir leid, aber Sie sind verrückt. ☐
   B. Es tut mir leid, aber Sie sprechen nicht Deutsch. ☐
   C. Es tut mir leid, aber wir haben keinen Platz. ☐

9. You want to say to someone that you are American and speak only a little German. You might say:
   A. Ich bin Amerikaner (Amerikanerin) und spreche nur ein bißchen Deutsch. ☐
   B. Ich spreche Englisch und bin kein Italiener. ☐
   C. Ich bin kein Italiener, ich bin Amerikaner. ☐

10. If someone were to ask you what nationality you are, he/she would *not* say:
   A. Sind Sie Kanadier? ☐
   B. Sind Sie Deutscher? ☐
   C. Sind Sie intelligent? ☐
   D. Sind Sie Spanier? ☐
   E. Sind Sie Franzose? ☐

11. You want to rent a car at a good rate. You might ask the clerk:
   A. Ich möchte einen sehr teuren Wagen mieten. ☐
   B. Ich möchte einen sehr preiswerten Wagen mieten. ☐
   C. Ich möchte einen neuen Wagen mieten. ☐

12. You want to fill up your car. You might say:
   A. Ein neues Auto, bitte. ☐
   B. Auffüllen, bitte! ☐
   C. Bitte, das kostet zu viel. ☐

ANSWERS

Situation 3.
5. A **6.** B **7.** A **8.** C **9.** A **10.** C **11.** B **12.** B

13. You have just been in a car accident and wish to ask how the other motorist is. You might say:
   A. Guten Tag, wie geht's ☐
   B. Sind Sie verletzt? ☐
   C. Wie heißen Sie? ☐

14. A service station attendant might tell you that your car needs repairs. He would *not* say:
   A. Ihr Auto ist schön. ☐
   B. Ihr Auto braucht eine neue Bremse. ☐
   C. Ihr Auto braucht einen neuen Motor. ☐

15. You ask a "camping employee" if there are essential services. You would not say:
   A. Gibt es hier Wasser? ☐
   B. Gibt es hier Toiletten? ☐
   C. Gibt es hier ein Kino? ☐
   D. Gibt es hier einen Spielplatz für Kinder? ☐

16. As an answer to "How much do you charge?" (Wieviel kostet das?), the clerk might respond:
   A. Hundert Mark ☐
   B. Fünfzig Dollar ☐
   C. Vierzehn Uhr ☐

17. If someone were to ask you about the weather back home, you would *not* say:
   A. Es kann nicht sprechen. ☐
   B. Es ist schönes Wetter. ☐
   C. Es ist schlechtes Wetter. ☐
   D. Es regnet immer. ☐
   E. Es schneit immer. ☐

18. As an answer to „Was ist das Datum heute?" (What's today's date?), you would not hear:
   A. Es ist der dreißigste März. ☐
   B. Es ist der zweite Tag. ☐
   C. Es ist der dritte Mai. ☐

19. At the airport, you might hear this over the loudspeaker:
   A. Der Flug 303 nach New York ist interessant. ☐
   B. Der Flug 303 nach New York kommt nicht an. ☐
   C. Der Flug 303 nach New York startet um 3.30. ☐

20. To ask an airline employee at what time your flight leaves, you would say:
   A. Entschuldigen Sie! Um wieviel Uhr fliegt meine Maschine ab? ☐
   B. Entschuldigen Sie! Wann kommt mein Flug an? ☐
   C. Entschuldigen Sie! Fliegen Sie oft? ☐

ANSWERS

Situation 3.
13. B **14.** A **15.** C **16.** A **17.** A **18.** B **19.** C **20.** A

SITUATION 4: Unterhaltung

Entertainment

1. You are at a ticket agency. The clerk would *not* ask you:
   A. Wollen Sie eine Karte für die Oper? ☐
   B. Wollen Sie eine Karte fürs Kino? ☐
   C. Wollen Sie eine Karte fürs Frühstück? ☐
   D. Wollen Sie eine Karte fürs Theater? ☐

2. If someone were to ask you what your favorite sport was („Was ist Ihr Lieblingssport?“), you would *not* say:
   A. Ich spiele gern Tennis. ☐
   B. Ich schwimme gern. ☐
   C. Ich spiele gern Fußball. ☐
   D. Ich spiele gern italienisch. ☐
   E. Ich wandere gern. ☐
   F. Ich fahre gern Rad. ☐

SITUATION 5: Essen bestellen

Ordering Food

1. You want to ask what kind of restaurants are available? You might ask:
   A. Ißt man in Deutschland gut? ☐
   B. Was für Restaurants gibt es hier? ☐
   C. Wo sind die Badezimmer? ☐

2. As a possible answer, you would *not* hear:
   A. Hier sind die besten Restaurants. ☐
   B. Hier sind die Bars. ☐
   C. Hier sind die Gasthäuser. ☐

3. When a waiter asks you to order, he might say:
   A. Möchten Sie schwimmen? ☐
   B. Was soll es sein? ☐
   C. Möchten Sie zahlen? ☐

4. To see the menu, you would say:
   A. Kann ich die Küche sehen? ☐
   B. Kann ich die Speisekarte sehen? ☐
   C. Kann ich den Direktor sehen? ☐

5. One of the following is not connected with eating:
   A. Frühstück ☐
   B. Mittagessen ☐
   C. Benzin ☐
   D. Abendessen ☐

ANSWERS

Situation 4.
1. C 2. D

Situation 5.
1. B 2. B 3. B 4. B 5. C

SITUATION 6: Im Geschäft

At the Store

1. Which of the following would you *not* say in a clothing store:
   A. Entschuldigen Sie! Wieviel kostet dieses Hemd? ☐
   B. Entschuldigen Sie! Wieviel kostet dieser Wagen? ☐
   C. Ich möchte die Schuhe, die Socken und die Krawatte. ☐

2. One of the following lists has nothing to do with clothing:
   A. blauer Anzug, rote Jacke, weißes Hemd ☐
   B. Wollanzug, Baumwolljacke, Seidenhemd ☐
   C. italienisch, deutsch, spanisch ☐

3. You would *not* hear which of the following in a supermarket:
   A. Wieviel kostet das Obst? ☐
   B. Wo sind die Erdbeeren? ☐
   C. Wieviel kostet das Kleid? ☐
   D. Das Fleisch kostet 13 Mark pro Kilo. ☐
   E. Der Fisch ist frisch. ☐
   F. Wir haben keinen Kuchen mehr. ☐

4. You want to order a drug at the pharmacy. You might say:
   A. Dieses Gemüse, bitte. ☐
   B. Diese Medizin, bitte. ☐
   C. Dieses Obst, bitte. ☐

5. A pharmacist would *not* ask you one of the following:
   A. Möchten Sie ein Glas Wein? ☐
   B. Brauchen Sie Aspirin? ☐
   C. Haben Sie ein Rezept für die Medizin? ☐

6. You are at the laundry. You would *not* ask one of the following:
   A. Wo ist der Trockenapparat? ☐
   B. Wieviel kostet es, diesen Anzug zu reinigen? ☐
   C. Wieviel kostet die Schokolade? ☐

7. You are at the barber's and want a haircut. You might say:
   A. Geben Sie mir bitte eine Packung Zigaretten. ☐
   B. Schneiden Sie mir bitte die Haare kurz. ☐
   C. Geben Sie mir bitte eine Karte. ☐

8. The hairdresser might ask you (choose three things):
   A. Soll ich Ihr Haar waschen? ☐
   B. Wollen Sie ein Stück Kuchen? ☐
   C. Soll ich das Haar tönen? ☐
   D. Soll ich das Haar schneiden? ☐

ANSWERS

Situation 6.
1. B **2.** C **3.** C **4.** B **5.** A **6.** C **7.** B **8.** A, C, D

Choose the store for each question: (Match them up.)

1. Können Sie diese Schuhe reparieren?
2. Wieviel kostet dieses Armband?
3. Ich brauche Briefpapier.
4. Ich nehme zwei Magazine und eine Zeitung.
5. Ich möchte eine rote Handtasche kaufen.
6. Geben Sie mir ein Kilo Äpfel.
7. Ich brauche einen Tisch und vier Stühle.
8. Ich nehme zwei Hemden und eine Krawatte.

A. Obsthandlung
B. Kiosk
C. Lederwaren
D. Schuhmacher
E. Möbelhandlung
F. Herrenmode
G. Papierwarenhandlung
H. Juwelier

SITUATION 7: Wichtige Dienstleistungen

Essential Services

1. You are at a bank and want to exchange a traveler's check.
   A. Entschuldigen Sie! Wieviel Uhr ist es? ☐
   B. Entschuldigen Sie! Können Sie mir diesen Reisescheck wechseln? ☐
   C. Entschuldigen Sie! Verkaufen Sie Briefmarken? ☐

ANSWERS

Matching.
1. D 2. H 3. G 4. B 5. C 6. A 7. E 8. F

Situation 7.
1. B

2. Now you want to deposit some money.
   A. Ich möchte Geld einzahlen. ☐
   B. Ich möchte eine Rechnung bezahlen. ☐
   C. Ich brauche etwas Geld. ☐

3. A bank employee would *not* ask you:
   A. Bitte unterschreiben Sie auf diesem Formular. ☐
   B. Bitte essen Sie den Kuchen. ☐
   C. Bitte füllen Sie dieses Formular aus. ☐

4. You want to buy stamps at a post office.
   A. Ich möche Erdbeeren kaufen. ☐
   B. Ich möchte Zeitungen kaufen. ☐
   C. Ich möchte Briefmarken kaufen. ☐

5. Which of the following would you *not* say in a post office?
   A. Bitte schicken Sie den Brief per Luftpost. ☐
   B. Einschreiben, bitte. ☐
   C. Können Sie den Brief jetzt schreiben? ☐

6. When you answer the telephone, you might say:
   A. Hallo, Miller hier. ☐
   B. Auf Wiedersehen. ☐
   C. Tschüß. ☐

7. You want to make a long distance phone call. You would say:
   A. Ich möchte meine Telefonrechnung bezahlen. ☐
   B. Ich möchte ein Ferngespräch machen. ☐
   C. Ich möchte Ihre Telephonnummer haben. ☐

8. You want to ask someone how to dial a number. You would say:
   A. Entschuldigen Sie bitte! Wie wähle ich die Nummer? ☐
   B. Entschuldigen Sie bitte! Wann kann ich telefonieren? ☐
   C. Entschuldigen Sie bitte! Wo ist das Telefon? ☐

9. Which of the following would *not* be used to seek help in an emergency?
   A. Bitte bestellen Sie einen Krankenwagen. ☐
   B. Bitte rufen Sie die Polizei an. ☐
   C. Bitte rufen Sie die Feuerwehr an. ☐
   D. Sagen Sie mir bitte, wo ich erste Hilfe bekommen kann? ☐
   E. Sagen Sie mir bitte, wo Sie wohnen? ☐

10. Which of the following would you *not* say to a doctor?
   A. Herr Doktor, ich habe Kopfweh. ☐
   B. Herr Doktor, Sie sind verrückt. ☐
   C. Herr Doktor, ich habe Magenschmerzen. ☐
   D. Herr Doktor, ich habe Fieber. ☐

ANSWERS

Situation 7.
2. A 3. B 4. C 5. C 6. A 7. B 8. A 9. E 10. B

haben

Was hat Kurt auf dem Kopf?

helfen

Was tut der Gepäckträger?

mögen

Warum ißt Franz kein Gemüse?

trinken

Was tut Hans?

essen - fressen

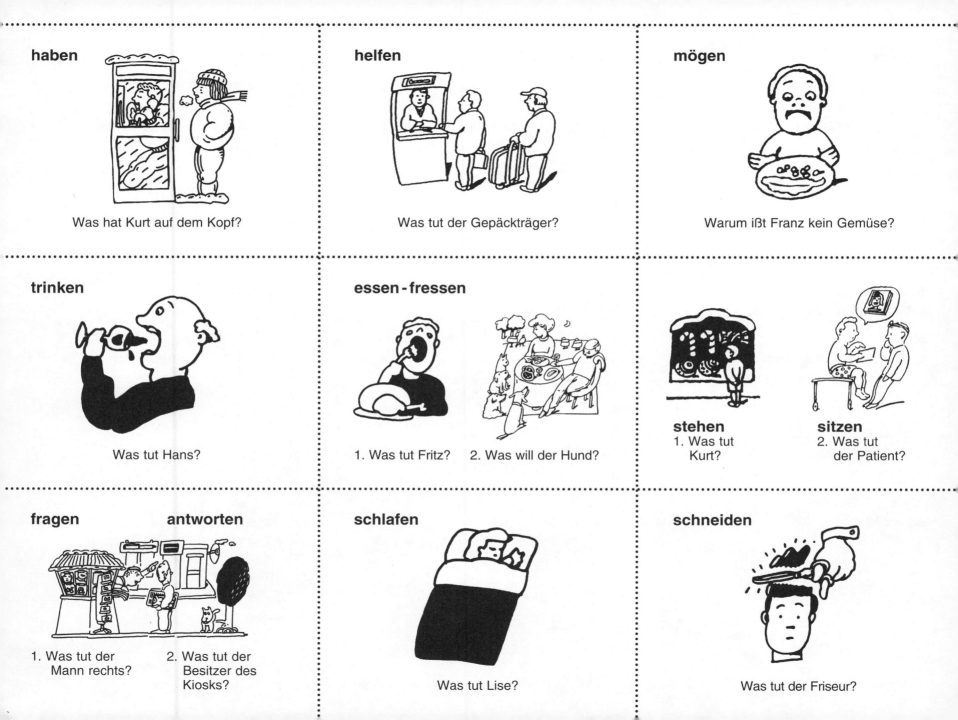

1. Was tut Fritz?
2. Was will der Hund?

stehen

1. Was tut Kurt?

sitzen

2. Was tut der Patient?

fragen **antworten**

1. Was tut der Mann rechts?
2. Was tut der Besitzer des Kiosks?

schlafen

Was tut Lise?

schneiden

Was tut der Friseur?

mögen

Weil er es nicht **mag.**

helfen

Der Gepäckträger **hilft** dem Fahrgast.

haben

Kurt **hat** eine Mütze auf dem Kopf.

der Kopf (-es, ¨-e)

stehen

1. Kurt **steht** vor dem Fenster.

sitzen

2. Der Patient **sitzt** auf dem Tisch.

essen
fressen

1. Fritz **ißt.**
2. Der Hund will **fressen.**

der Hund (-es, -e)

trinken

Hans **trinkt** Wein.

der Wein (-es, -e)

schneiden

Er **schneidet** die Haare.

der Friseur (-s, -e)

schlafen

Lise **schläft.**

fragen

1. Der Mann **fragt** nach Auskunft.

antworten

2. Der Besitzer des Kiosks **antwortet** dem Mann.

gehen-kommen

Die Kinder ______, aber die Leute _______.

wiegen

Was tun die Männer?

bringen

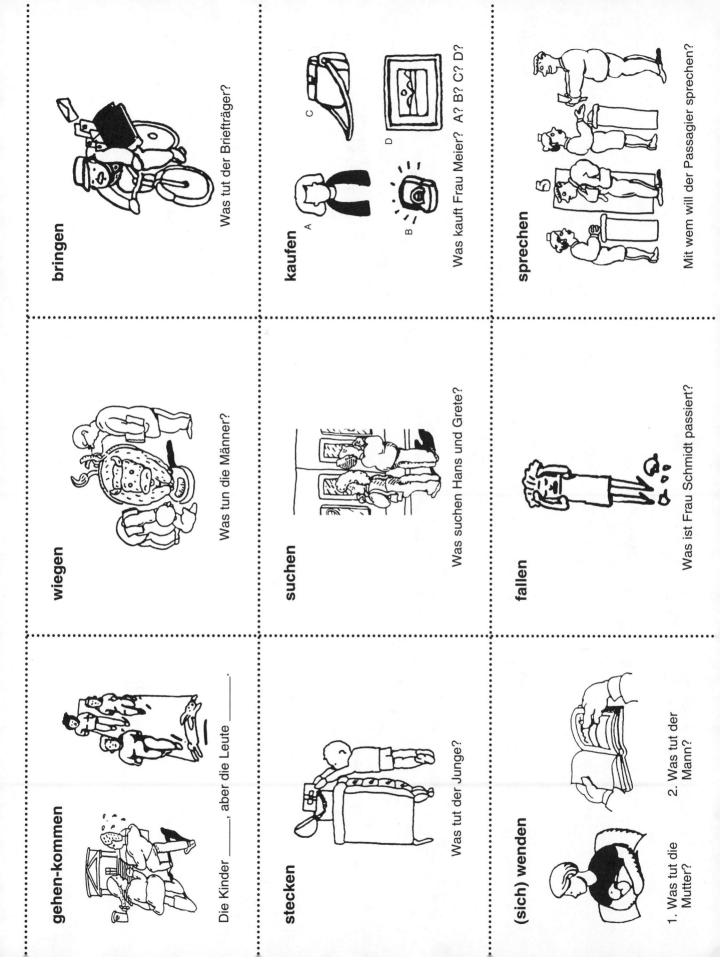

Was tut der Briefträger?

stecken

Was tut der Junge?

suchen

Was suchen Hans und Grete?

kaufen

Was kauft Frau Meier? A? B? C? D?

(sich) wenden

1. Was tut die Mutter?
2. Was tut der Mann?

fallen

Was ist Frau Schmidt passiert?

sprechen

Mit wem will der Passagier sprechen?

bringen

Er **bringt** die Post.

der Briefträger (-s, -)

wiegen

Die Männer **wiegen** das Tier.

gehen-kommen

Die Kinder **gehen,** aber die Leute **Kommen.**

kaufen

A. Frau Meier kauft **einen Schal.**
der Schal (-es, -s)

B. Frau Meier kauft **einen Ring.**
der Ring (-es, -e)

C. Frau Meier kauft **eine Handtasche.**
die Handtasche (-, -n)

D. Frau Meier kauft **ein Bild.**
das Bild (-es, -er)

suchen

Hans und Grete **suchen** das Lebensmittelgeschäft.

das Lebensmittelgeschäft (-es, -e)

stecken

Der Junge **steckt** die Briefe in den Kasten.

sprechen

Der Passagier will mit der Flugbegleiterin **sprechen.**

fallen

Frau Schmidt hat die Vase **fallen** lassen.

die Vase (-, -n)

(sich) wenden

1. Die Mutter **wendet sich.**
2. Der Mann **wendet** die Seiten im Buch.

der Mann (-es, ¨-er)

tragen

1. Was tut Fritz?

2. Was tut Lise?

(sich) waschen

1. Was tut Olga?

2. Was tut die Frau?

schwimmen

Was tut Hans?

anrufen

Was tut Erika?

auf

Wo sitzt die Familie?

für

Für wen kauft Frau Meier den Schal?

vor

Wo stehen die Leute?

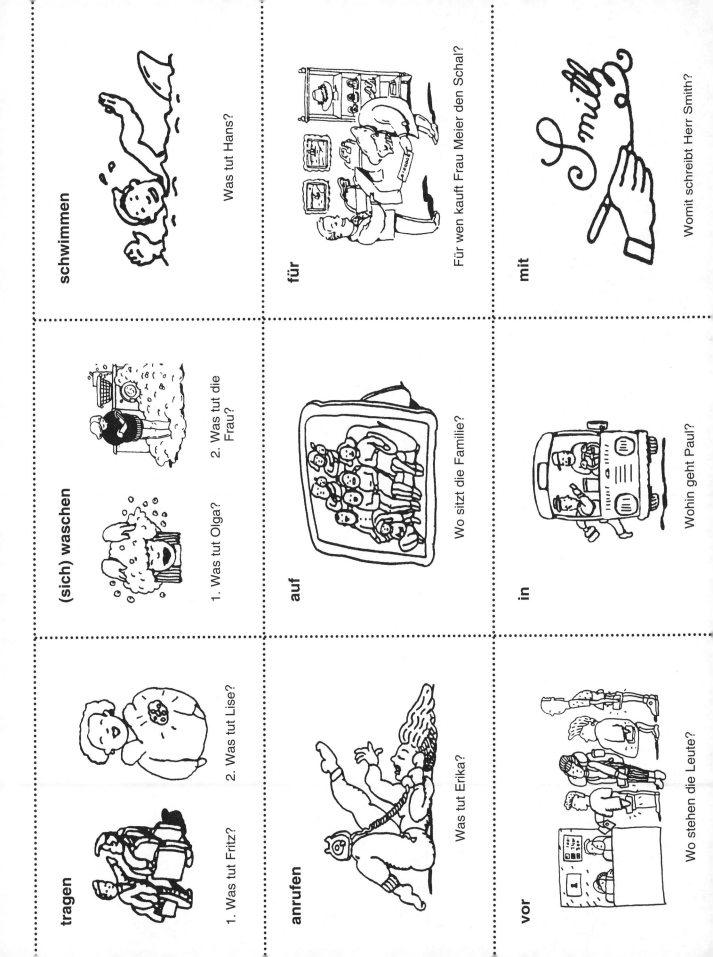

in

Wohin geht Paul?

mit

Womit schreibt Herr Smith?

schwimmen

Er **schwimmt** im Wasser.

(sich) waschen

1. Olga **wäscht sich** die Haare.
2. Die Frau **wäscht** die Wasche.

tragen

1. Fritz **trägt** die Koffer.
2. Lise **trägt** eine Brosche.

der Koffer (-s, -)
die Brosche (-, -n)

für + *accusative*

Sie kauft ihn **für** ihre Tochter.

auf + *dative*

Die Familie sitzt **auf** dem Sofa.

anrufen

Sie **ruft** ihre Freundin **an.**

mit + *dative*

Herr Smith schreibt **mit** dem Kugelschreiber.

der Kugelschreiber (-s, -)

in + *accusative*

Paul geht **in** den Bus.

der Bus (-ses, -se)

vor + *dative*

Die Leute stehen **vor** dem Schalter.

neben

Wo steht das Mädchen?

nur

Trägt Karin 6 Bücher?

um

Wohin legt die Mutter ihren Arm?

unter

Wo sitzt Frau Schmidt?

offen (auf)

Der Kofferraum ist **offen (auf),** aber die Motorhaube ist __________ .

hübsch

Das Mädchen ist **hübsch,** aber der Mann ist __________ .

spielen

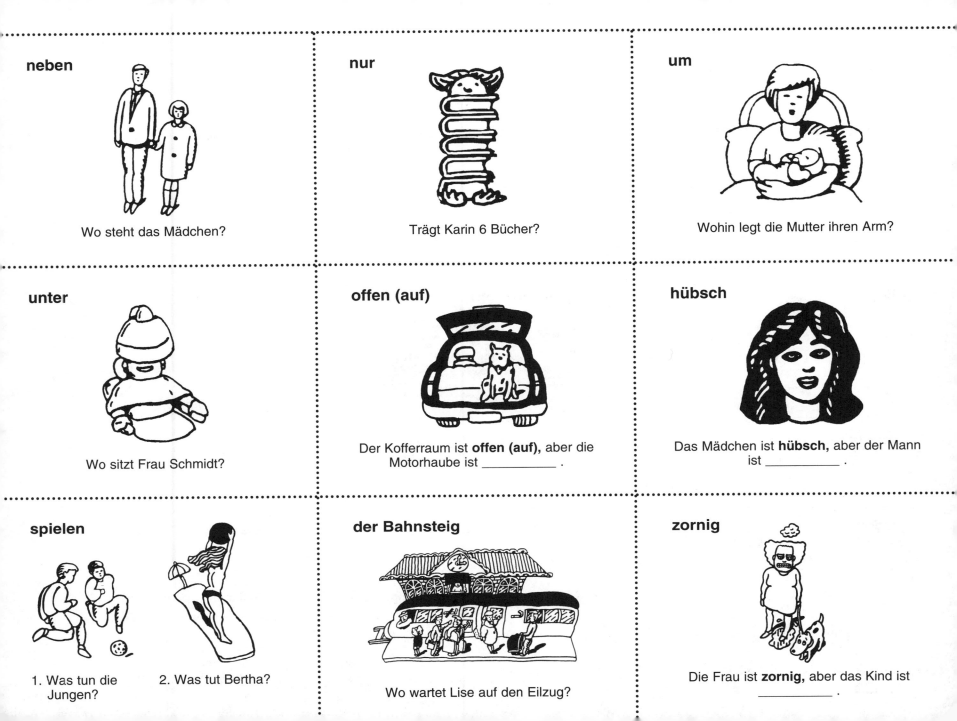

1. Was tun die Jungen?
2. Was tut Bertha?

der Bahnsteig

Wo wartet Lise auf den Eilzug?

zornig

Die Frau ist **zornig,** aber das Kind ist __________ .

um + *accusative*

Die Mutter legt ihren Arm **um** das Kind.

das Kind (-es, -er)

nur

Nein, sie trägt **nur** 5 Bücher.

neben + *dative*

Das Mädchen steht **neben** dem Vater.

häßlich

Der Mann ist **häßlich,** aber das Mädchen ist __________ .

zu (geschlossen)

Die Motorhaube ist **zu (geschlossen)**, aber die Tür ist __________ .

unter + *dative*

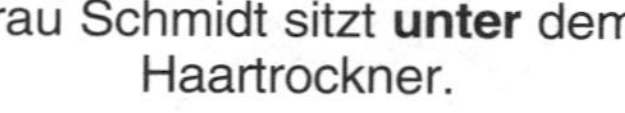

Frau Schmidt sitzt **unter** dem Haartrockner.

zufrieden

Das Kind ist **zufrieden,** aber die Frau ist __________ .

der Bahnsteig (-es, -e)

Sie wartet auf **dem Bahnsteig.**

spielen

1. Die Jungen **spielen** zusammen.
2. Bertha **spielt** mit dem Ball.

schwer

Der Koffer ist **schwer**, aber der Korb ist ________ .

klein-groß

1. Wie ist Brigitte?
2. Wie ist Herr Schmidt?

hoch-tief

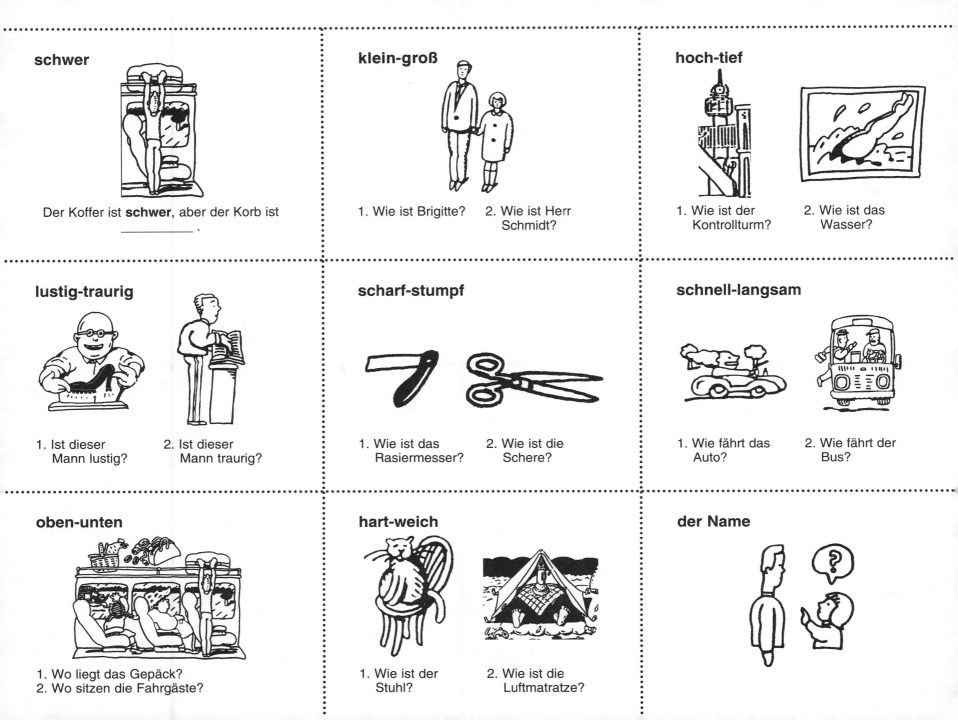

1. Wie ist der Kontrollturm?
2. Wie ist das Wasser?

lustig-traurig

1. Ist dieser Mann lustig?
2. Ist dieser Mann traurig?

scharf-stumpf

1. Wie ist das Rasiermesser?
2. Wie ist die Schere?

schnell-langsam

1. Wie fährt das Auto?
2. Wie fährt der Bus?

oben-unten

1. Wo liegt das Gepäck?
2. Wo sitzen die Fahrgäste?

hart-weich

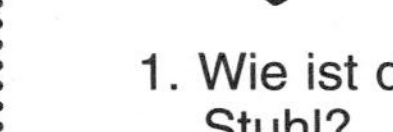

1. Wie ist der Stuhl?
2. Wie ist die Luftmatratze?

der Name

hoch-tief

1. Der Kontrollturm ist **hoch.**
2. Das Wasser ist **tief.**

klein-groß

1. Brigitte ist **klein.**
2. Herr Schmidt ist **groß.**

leicht

Der Korb ist **leicht,** aber der Koffer ist __________ .

schnell-langsam

1. Das Auto fährt **schnell.**
2. Der Bus fährt **langsam.**

scharf-stumpf

1. Das Rasiermesser ist **scharf.**
2. Die Schere ist **stumpf.**

lustig-traurig

1. Ja, dieser Mann ist **lustig.**
2. Ja, dieser Mann ist **traurig.**

der Mann (-es, ¨er)

der Name, (-ns, -n)

Mein **Name** ist __________________ .
your name

hart-weich

1. Der Stuhl ist **hart.**
2. Die Luftmatratze ist **weich.**

oben-unten

1. Das Gepäck liegt **oben.**
2. Die Fahrgäste sitzen **unten.**

die Kundin

Was macht die Kundin?

die Schwester
der Bruder

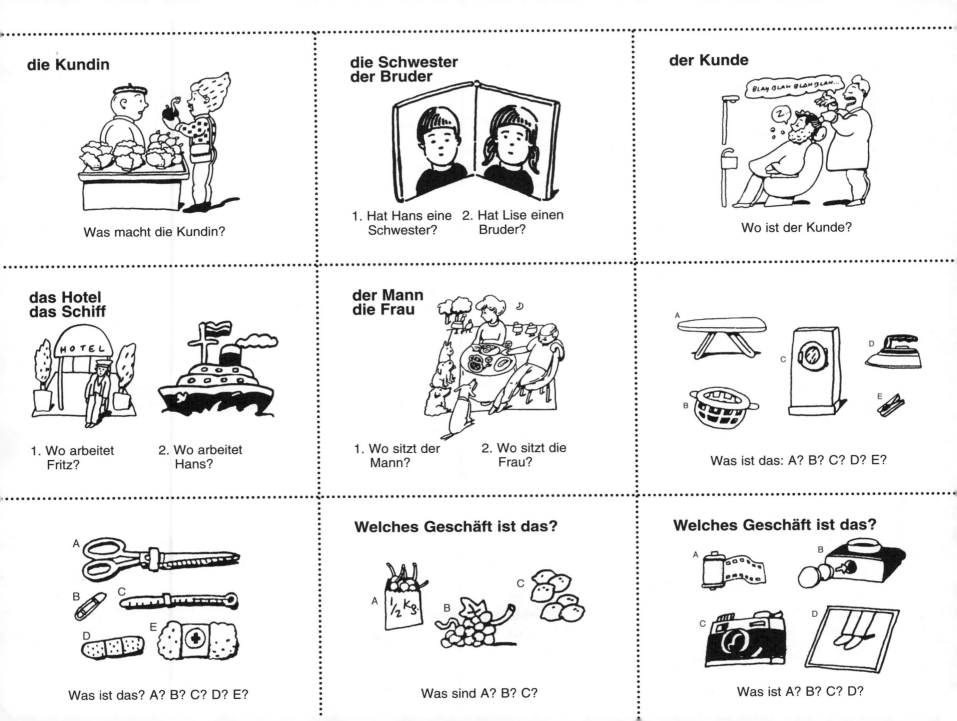

1. Hat Hans eine Schwester?
2. Hat Lise einen Bruder?

der Kunde

Wo ist der Kunde?

das Hotel
das Schiff

HOTEL

1. Wo arbeitet Fritz?
2. Wo arbeitet Hans?

der Mann
die Frau

1. Wo sitzt der Mann?
2. Wo sitzt die Frau?

A B C D E

Was ist das: A? B? C? D? E?

A B C D E

Was ist das? A? B? C? D? E?

Welches Geschäft ist das?

A

B C

Was sind A? B? C?

Welches Geschäft ist das?

A

B

C D

Was ist A? B? C? D?

der Kunde (-n, -n)

Der Kunde ist im Herrensalon.

die Schwester, (-, -n)
der Bruder, (-s, ¨-)

1. Ja, Hans hat eine Schwester.
2. Ja, Lise hat einen Bruder.

die Kundin, (-, -nen)

Die Kundin kauft einen Apfel.

A. Das ist **ein Bügelbrett.**
das Bügelbrett (-es, -er)

B. Das ist **ein Waschkorb.**
der Waschkorb (-es, ¨-e)

C. Das ist **eine Waschmaschine.**
die Waschmaschine (-, -n)

D. Das ist **ein Bügeleisen.**
das Bügeleisen (-s, -)

E. Das ist **eine Wäscheklammer.**
die Wäscheklammer (-, -n)

der Mann, (-es, ¨-er)
die Frau, (-, -en)

1. **Der Mann** sitzt vorm (vor + dem) Tisch.
2. **Die Frau** sitzt hinter dem Tisch.

das Hotel (-s, -s)
das Schiff (-es, -e)

1. Fritz arbeitet **in einem Hotel.**
2. Hans arbeitet **auf dem Schiff.**

Das ist das Photogeschäft.

A ist **der Film.** (-es, -e)
B ist **die Batterie.** (-, -n)
C ist **die Kamera.** (-, -s)
D ist **der Abzug.** (-es, ¨-e)

Das ist die Obsthandlung. (-, -n)

A sind **Kirschen.**
B sind **Weintrauben.**
C sind **Zitronen.**

A. Das ist **eine Schere.**
die Schere (-, -n)

B. Das ist **eine Sicherheitsnadel.**
die Sicherheitsnadel (-, -n)

C. Das ist **ein Thermometer.**
das Thermometer (-s, -)

D. Das ist **ein Heftpflaster.**
das Heftpflaster (-s, -)

E. Das ist **ein Paket Watte.**
die Watte (-, -)

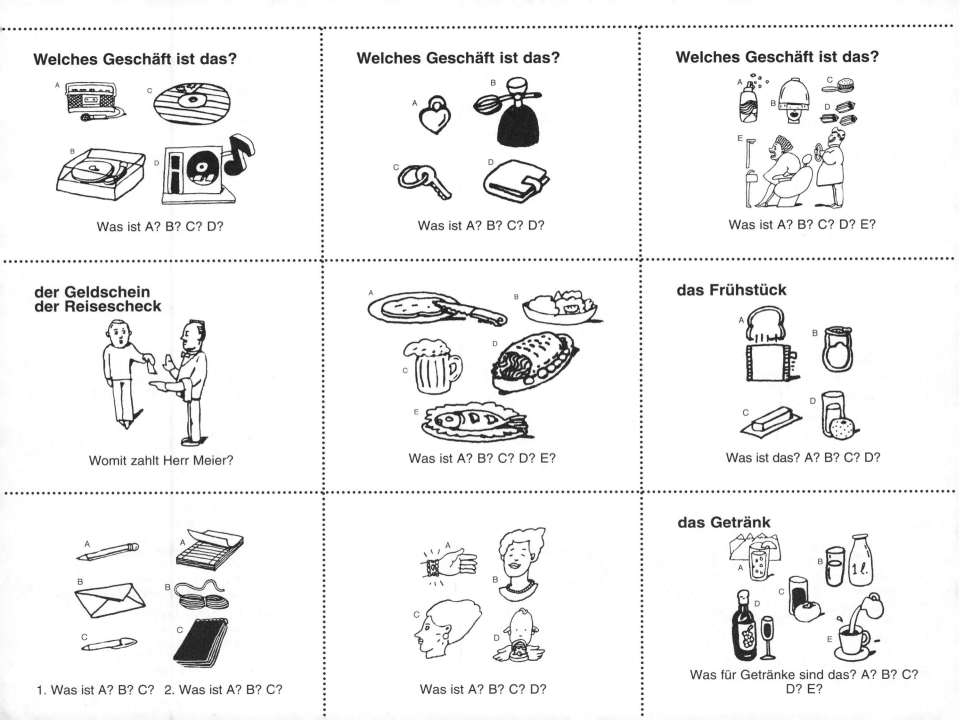

Welches Geschäft ist das?

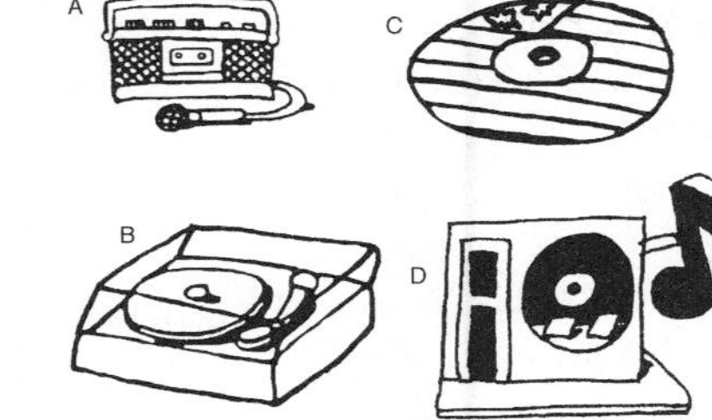

Was ist A? B? C? D?

Welches Geschäft ist das?

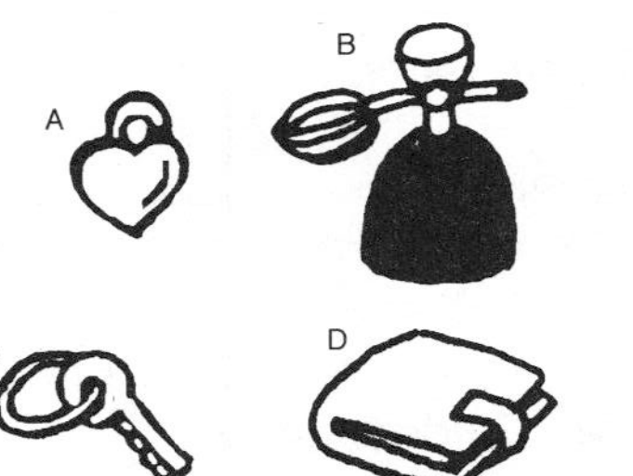

Was ist A? B? C? D?

Welches Geschäft ist das?

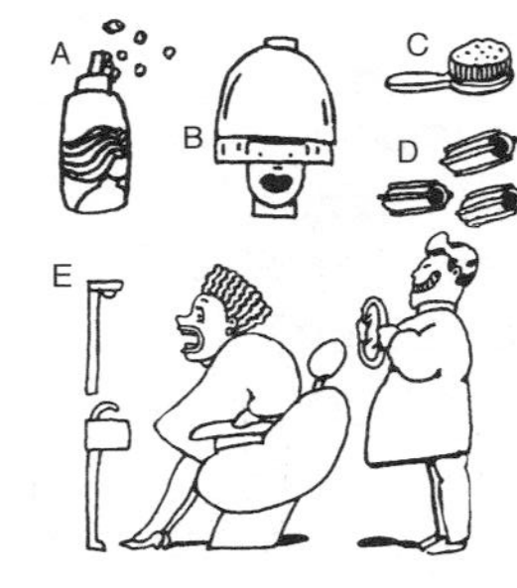

Was ist A? B? C? D? E?

der Geldschein
der Reisescheck

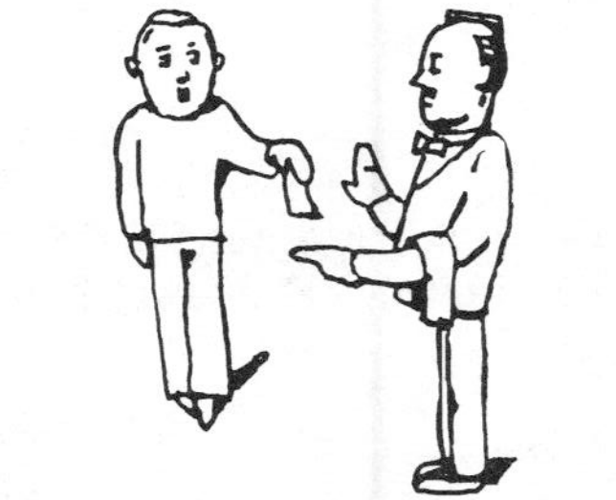

Womit zahlt Herr Meier?

Was ist A? B? C? D? E?

das Frühstück

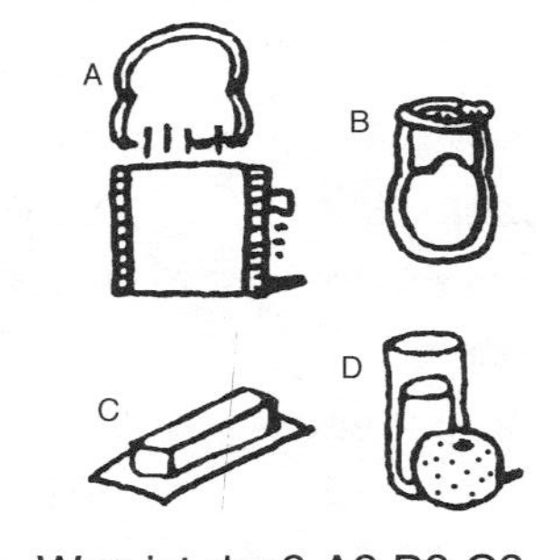
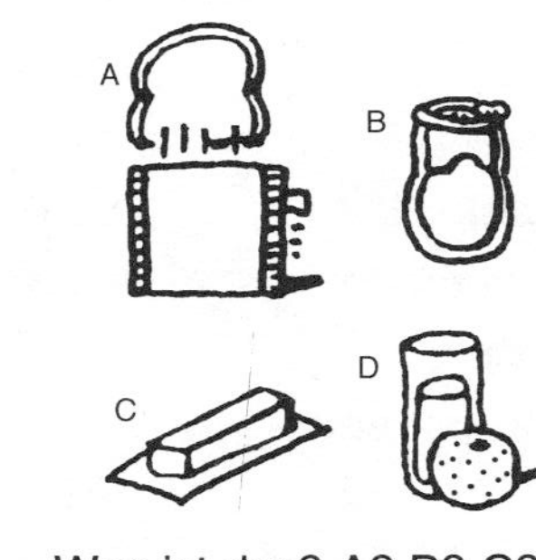
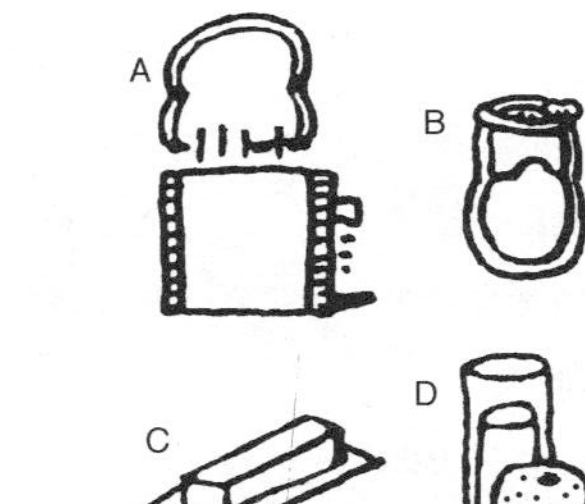

Was ist das? A? B? C? D?

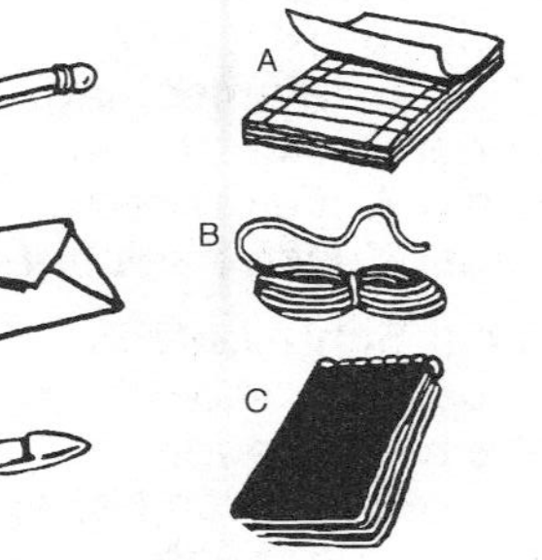

1. Was ist A? B? C?   2. Was ist A? B? C?

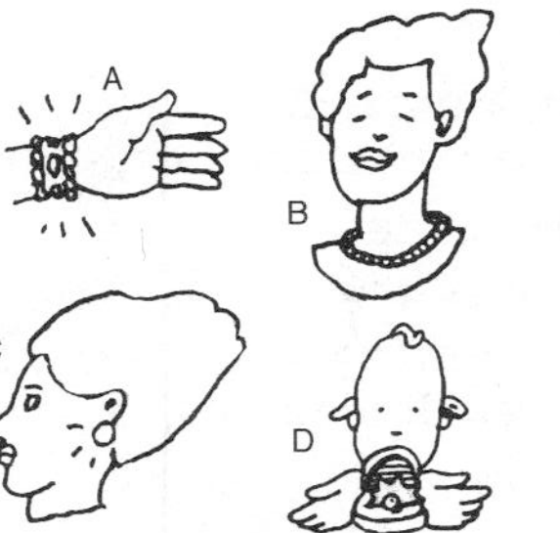

Was ist A? B? C? D?

das Getränk

Was für Getränke sind das? A? B? C? D? E?

Das ist der Damensalon.

A ist **ein Shampoo.**
(das Shampoo, -s, -s)
B ist **ein Haartrockner.**
(der Haartrockner, -s, -)
C ist **eine Haarbürste.**
(die Haarbürste, -, -n)
D ist **ein Lockenwickel.**
(der Lockenwickel, -s, -)
E ist **ein Spiegel.**
(der Spiegel, -s, -)

Das ist der Geschenkartikelladen.

A ist **ein Anhänger.**
(der Anhänger, -s, -)
B ist **ein Parfümzerstäuber.**
(der Parfümzerstäuber, -s, -)
C ist **ein Schlüsselring.**
(der Schlüsselring, -s, -e)
D ist **eine Geldtasche.**
(die Geldtasche, -, -n)

Das ist das Musikgeschäft.

A ist **ein Mikrophon.**
(das Mikrophon, -es, -e)
B ist **ein Plattenspieler.**
(der Plattenspieler, -s, -)
C ist **eine Schallplatte.**
(die Schallplatte, -, -n)
D ist **eine Stereoanlage.**
(die Stereoanlage, -, -n)

das Frühstück (-s, -)

A. Es ist **Toast.**
B. Es ist **Marmelade.**
C. Es ist **Butter.**
D. Es ist **Orangensaft.**

A ist **ein Brot.** (das Brot, -es, -e)
B ist **ein Salat.** (der Salat, -es, -e)
C ist **ein Bier.** (das Bier, -es, -e)
D ist **ein Schweinebraten.**
(der Schweinebraten, -s, -)
E ist **ein Fisch.** (der Fisch, -es, -e)

der Geldschein (-es, -e)
der Reisescheck (-s, -s)

Herr Meier zahlt mit **einem Geldschein** oder mit **einem Reisescheck.**

das Getränk, (-s, -e)

A ist **Mineralwasser.**
das Mineralwasser (-s, -)
B ist **Milch.**
die Milch (-, -)
C ist **Tomatensaft.**
der Tomatensaft (-es, ⸚e)
D ist **Rheinwein.**
der Rheinwein (-es, -e)
E ist **Kaffee.**
der Kaffee (-s, -)

A ist **ein Armband.**
das Armband (-es, ⸚er)
B ist **eine Kette.**
die Kette (-, -n)
C ist **ein Ohrring.**
der Ohrring (-es, -e)
D ist **eine Perle.**
die Perle (-, -n)

1. A ist **ein Bleistift.**
der Bleistift (-es, -e)
B ist **ein Briefumschlag.**
der Briefumschlag (-es, ⸚e)
C ist **ein Kugelschreiber.**
der Kugelschreiber (-s, -)
2. A ist **ein Schreibblock.**
der Schreibblock (-es, ⸚e)
B ist **ein Bindfaden.**
der Bindfaden (-s, ⸚)
C ist **ein Notizbuch.**
das Notizbuch (-es, ⸚er)

das Schwarzbrot

Was liegt auf dem Teller?

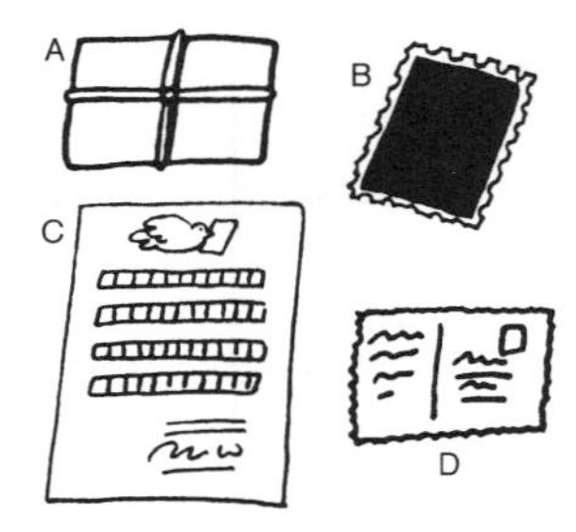

Was ist A? B? C? D?

die Waage

Was liegt auf der Waage?

leicht-reichlich

1. Wie ist das Abendessen?
2. Wie ist das Mittagessen?

die Idee

Was hat Herbert?

das Fieber

Was hat Michael?

Was ist das?

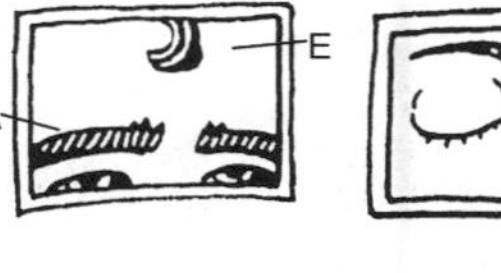

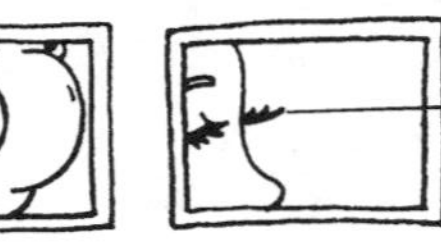

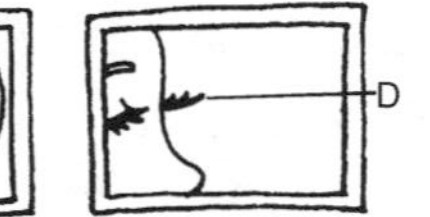

Nennen Sie die Teile des Gesichtes!

die inneren Körperteile

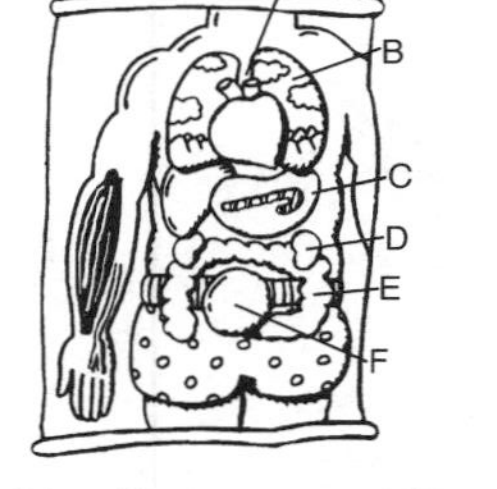

Nennen Sie die inneren Körperteile!
A? B? C? D? E? F?

Was ist das?

Nennen Sie die Körperteile! A? B? C? D?

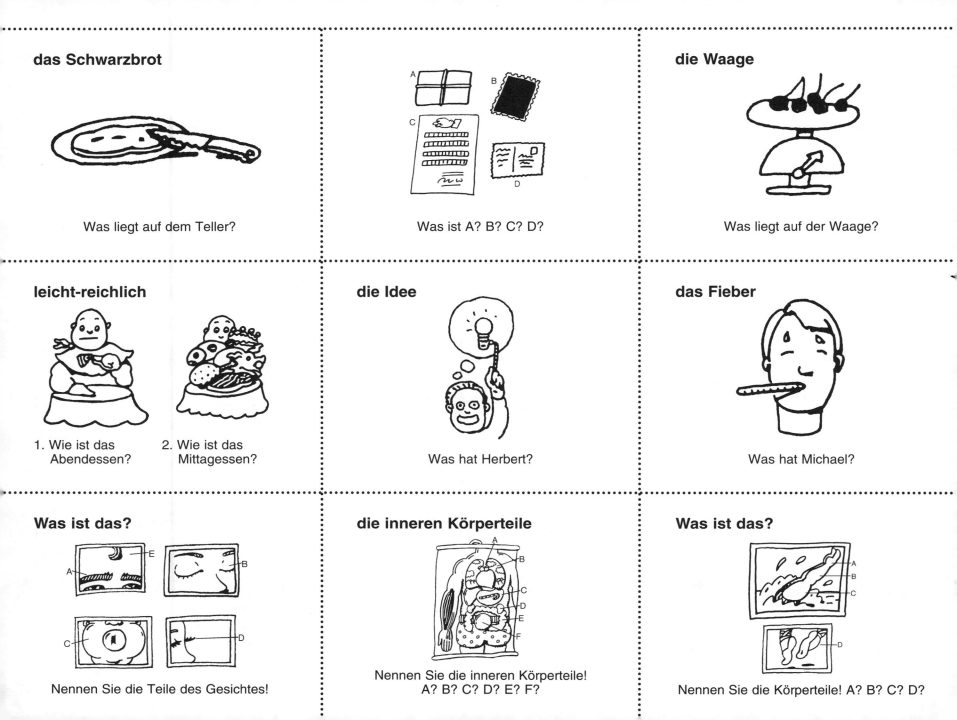

die Waage (-, -n)

Die Kirschen liegen auf der Waage.

die Kirsche (-, -n)

A ist **ein Paket.**
das Paket (-es, -e)
B ist **eine Briefmarke.**
die Briefmarke (-, -n)
C ist **ein Telegramm.**
das Telegramm (-es, -e)
D ist **eine Postkarte.**
die Postkarte (-, -n)

das Schwarzbrot (-es, -e)

Das Schwarzbrot liegt auf dem Teller.

das Fieber (-s, -)

Michael hat **Fieber**.
or:
Michael hat hohes **Fieber**.

die Idee (-, -n)

Herbert hat eine **Idee.**
or:
Herbert hat eine gute **Idee.**

leicht - reichlich

1. Das Abendessen ist **leicht.**
2. Das Mittagessen ist **reichlich.**

das Mittagessen (-s, -)

Das ist das Bein. (-es, -e)

A ist **der Knöchel.** (-s, -)
B ist **die Wade.** (-, -n)
C ist **die Schenkel**. (-s, -)
D ist **der Fuß**. (-es, ¨-e)

die inneren Körperteile (-, -)

A ist **das Herz.** (-ens, -en)
B ist **die Lunge.** (-, -n)
C ist **der Magen.** (-s, -)
D ist **die Niere.** (-, -n)
E ist **der Darm.** (-es, ¨-e)
F ist **die Blase.** (-, -n)

Das ist das Gesicht.

A ist **die Augenbraue.** (-, -n)
B ist **das Augenlid.** (-es, -er)
C ist **die Wange.** (-, -n)
D ist **die Wimper.** (-, -n)
E ist **die Stirn.** (-, -en)

die Krankenhaushierarchie

Wer arbeitet im Krankenhaus?
A? B? C? D?

der Bahnsteig

Was sieht Lotte auf dem Bahnsteig?
A? B? C? D?

die Jahreszeiten II

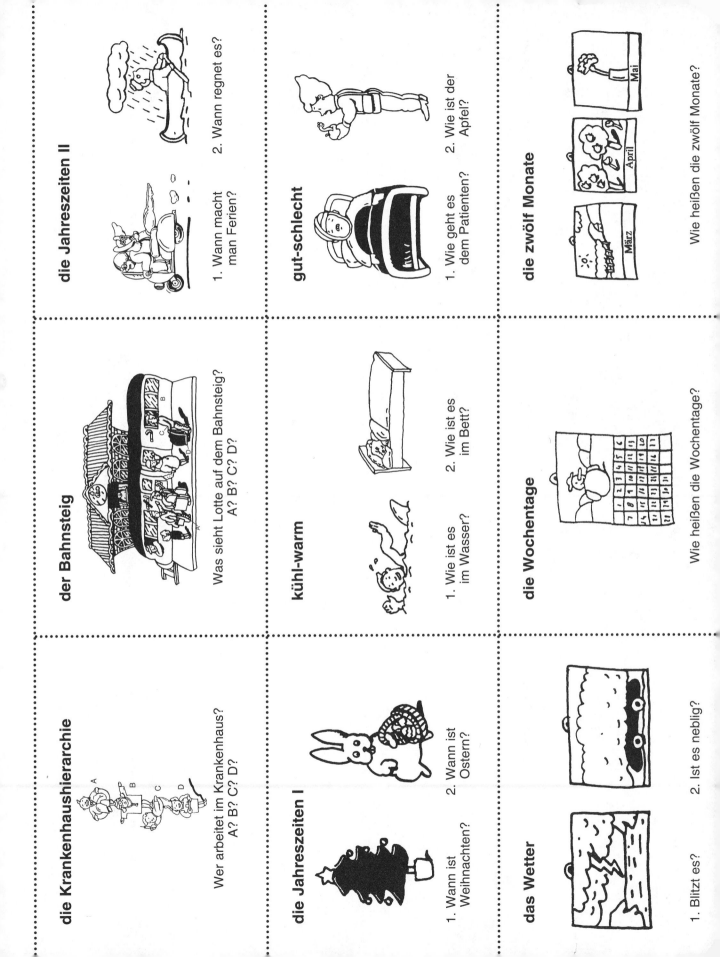

1. Wann macht man Ferien?
2. Wann regnet es?

die Jahreszeiten I

1. Wann ist Weihnachten?
2. Wann ist Ostern?

kühl-warm

1. Wie ist es im Wasser?
2. Wie ist es im Bett?

gut-schlecht

1. Wie geht es dem Patienten?
2. Wie ist der Apfel?

das Wetter

1. Blitzt es?
2. Ist es neblig?

die Wochentage

Wie heißen die Wochentage?

die zwölf Monate

Wie heißen die zwölf Monate?

der Sommer-der Herbst

1. **Im Sommer** macht man Ferien.
2. **Im Herbst** regnet es.

der Bahnsteig

A. Lotte sieht **einen Fahrgast.**
der Fahrgast (-es, ¨-e)

B. Lotte sieht **einen Eisenbahnwagen.**
der Eisenbahnwagen (-s, -)

C. Lotte sieht **einen Gepäckträger.**
der Gepäckträger (-s, -)

D. Lotte sieht **einen Koffer-Kuli.**
der Koffer-Kuli (-s, -s)

die Krankenhaushierarchie

A. der Chefarzt (-es, ¨-e)
B. die Oberärztin (-, -nen)
C. der Pflichtassistent (-en, -en)
D. die Krankenschwester (-, -n)

gut-schlecht

1. Dem Patienten geht es **gut.**
2. Der Apfel ist **schlecht.**

kühl-warm

1. Im Wasser ist es **kühl.**
2. Im Bett ist es **warm.**

das Bett (-es, -en)

der Winter-der Frühling

1. Weihnachten ist **im Winter.**
2. Ostern ist **im Frühling.**

der Monat, (-es, -e)

Die zwölf Monate heißen:

Januar	Juli
Februar	August
März	September
April	Oktober
Mai	November
Juni	Dezember

der Wochentag, (-es, -e)

Die Wochentage heißen:
Sonntag
Montag
Dienstag
Mittwoch
Donnerstag
Freitag
Samstag (oder: Sonnabend)

blitzen-neblig

1. Ja, es **blitzt.**
2. Ja, es ist **neblig.**

der Blitz
der Nebel